ALASKA

Publisher:	Aileen Lau
Project Editor:	Wong Ee Ling
Assisting Editor:	Catherine Khoo
	Vanita Jayaram
Design/DTP:	Sares Kanapathy
	Sarina Afandie
	Michelle Ng
Production:	Brian Wyreweden
Illustrations:	Mohamed Nasuhar
Cover Artwork:	Susan Harmer
Maps:	Hong Li

Published in the United States by
PRENTICE HALL GENERAL REFERENCE
15 Columbus Circle
New York, New York, 10023

Copyright © Sun Tree Publishing Ltd 1994

All rights reserved,
including the right of reproduction in whole or in part in any form.

PRENTICE HALL is a registered trademark and colophon is a trademark of Prentice-Hall, Inc.

ISBN 0-671-88274-0

Titles in the series:
Alaska - American Southwest - Australia - Bali - California - Canada - Caribbean - China - England - Florida - France - Germany - Greece - Hawaii - India - Indonesia - Italy - Ireland - Japan - Kenya - Malaysia - Mexico - Nepal - New England - New York - Pacific Northwest - USA - Singapore - Spain - Thailand - Turkey - Vietnam

USA MAINLAND SPECIAL SALES
Bulk purchases (10+copies) of the Travel Bugs series are available at special discounts for corporate use. The publishers can produce custom publications for corporate clients to be used as premiums or for sales promotion. Copies can be produced with custom cover imprints. For more information write to Special Sales, Prentice Hall Travel, Paramount Communications Building, 15th floor, 15 Columbus Circle, New York, NY 10023.

Printed in Singapore

A DISCLAMER
Readers are advised that prices fluctuate in the course of time and travel information changes under the impact of the varied and volatile factors that affect the travel industry. Neither the author nor the publisher can be held responsible for the experiences of readers while traveling. Readers are invited to write to the publisher with ideas, comments, and suggestions for future editions. The publisher and the author expressly disclaim any responsibility for any liability, loss or risk, personal or otherwise which is incurred as a consequence, directly or indirectly, in the use of this book.

SAFETY ADVISORY
Whenever you're traveling in an unfamiliar city or country, stay alert. Be aware of your immediate surroundings. Wear a moneybelt and keep a close eye on your possessions. Be particularly careful with cameras, purses, and wallets, all favorite targets of thieves and pickpockets.

ALASKA

Text by Tom Reale

Project Editor
Wong Ee Ling

Prentice Hall Travel

New York   London   Toronto   Sydney   Tokyo   Singapore

CONTENTS

INTRODUCTION

"Alyeska" – The Great Land 1
The Final Frontier - Awe-inspiring Landscapes - Touring Alaska
    Fast Facts 4

HISTORY, GOVERNMENT & ECONOMY

Once Upon A Time – History 9
The Ancestors - The Eskimos and the Indians - Russian Explorer and the Fur Trade - European Voyages - "Seward's Folly": The US Buys Alaska - Gold !
    Klondike Gold Rush 12
    The Problem of Subsistence 18

Settlements to Statehood – Government 25
World War II - Post-War Construction - Statehood - Alaska Native Claims Settlement Act - ANILCA
    The Matanuska Colony 28
    Environmentalists & Economists 32

Jewels of the Snow – Economy 35
Commercial Fishing - Mining - Logging - Tourism
    Natural Resources of Alaska 39
    Alaska's Fishing Industry 42

PHYSICAL PROFILE

Land of Extremes – Geography & Climate 47
The Good Friday Earthquake - Mountains - Greens - Wetlands - The Aleutians - Daylight (or lack thereof)
    Avoiding Hypothermia 52
    Beauty of the Fjords 57

The Great Land's Untamed – Flora & Fauna 63
Marine Mammals - The Great Land's Untamed - The Ubiquitous Deer - "Grizzly" and Cousins - Other mammals - Flight of the Fair Birds - Hunting seasons - The Pristine Forest - Wildflowers - Wild Berries
    Bears & You 66
    Birding in Alaska by Morten Strange 68

CONTENTS

Hazards of Oil Spills 74

MEET THE PEOPLE

Native Peoples – People 81
The Yup'iks - The Aleuts & Athabascans - The Tlingit & Haida - Subsistence Styles - Housing - Social Organization - First Contact with Europeans - Who Owns the Land?
    The Utqiagvik Find 87
    Evolving Hunting Lores 90

Rituals & Reverence – Religion 95
Russian Orthodoxy - 'The Three Saints' - Mission Schools and Hospitals - Influx of Protestantism - Reverend Sheldon Jackson - The Nuns - Today's Alaska: Flourishing Faiths
    Native Religions 98
    Totem Poles 102

The Heat of Winterfest – Culture & Festivals 107
Winter Festivals - Spring Festivals - Summer Festivals - Autumn Festivals - The Arts - Museums

    Anchorage's Fur Rendezvous ... 113
    The Wonder of Alaskan Story Telling
    118

Native Inspirations – Handicrafts ....
.... 121
Eskimo Carvings and Clothes - Aleutians Basket-weaving - 'Status Symbols' of Coast Indians - Athabascan Accessories
    Eskimo Ivory Carving 126
    Making Utensils for the Home . 128

FOLLOW THAT BUG

Capital City – Juneau & Environs ....
.... 135
Visiting Juneau - Cruising - Fly Away - On the Road
    The Alaska Marine Highway ... 138
    Mendenhall Glacier 148

Panhandle Country – Southeast Alaska 151
Misty Fjords - Wrangell - Petersburg - Sitka - Glacier Bay
    Gold Panning 156

CONTENTS

Pack Creek - Meeting Bears in the Wild 162
Canada-US Border Crossings ... 168

Scenic Sounds – Southcentral Alaska 173
Prince William Sound - The Kenai Peninsula - Halibut Fishing in Homer - Seward - (Southcentral) North of Anchorage
Public Use Cabins 178
Columbia Glacier 186

Sport Fishing in Bear Country – Kodiak Island 191
Getting there - Kodiak History and Culture - Kodiak Wilds - The Surrounding Waters of Kodiak - Beachcombing
Kodiak Bears 196
A Day in the life of a Kodiak Fisherman 202

Anchorage Affluence – Anchorage 207
Downtown - Chugach State Park - Anchorage Outskirts - Alyeska Ski Resort
Anchorage Fishing Opportunities 216

Glorious Summers – Fairbanks & the Interior 219
Highway 'Hike' - Water and Air Travel - Hot Springs Resorts - The Denali Highway - Wrangell-St Elias National Park
Archeological Finds at the Campus Site 222
Denali National Park 228
E.T. Barnette and the founding of Fairbanks 230

Tip of the Iceberg – The Bush 237
Travel by Flying - Accomodations - Backcountry Travel
The Aurora Borealis 241
Pilots of the Bush 246

WHAT TO DO

Fast & Fun – Sports & Recreation 251
River Sports - Fishing Charters - Whale-watching - Camping - Clamming - Ball Games - Winter Sports
The Iditarod: The Last Great Race 254

CONTENTS

The World Eskimo Indian Olympics 260

All Kinds of Alaskana – Shopping 265
The Price Spectrum - Guide Books - "Two Bears and a Silver Hand"-Souvenir Shopping - Alaskan Art Galleries - Fish Taxidermy
    Fur Shops 268

Sumptuous Seafood – Cuisine 273
    Clams Recipe 275
    Salmon Recipe 277
    Halibut in Cheese Sauce 277

In Pace with the World –
    Entertainment 281
Arctic Escapades-Juneau - Ketchikan - Fairbanks - Anchorage
    The Fly by Night Club 284

EASY REFERENCE

Travel Tips 289
Supplement essential for travel planning

Directory 297

Photo Credit 308

Index 309

MAPS

Alaska 133
Juneau 142
Southeast Alaska 152
Prince William Sound 174
Downtown Anchorage 212
Anchorage & Fairbanks 220
Downtown Fairbanks 224
Arctic Circle Area 238

Alaska awakes from her winter slumber.....

with a rhapsody of Forget-me-nots, Firewoods and Buttercups.

Modern day damsels, Skagway gentleman, Chilkat Indian

..... people of different eras living in harmony on the Great Land.

The silent gaze of totem poles seem to reminisce.....

..... of a distant past when Alaskan Indians first crossed the Beringia.

"ALYESKA" – THE GREAT LAND

Introduction

The mere mention of "Alaska" conjures up a multitude of images and ideas about the Great Land, some of them romantic and fascinating, others fanciful or simply inaccurate. However, these images and the legends that enshroud the native land, are all a part of the mystique surrounding this Final Frontier.

Of all the common misconceptions, probably the most enduring and widespread is that Alaska is covered by snow and ice all year round and inhabited by Eskimos living in igloos, and that the sun shines for six months, then is abruptly turned off, leaving six months of darkness.

As is the case with most myths, there is a grain of truth buried in there to see where the idea came from. For one thing, there is really a lot of snow and ice in Alaska. In nearly 600,000 sq miles (1,554,000 sq km), Alaska contains over 51,000 sq miles (131,580 sq km) of glaciers and snowfields, about two-thirds of North America's glacial ice.

Totem poles mark the Great Land and recalls old Indian legends.

Ice-blue glaciers and rugged terrains, quintessentially Alaska's Inside Passage.

However, it should be noted that summer temperatures in the interior can approach 100° F (37.7°C), and Alaska Natives live in just about every kind of housing known to the modern world and traditional cultures *except* igloos. (Igloos were only the temporary housing used by the Inuit people of northern Canada.)

The amount of daylight, and lack thereof, varies considerably from the top of the state to the bottom. Contrary to popular belief, it does not stay dark for six months in a year anywhere in Alaska, although at Point Barrow, the northernmost point of land in the American continent, the sun sets for more than two months from around November 18 to January 24.

The Final Frontier

Alaska has been called a land of extremes, and rightly so. There are extremes of environment, including geographic features and ecosystems, extremes of climate, from high temperatures that can creep into triple figures to low temperatures that test the lower limits of contemporary thermometer technology. Extremes of sheer size exist as well, from the size of the state itself, to the size of the mountains, glaciers, wide rivers, and lakes.

On the other spectrum, this Final Frontier can be a very civilized place. The cities and larger towns have every convenience and most of the luxuries

An Alaskan girl snug in furs.

that other cities in the Western world have to offer – fine dining, modern telecommunications, limousines, electricity and all the trappings of high-living.

You can park yourself down in a luxury hotel in Anchorage and be every bit as sealed off and distant from the natural world as the average Manhattanite. Or, you can leave the trappings of the late 20th century behind, and embark on an adventure in the biggest expanse of true wilderness in the United States and become a part of the natural world – feeling cold when it's cold, hot when it's hot, and adjusting your daily routine to accommodate the whims of the sub-artic Alaskan weather.

Once you get away from the cities, Alaska's rough edges become more apparent, and more of the distinctive character of the place comes through. To make up for the inconveniences of Alaska's harsh environment, the people are among the friendliest and most helpful you will find anywhere. It's a rare Alaskan indeed who is not willing and able to lend a hand in a highway emergency, point you in the direction of your next destination, or even to give you tips on how and where to catch that big salmon you came here to find.

All of these factors combine to draw hundreds of thousands of visitors to the state every year. People come from all over the world, by air, by ship, by ferry boat, by bus, car, and motorhome, to see the spectacle. Some visitors save up all their lives for one chance to visit

Fast Facts

Area: 586,412 sq miles (1,518,807 sq km). Alaska measures approximately 1,420 miles (2,286 km) north to south, and over 2,400 miles (3,864 km) east to west.
Population: 500,000 (1990 census).
Capital: Juneau
Government: United States Congress – two senators, one representative.
State legislature: 20 senators, 40 representatives.
Religions: Protestant, Roman Catholic, Byzantine Catholic, Russian Orthodox, Jewish, and Native Alaskan religious traditions.
People: Athabascan, Haida, Tlingit, and Tsimshian Indians, Inupiat and Yup'ik Eskimos, Aleut, Caucasian, African-American, Asian, Latino, Pacific Islanders.
Economy: Tourism, oil and gas, fishing, timber, mining, and agriculture.
Language: English in the cities, Native languages such as Inupiak and Yup'ik in the Bush villages.
Main IIndustry: Oil and gas exploration and production.
State Flower: Forget-me-not
State bird: Willow ptarmigan
State song: "Alaska's Flag"
Time zones: Most of the state is in the Alaska Time Zone, one hour behind Pacific Time, and the westernmost Aleutians and St. Lawrence Island are on Hawaii-Aleutian Time.
Access: The major cities are accessible by highway with the exceptions of the towns in Southeast Alaska. Anchorage, Fairbanks, Homer, Seward and many smaller towns in between are linked together by road, and to the North American road system by way of the Alaska Highway. However, the vast majority of Alaska's land area is reachable only by airplane, and the coastal and river communities by boat. The towns of Southeast Alaska are linked together to Bellingham, Washington and to the road system at Haines and Skagway by the Alaska Marine Highway, the state-run ferry system. The ferries also serve communities on Prince William Sound on the Kenai Peninsula, Kodiak Island, and the Alaska Peninsula and the Aleutians.
National Parks: There are more than 50 million acres of Alaska under the jurisdiction of the National Park Service, including national parks, preserves, and monuments. The most popular is Denali National Park, and the largest national park in the United States is Wrangell-St. Elias National Park, measuring 12 million acres.
Highest point: 20,320 feet (6,198 m), Mt. McKinley, the highest point in North America.
Coastline: Over 33,000 miles (53,130 km) of shoreline, more than the total for the lower 48 states of the continent.
Mountains: Of the 20 tallest mountains in the United States, 17 are found in Alaska.
Bodies of water: The third-longest river in the United States, the Yukon, is nearly 2,000 miles (3,220 km) in length. Alaska has more than 3,000 rivers, and more than 3,000,000 lakes.
Glaciers: There are more glaciers and ice fields in Alaska than in the rest of the populated world. Malaspina Glacier in Southeast Alaska measures

---

Alaska, others make annual pilgrimages and still do not grow tired of the many sights and sounds that Alaska has to offer.

Awe-inspiring Landscapes

Alaska has some of the most spectacular sceneries ever to grace the planet, in a variety of landforms, ecosystems and environments beyond the ordinary. There are magnificent mountain ranges, including the tallest peak in North America; vast tracts of tundra and open plains at times covered with caribou herds numbering in the tens of thousands; impenetrable forests of huge old growth trees, growing at the edge of deep fjords; over 33,000 miles (53,130

more than 850 sq miles (2,202 sq km).

Volcanoes: There are more than 70 active volcanoes in the state, many of them in the Aleutian Islands and on the Alaska Peninsula. Recent volcanic eruptions that have affected Alaska's populated areas include Mt. Spur in 1992 and Mt. Redoubt in 1989, both peaks are visible from Anchorage, and Augustine Volcano near Homer in 1986, the ash from which reached much of the Kenai Peninsula.

Earthquake: The Good Friday earthquake of March 27, 1964, measured a high of 8.4 on the Richter scale, the strongest quake ever measured in North America. Property damage from the earthquake was estimated at between 380 and 500 million US dollars, and at least 115 people lost their lives. Alaska is still geologically active today, and small to moderate quakes are not uncommon.

Extremes of climate: The highest recorded temperature in the state was 100°F (37.7°C), in Fort Yukon in 1915, the coldest -80°F (-2°C), set in 1971.

Daylight: Extremes of daylight hours, and also the lack of daylight, are the rule in Alaska. At Point Barrow, the northernmost point in the state, the sun sets on May 10, and rises again on August 2 for 84 day of continuous daylight.

From November 18 until January 24, for 67 days, the sun never rises above the horizon. In Ketchikan, more than 1,200 miles (1,932 km) to the south, daylight hours can vary from 17 1/2 hours on June 21 to just over seven hours on December 21.

St Nicholas Orthodox Church at a cosy corner of Juneau.

km) of shoreline, including sandy beaches, rock-strewn islands and sheer cliffsides covered with nesting sea birds; glaciers and icefields devoid of any signs of life with lakes and rivers too numerous to finger-count.

To inhabit this scenery, Alaska presents an array of living creatures to match the geography. On land, watching and keeping track of the large mammals alone can provide a lifetime's worth of delightful diversions. The caribou herds number more than three-quarters of a million animals; the moose, the largest member of the deer family, is found in most of the state's ecosystems, from the remote and forbidding Brooks Range to within sight of the skyscrapers of downtown Anchorage; clinging to cliffs and living in high mountain meadows are the snow white Dall sheep and mountain goats. Bears of three species, polar, black and brown/grizzly, are even more widely distributed than the ubiquitous moose, with very few exceptions, all of Alaska is bear country.

On and in the sea, more animals proliferate. Walruses, sea lions, and several species of seals live in Alaskan wa

Rocky pine covered cliffs rise above the waters of Resurrection Bay.

Touring Alaska

There are many number of different ways to see Alaska. You can arrange a pre-packaged tour, visiting another venue every other day, watching Alaska whiz past the windows of your airplane, train car, or bus. Or arrange a series of guided adventures, taking a helicopter ride to the top of a glacier one day, white-water rafting the next, followed by a fly-in fishing trip. You could also rent a motorhome and visit the road accessible portions of the state, self-contained and changing locations when it suits your mood. Or do everything yourself, climbing, hiking, skiing, fishing, camping, sightseeing, shopping, all to your own rhythms and desires.

While the vast majority of visitors thoroughly enjoy their Alaska vacations, there are occasional grumbles heard from a few dissatisfied customers. To fully appreciate all that the state has to offer, and to make sure that your stay is an enjoyable one, it's important to know what to expect, and what not to expect, during your visit.

For one thing, while Alaska is huge almost beyond comprehension, there are crowds in the more popular locations. During the summer, visitors arrive from all over the world to experience their desired chunk of the Alaska mystique, and residents do everything in their power to enjoy as much of the short intense summer as possible. This results in a concentration of effort,

ters, and often haul themselves onto beaches and rocks to bask in the sun; sea otters abound along much of the shoreline; whales of 14 species have been sighted in Alaska, with orcas (killer whales) and humpbacks, the most often seen by visitors; sea birds, waterfowl and shorebirds live on the shores or on the surface of the sea, gathering food and congregating noisily. Underwater, numbering in the millions, unseen except for when they are pulled to the surface by commercial or sport fishermen, there are fishes in fresh and salt water, fishes large and small, fishes of an amazing number of species and configurations, fishes everywhere. The waters of Alaska certainly present a challenge to the eager fishermen.

The serene smiles of young native Alaskans tell of a simple and harmonious life.

whether it is for fishing holes, hotel and car reservations, or air taxi and remote lodge accommodations. For these reasons, plan ahead before embarking on your journey.

If you are going to be backpacking in the Brooks Range, finding a spot to put up your tent north of the Arctic Circle would not be a problem. However, if you need a hotel room in Fairbanks on either end of the trip, a rental car while you are in town, and a flight service to take you to the mountains, you would have to arrange for these things as far in advance as is practical for you.

Nevertheless, there are still methods of getting away from the crowd – money and muscle. If you want to experience the solitude beyond the Gates of the Arctic National Park, prepare to spend on air power. The more you spend, the farther you fly and the less company you are likely to have. Or if you are limited to traveling on the road system, the more physical effort you put into getting away from the road, the lesser the likelihood of meeting someone. This is not to say that there are not lots of opportunities for contemplating the wonders of the Far North within reach of the "budgetarily challenged" or non-athletes, opportunities abound for the adventurous. So make your plans, dream your dreams, and enjoy your stay. The more of Alaska you see, the more you would want to see. You can never see it all, but it's worth trying.

History

During the Ice Age of the Pleistocene era, a period from 10,000 to 1,000,000 years ago, enormous ice sheets had covered large areas of North America. However, a lack of moisture in the region had prevented total ice coverage in Alaska. The Arctic coast including much of the interior have never been glaciated. The ice sheets that did exist, though, were massive, with depths estimated at up to a mile. This locking up of such a huge quantity of moisture lowered the depth of the surrounding seas by approximately 300 ft (92 m), exposing a land bridge across the Bering Strait. With the successive formation and melting of glacial ice sheets, it is postulated that the land bridge has been exposed for at least three different periods.

Pioneers monument in the old town of Sitka.

The Ancestors

When the Beringia land bridge existed, it served as a thousand-mile wide connection to the Asian conti

A tribute to the Eskimo families who braved the land.

Totem Heritage Center, Ketchikan.

nent, a pathway for animals and people. According to some anthropological theories, human migrations took place in three separate stages. Between 15,000 and 25,000 years ago the first migration brought the ancestors of most of the Indian tribes in the lower 48 states of present day America. Between 9,000 and 14,000 years ago, the second migration brought the ancestors of Alaskan Indians, and the final migration, from 5,000 to 10,000 years ago, the ancestors of Eskimo and Aleut peoples.

A division between coastal and interior Eskimos developed. While both groups still hunted caribou, coastal residents had greater access to the wide variety of marine life while interior Eskimos depended largely on salmon for their fish supplies.

This caused the lifestyles of the two groups to evolve differently, as interior residents were forced to stay on the move in order to maintain contact with the herds of caribou, while coastal peoples were able to establish more permanent settlements and to pursue whales, seal, and walruses from their villages. The two groups were not entirely separate, though, and evidence exists of contact and trade between them.

The Eskimos and the Indians

Today, Eskimos are divided into two main groupings, the Inupiat Eskimos of

Klondike Gold Rush

Klondike Gold Company – a memorabilia of the gold rush days.

In 1896 a gold strike at Bonanza Creek in Canada's Klondike region started one of the world's largest gold rushes. When the ships carrying the first of the lucky prospectors arrived at Seattle and San Francisco in 1897, word of the Klondike gold strikes had spread like wild fire across the continent. The town of Dawson was established at the junction of the Yukon and Klondike Rivers, and became the center for mining activity in the area. Dawson grew to accommodate over 40,000 people, the largest city west of Chicago and north of San Francisco.

Access to the gold fields was by way of overland trails beginning in Southeast Alaska including the Chilkoot Trail from Dyea, the White Pass Trail from Skagway, the Dalton or Chilkat Trail from Haines, the Stikine River Trail to Telegraph, and the Valdez Glacier Trail from Valdez, nick-named the "all-American" trail. Over 4,000 people landed at the Valdez trailhead alone in 1898.

The Chilkoot Trail from Dyea and the White Pass Trail from Skagway were the most popular routes to the gold fields. The Chilkoot Trail is shorter but steeper, and prospectors could use pack animals on the White Pass Trail. To ensure that the gold seekers were adequately provisioned, the Canadian government required that each person carry one year's worth of supplies with him into the region. In the days long before the invention of freeze-dried food, aluminum pack frames, and lightweight cold weather clothing, such a load could easily weigh tons, and the trips over the passes were, to say the least, strenuous.

Towns such as Nome and Dawson were established in the gold regions. Supply points such as Haines, Valdez, and Juneau grew into cities, and boom conditions dictated the growth of the local population and the services that followed. While few of the prospectors struck it rich, the merchants and camp followers who

the north, and the Yup'ik Eskimos of western Alaska. The other native peoples of Alaska include the Athabascan Indians of the interior, the Aleuts, and the Tlingit and Haida Indians of Southeast Alaska.

The Aleut people of the Aleutian Islands are closely related to the Eskimos, both physically and culturally. Over a period of three to six thousand years, the Aleuts evolved separately from the Eskimos. By the time the first Russians chanced upon the Aleutian Islands, there were Aleut villages on all of the habitable Aleutian islands, their total population estimated at 15-20,000 people. Contact with foreigners was disastrous for the Aleuts and by 1840 the population was decimated, declining to an estimated 4,000 individuals due to

provided supplies and services did quite well. Real estate speculators sold and re-sold plots of land. Packers rented out pack stock at exorbitant rates. Gamblers and dance hall girls eventually followed, eager to relieve the newly rich of their gold dust and nuggets.

Disappointed gold miners who failed to make their fortune in the Klondike spread out all over Alaska looking for the next bonanza. Some of them actually hit pay dirt. Gold was found near Fairbanks, on the Kenai Peninsula, and on the beaches at Nome, among many other places. The Nome strike in 1900 became the next major gold rush, drawing most of the prospectors away from the Klondike and leaving the development of mines in the region to the large and established corporations.

The route from Skagway to the Yukon over White Pass appealed to a group of investors who saw the need for a railroad. They secured financing, and with little pre-construction surveying, sent their crews to the area. The construction of the 110 mile-long (177 km) narrow gauge railway posed a formidable technical challenge to the builders, but they overcame the problems of steep cliffs, massive rocks, terrible weather, labor unrest, and pesky bears to complete the project. The route from Skagway to Whitehorse was celebrated with a ceremonial driving of a golden spike on July 29, 1900. The first railroad built in Alaska survives to this day, and the passenger service on the White Pass at Yukon Route to White Pass Summit is a popular tourist attraction.

disease and harsh treatment at the hands of the Russians.

The panhandle region of Southeast Alaska is dotted with islands separated by deep, fast tidal waters, and the mainland is steep and heavily forested. Natives in the region developed a lifestyle dependent on boats and access to the coastal waters. The Tlingit Indians moved south to the area from mainland

Nunamiut Eskimo Cemetery – in the embrace of blue skies.

Alaska, and the Haidas moved north from the Queen Charlotte Island region of coastal British Columbia. The land and the sea provided a rich variety of food sources, and trade and contact between Haidas and Tlingits were common. They also discovered access routes through the coastal mountain ranges by which they traded with Indians in the interior. Their societies differed from many other native cultures in that much emphasis was placed on the acquiring of personal wealth. Most native cultures practiced a form of socialism but the Indians of Southeast Alaska were more attuned to a capitalistic lifestyle.

The Athabascan Indians are thought to be related to the Indians of the American Southwest. They inhab-

Nunamiut Eskimos go through thick and thin together.

ited the great forests of the interior, and have traditionally depended on caribou, fresh water fish, and small game as food sources. With a range spreading from northwestern Canada to the lower Yukon and Kuskokwim Rivers in western Alaska, the 11 different groups of Athabascans adapted well to a wide variety of sub-arctic environments. They used the network of rivers to move nomadically to follow the caribou, and to trade with one another as well as with interior and coastal Eskimos.

Russian Explorers and the Fur Trade

When Peter the Great ascended to the throne of Russia, a scholarly debate over the question of Asia's connection to the American mainland was unresolved. To settle the question, and to undertake a voyage of discovery, Peter commissioned Vitus Bering, a Dane in Russian service, to explore the area east of Russia's Kamchatka peninsula. Peter never got to see the fruits of his royal plan – he died very soon after assigning Bering to the formidable task of exploration, and his widow, Catherine I, continued to support the Bering expedition.

In 1741, Vitus Bering and Aleksei Chirikov, commanding the ships *St. Peter* and *St. Paul*, left from their base at Avacha Bay on the Kamchatka peninsula to explore the American coast and to determine if Asia and America were

A portrait of early Russian explorer, Baranov on the walls of Baranov Museum, Kodiak.

indeed joined together. As they neared America, the ships were separated in the fog, and soon lost track of one another. On July 15, Chirikov's party sighted land, and the captain sent a small boat ashore for fresh water. When that boat failed to return, he sent another, which also disappeared. After waiting several days for the missing crewmen, and low on water, Chirikov gave up and returned to Kamchatka, assuming that his men had been killed by "savages".

Meanwhile, Captain Bering sighted the mainland on July 16, most probably at Mt. St. Elias. He sent two parties ashore on an island to explore and to find water. The parties discovered Native-built structures, hastily abandoned by their occupants, and took some dried salmon they found there, leaving behind tobacco and a pipe in payment. George Steller, scientist and natural historian had headed one of the parties. He was however, unable to indulge his scientific curiosity to his satisfaction as Bering abruptly ordered the shore parties aboard and cast off for home before even filling his water casks to capacity.

Bering's ship made contact with some Alaska Natives on September 4 as the ship island-hopped around the Aleutian chain. After a shore crew's near escape from the Natives, the ship continued on its way towards home port. By this time, low on water and with a crew beset by scurvy, things looked grim indeed for the *St. Peter*. Eventually the ship

The sea otter fur trade brought about the first wave of colonisation.

ran aground on an island east of Kamchatka. The crew was forced to stay over winter. Captain Bering and most of the remaining crew died there. During the time they were forced to remain, the crew discovered a large sea otter population, a discovery that were to have enormous ramifications for the fur trade, and for the further exploration of the north Pacific.

When the survivors reached Kamchatka the following spring, they brought news of Bering's death and of the sea otter discovery. The island was named "Bering" in honor of their commander. Soon, ships seeking their fortune in fur set out for Bering Island and proceeded from there to the Aleutian Islands. The Russians eventually established a profitable trade in furs, and Aleut Natives often paid the price for resisting the armed foreigners. By 1783, when Russians discovered Prince William Sound, the fur trade in the Aleutians was brisk indeed. Eventually, the Russians worked their way down the coast of the mainland, following the range of the sea otter into present-day southeast Alaska. They soon discovered fur seals to add to their list of prey species, as well as arctic foxes and river otters. The foxes were so docile that they could be taken by hand. The Russians also took walrus for their ivory, and whales for whalebone.

In 1799, the Russian American Company was formed as Russia's unofficial arm in Alaska. The company was

A tale of tradition – Russian dancer in red scarf.

granted a charter to do business in Alaska, to trade with foreign governments, and to colonize the area and spread Russian influence. The charter was renewable every 20 years and operated in Alaska until the sale to the United States in 1867.

European Voyages

News of the riches to be had in the far northwest corner of America soon reached Europe, and the Spanish, French and English sent ships to investigate Alaska's potential. Several French and Spanish expeditions visited the area in the years between 1775 and 1792.

The Spanish sent ships in 1774 and 1775 and one of them reached the area near Sitka in 1775. The Spaniards explored Southeast Alaska, encountering natives near Chichagof Island and claiming Prince of Wales Island for Spain. But Spain's position as a world power was declining and the Spaniards influence on the region was slight. Eventually Spain ceded the rights of her Alaskan interests to England. Today the names of Malaspina Glacier, Revillagigedo Island and the town names of Valdez and Cordova commemorate the early Spanish explorers.

French explorers also visited the Alaskan waters, although their eventual influence was negligible. The French explorer La Perouse visited Alaskan waters in 1786, making landfall near Mount St. Elias. After some coastal explorations and losing two shore boats and crews to the treacherous tidal currents, La Perouse left Alaska for Mexico.

The English, still searching for the elusive northwest passage, sent Captain James Cook up the Pacific coast. He reached Prince William Sound in May of 1778, and from there proceeded around the Kenai Peninsula

The Problem of Subsistence

Gold panning! A young man's dream.

The question of subsistence, what exactly constitutes subsistence and who may choose to pursue such a way of living continue to bedevil Alaskans. In "the old days", there was no question about this issue. If a person chose to live in the Bush, away from the trappings of civilization, he or she took whatever forms of food from the land that were available. Natives lived this way for thousands of years, living off the land, feasting in times of abundance, starving or moving on when supplies of fish or meat became scarce. With the coming of the white man, things began to get complicated, which should come as no surprise to anyone. While the occasional trapper or gold miner could live in a remote cabin and harvest fish, game, and other wild foods without having much impact on the land, large numbers of white men concentrated in cities changed the situation radically. Before too long, concepts like hunting and fishing seasons and bag limits became necessary. There was not adequate stocks of fish and game around to allow everyone to take all the wild food he or she wanted all the time. Eventually the situation stabilized to the point where people living in urban areas were considered sport hunters and fishers, and were governed by strict laws concerning seasons, bag limits, and other restrictions to limit the number of animals taken. People who lived in the Bush were considered subsistence users, and were allowed more leeway in the hunting and fishing regulations. This took into account the assumption that every one, Native and non-Native, living in the Bush was taking fish and game for food, and not for sport purposes.

A provision of the 1980 passage of the Alaska National Interest Lands Conservation ACT (ANILCA) stated that rural residents were to be given priority in the taking of fish and game when supplies became scarce. Federal law cannot grant preferences based on race, so allowing only Alaska Natives to live the subsistence lifestyle was not an option. At first, this

looking for a route north. He went on to explore what is now known as Cook Inlet near Anchorage, headed south out of the Inlet and up the west coast of Alaska, eventually exploring parts of the Aleutians, and as far north as Icy Cape, above 70 degrees north latitude. Captain Cook then went south, bound for the Hawaiian Islands where he met his death.

The Russians eventually established cities, hospitals, and missions in the southeast, the Aleutians, and on Kodiak island, to support the fur trade. From 1741 until 1867, when Alaska was sold to the United States, the hospitals had

meshed well with state laws. However, distinctions based on location present an oversimplification. Urban residents eat the fish and game they take, while many rural residents now have access to stores and money. Should a school teacher who makes US$50,000 a year and lives in one of the larger villages, complete with access to electricity, running water, grocery stores, television, telephones, and daily jet service to Anchorage and Outside, be considered a subsistence user just because he shoots a moose once in a while?

Further complicating the picture is the Alaska constitution, which guarantees equal treatment under the law to all Alaskans – both Natives and non-Natives. When a group of urban sportsmen brought suit claiming that they were discriminated against because they were denied access to fish and game based on where they chose to live, the issue had to be brought to the court. Now the question facing the courts and the Alaska legislature is that since the state constitution is in direct conflict with ANILCA, therefore something has got to give. Changing the provisions of a federal law so that Anchorage hunters can shoot more moose is not likely to sail through congress. On the other hand, amending the state constitution in the face of perceived bullying by the feds is not a very likely scenario given the Alaskan resistance to federal control, either. So, with the federal government, state government, federal and state courts, Native corporations, and urban hunters and fishers all thrown together into a complicated situation, only time will tell who "wins". Besides the lawyers, that is.

offered free treatment to the local natives, including smallpox vaccine.

"Seward's Folly": The US Buys Alaska

Declining sea otter populations and in-

Captain James Cook heralded the arrival of the English.

creasing logistical costs made the Russian government reconsider its objectives in Alaska. The ventures in Alaska were no longer profitable, and as the United States continued its growth, defending Russian interests in Alaska became almost impractical. After negotiations with the U.S. government on April 9, 1867 the United States Senate voted to purchase Alaska from Russia for US$7.2 million. Widely criticized at the time as a waste of money, Alaska was referred to as "Seward's Folly" and "Seward's Icebox", after William Seward, the American Secretary of State. The U.S. took possession of Alaska in Sitka on October 18, 1867, and the region was placed under military rule. After the transfer, the U.S. Army sent troops to the

Robust-looking buildings that once housed the gold-seekers of Skagway.

former Russian settlements at Sitka, Wrangell, Tongass Island, Kenai, Kodiak, and the Pribilofs. These posts were soon abandoned in an economic move, and by 1870, Sitka was the only garrison left.

American companies soon realized the potential of Alaska's plentiful salmon resource. Canneries were built in the southeast, at Cook Inlet, and in 1884 the first cannery in Bristol Bay was built. By 1896 there were altogether 35 canneries in Alaska.

Gold!

Gold was first discovered in the Cassiar district of Canada in 1873. A gold strike on Bonanza Creek in the Klondike region started the largest of the Canadian gold rushes in 1896. The Klondike gold rush, popularly known as 'the last grand adventure' in those days, came at an opportune time when the world was hit by a severe recession. A large number of people simply threw in their lot in search of a fast fortune, and joined the gold rush trails across miles of highlands to Southeast Alaska. Of course, while prospectors were many, not all were gratified and quite a number had to return home, broke and disillusioned. Access to the gold fields was by way of overland trails beginning in southeast Alaska, including the Chilkoot Trail from Dyea, the White Pass Trail from Skagway, the Dalton or Chilkat Trail from Haines, the

The Alaska Railway – a major boost to the economy.

occupy the territory to protect American interests, since the exact location of the border with Canada was in dispute. The Army established garrisons at Dyea in 1897 and in the interior at Forts Gibbon and Egbert in 1899.

By 1881, Juneau was a boom town, and the locals began to see a need for some form of government. A representative was chosen to travel to Washington and present the case for the institution of a territorial government. After two years of lobbying, military rule in Alaska came to an end with the passage of the First Organic Act in 1884, establishing a civil and judicial district with Sitka as the seat of government. The laws of the state of Oregon were to be the laws of the district where applicable. However, Alas-

Stikine River Trail to Telegraph, and the Valdez Glacier Trail from Valdez. Over 4,000 people landed at the Valdez trailhead alone in 1898. Boom conditions dictated the growth of the local population and the services that followed as towns such as Nome, Fairbanks, and Dawson were established in the gold regions, and supply points such as Haines, Valdez, and Juneau quickly grew into cities.

In 1880, a major Alaskan gold strike near the present-day location of Juneau, led to that town's establishment. Subsequent gold strikes near Sitka, on the Kenai peninsula, and near the mouth of the Fortymile River off the Yukon River encouraged further exploration. The United States ordered Army troops to

Ruins of the Alaska-Juneau Gold Mine, a shade of past glory.

HISTORY

21

Soapy Smith

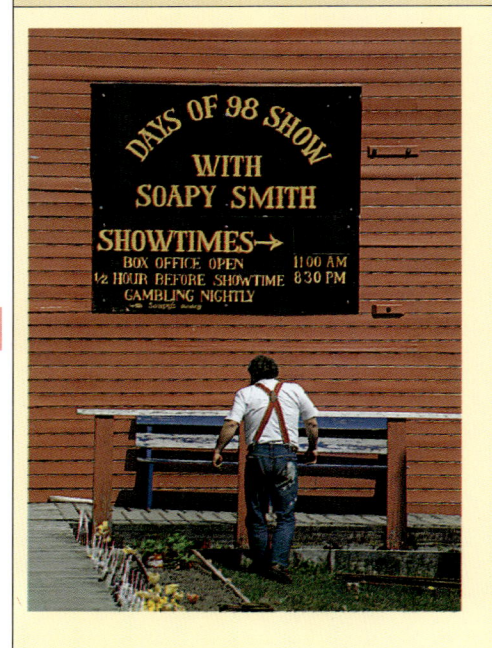

"Soapy's place."

When the eager "cheechakos", or newcomers to Alaska, hit the town of Skagway on their way to the Klondike, many of them were outfitted with fresh new clothes from Seattle and San Francisco, and were ready to head over the passes to the gold fields. As they saw it, they would soon join ranks with successful prospectors who had made their fortunes. All they needed, or so they thought, were some provisions and a little luck, and they would be on their way to lifelong financial security.

However, for the vast majority of the hopeful, this was not to be. Before they could begin prospecting, there was the enormous physical hardship of getting their small mountains of gear over the steep and treacherous White Pass Trail. They arrived in Skagway at the foot of the trail, often with full wallets, gullible and wide-eyed over their prospects.

Before they could even hope to begin their trip to the riches of the Klondike, they had to first get past the temptations and hazards of the town of Skagway. This was no easy task. Thanks in a large part to the efforts of one Jefferson Randolph "Soapy" Smith.

Soapy Smith was a confidence man, gang leader, gambler, and self-styled civic leader. He arrived in Skagway in 1897 to find a lawless, boisterous town of nearly 10,000 occupants. There were a few legitimate local businesses catering to the prospectors, as well as saloons, prostitutes, money lenders and other such camp followers as would usually found themselves ensconced in boom towns.

Conditions were ripe for Soapy's brand of opportunism. Since the town provided the only access to the White Pass Trail, Smith had a captive audience for his shenanigans. Many of the gold rushers were stuck in town due to winter trail conditions, making for easy pickings by an accomplished criminal and he was able to fleece his subjects both coming and going.

Soapy and his henchmen were adept at criminal enterprises of every sort, from selling illegal liquor and setting up a bogus telegraph shop to the less refined art of strong-arm robbery. While he was surreptitiously controlling his criminal empire, he was also paying lip service to the cause of law and order, as well as performing civic good deeds such as taking up collections for widows, adopting stray dogs, and organizing a "law and order" committee. His public persona differed significantly from his behind-the-scenes deeds, and he carried on his daily life on two levels. He justified his fleecing of newcomers and then sending them on their way back to where they had come from as a sort of weeding out of the weak from the strong. He was actually doing these men a favor by saving them from the ravages of the North, for which they were obviously unprepared!

Smith's reign in Skagway peaked when he installed himself as grand marshal of the Fourth of July parade in 1898, leading a parade of prospective Spanish-American War volunteers down the main street on the back of a majestic gray horse.

Nevertheless, Smith's reign was short, ending just four day later in the only too common shoot-out spree of the wild west.

The end of his reign came when a successful prospector returning from the Klondike took his pouch of hard-earned gold to Smith's place of business for appraisal. An invitation to go out back of the store, supposedly to have a look at Soapy's "famous stuffed eagle" resulted in a scuffle, much confusion, and the disappearance of the young man's sack. Soapy protested his innocence, but the man was not mollified.

After an unsuccessful plea to the town marshal, who was in Soapy's employ, he took his grievance to a vigilante committee. A mob soon formed, and a drunken Soapy Smith confronted one of the leaders, Frank Reid, armed with a rifle and a pair of revolvers. The resulting shoot-out killed Soapy outright, and a mortally wounded Reid who died 12 days later. Soapy Smith's days as the scourge of Skagway were over.

However, his legend lives on, commemorated annually in Skagway on July 8 with Soapy Smith's Wake, held in the graveyard where he was buried.

The end of Soapy Smith's reign.

ka's ability to rule itself was quite limited, and with no congressional representation, had little way to make the wants and desires of its residents known in Washington.

As the region grew with population increases from gold exploration and mining, Juneau eclipsed Sitka as the population center of the southeast, and in 1905, Juneau was established as Alaska's capital. Desire for home rule gathered momentum, and in 1912, Congress established Alaska as an organized territory with the passage of the Second Organic Act.

When the territorial legislature of eight senators and 16 representatives met, the issue of revenue came up early. Mining interests predominated among the legislators, so of course the first industry they sought to tax was fishing. By taxing salmon packaged by canneries, and by levying occupational taxes, the legislature sought to provide sufficient revenue for the new government entities. The salmon industry fought the taxation on legal grounds for many years, but eventually, as is so often the case, the government won.

Not content with the restrictions placed on them as a territorial entity, many Alaskans began to see the benefits of statehood as the answer to dealing with the federal government in faraway Washington D.C. In 1916, Delegate James Wickersham introduced the first of many Alaska statehood bills as a way for the residents of Alaska to control their own destinies and resources.

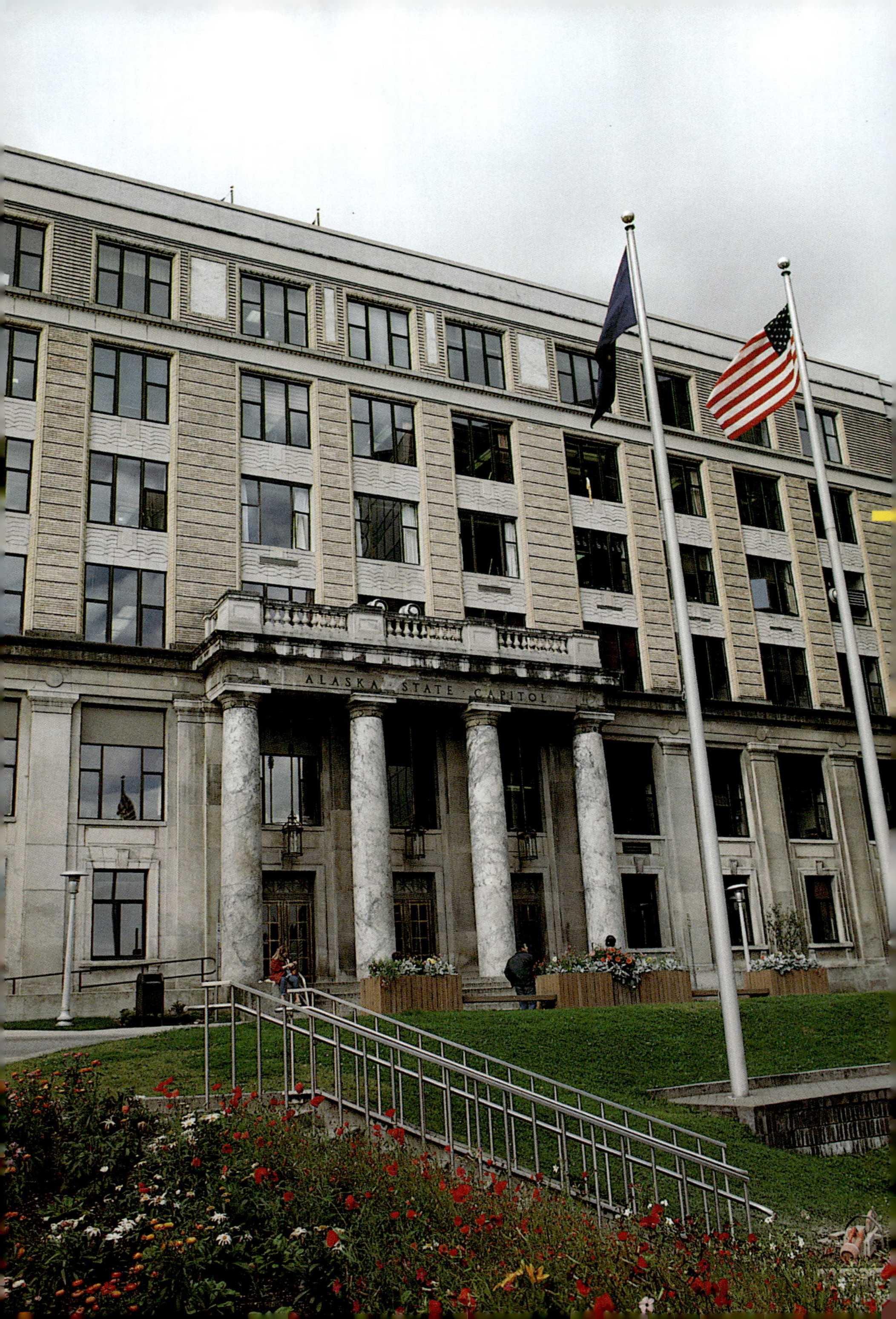
ALASKA STATE CAPITOL

SETTLEMENTS TO STATEHOOD

Government

The first significant settlement in the upper Cook Inlet area was Knik, on the west side of Knik Arm. Advertising itself with the slogan, "Travel by way of 'Sunny Knik', the California of Alaska," it was the primary jumping-off point for travelers to the Interior. However, when the federal government built a railroad connecting Fairbanks to Seward, the selection of a Cook Inlet railhead site on the west side of the inlet put an end to Knik's growth prospects. The railhead which had started out as a tent city called Ship Creek for its location at the mouth of that stream, soon evolved into the popular town of Anchorage. The town of Knik withered away with the ascendancy of Anchorage but a small rural community remains to this day along a spur road leading from Wasilla.

The construction of the government-owned railroad did much to provide access to Alaska's interior. The coal fields of the Matanuska Valley were opened up to mining, and by 1923

Alaska State Capitol building standing tall and proud in Juneau.

The Alaskan State Flag braving the cold winds.

the route linking Seward and Anchorage to Fairbanks was completed. The new railroad was not successful (operated under government subsidy). In the 1980s, the operation was turned over to the state of Alaska, and the 470 mile-long system between Seward and Fairbanks continues today to provide freight and passenger services along its historic route.

By 1940, Alaska's population stood at 72,000 and military presence in the territory consisted of a garrison of 200 infantry soldiers at Fort Seward near Haines. At that time, Haines was not connected by road to the Interior, and the soldiers depended on an asthmatic old harbor tug for transportation. However, with the advent of the Second World War, Alaska's military significance altered profoundly, and had a lasting impact on development and population dynamics.

World War II

As world tensions increased with the German and Japanese military build-ups, military leaders and Alaska's lone Congressional Delegate emphasized Alaska's strategic location, and agitated for additional military presence. The Navy began work on submarine and seaplane bases at Kodiak and at Dutch Harbor in the Aleutians, but a proposed Army base for Anchorage was denied by Congress in April of 1940. When Hitler invaded Denmark and Norway later that month, the Senate Appropriations Committee reconsidered, and the following month, approved the spending for the initial construction of Fort Richardson and Elmendorf Field. However, by December 7, 1941 when the Japanese attacked Pearl Harbor, no army or navy facility in Alaska was ready for war. Furthermore, the Territory still had no road or rail links to the rest of the United States.

In June of 1942, airplanes from a Japanese aircraft carrier bombed the Dutch Harbor in the Aleutians and the accompanying task force sent ground forces ashore to occupy Attu and Kiska Islands. A patrol plane had spotted the carrier force proceeding towards the Aleutians the day before the bombing attack, and the alerted submarine base met the planes with anti-aircraft fire. Little damage was done to the base, but foreign forces had launched an attack on American soil.

The battle for the Aleutians continued until August of 1943, with American forces eventually landing on and re-taking both Attu and Kiska. Casualties were high for the Japanese and the Americans, numbering in thousands for both sides.

The logistical difficulties of defending an area nearly 2,000 miles from Seattle emphasized the need for a highway link. In nine months ending in November of 1942, a combined military and civilian effort managed to construct a 1,420 mile (2,286 km) long road through the Alaskan and Canadian wilderness. Dubbed the Alcan Highway, the initial effort was crude but effective. For the first time, Alaska was joined with the rest of the North American road system.

After the threat to the Aleutians ended, American military efforts were directed elsewhere. Unlike the experiences of other combatant nations, the lasting effects of the war here consisted largely of improvements rather than devastation. Many roads, railroads, airfields, and marine facilities were turned over to the Territory for civilian use, and a large number of military personnel decided either to stay in Alaska or to return someday. The permanent population increased significantly, and the population center shifted from Southeast Alaska to Anchorage.

Post-War Construction

After the war, the civilian economy returned to a peacetime, seasonal basis, and the military economy boomed with Cold War construction projects. With America's former ally the Soviet Union now a very close presence just across the Bering Strait, Alaska retained its strategic military importance. Army and Air Force bases were built or expanded, communications and radar networks were developed, and military personnel and civilian workers arrived in large numbers. The 1950 census showed 128,600 residents, and Anchorage's population

GOVERNMENT

The Matanuska Colony

Summer blossoms at Matanuska Valley.

As a prospective site for an agricultural project, Alaska seems about as likely a place as the moon for growing crops. However, Alaska does have a farm economy, and although it has seen better days, a few hardy folks manage to make a living coaxing life out of the soil.

The two main agricultural areas are the Tanana Valley near Fairbanks, and the Matanuska Valley north of Anchorage. The primary crop in the Tanana area is barley, grown mainly as agricultural feed. The Mat Valley is home to vegetable farms, producing potatoes and the giant-sized cabbages beloved by photographers and postcard printers.

Cabbages and other plenteous produce illustrate the fact that, while Alaska's climate is not conducive to growing some kinds of vegetables, the ones that do grow here grow very well. The good soil, ample rainfall, and very long days are just the ticket for cole crops such as cabbage, broccoli, and cauliflower, and for growing potatoes. Plants that require high temperatures such as corn and tomatoes will only grow with the aid of greenhouses or with a lot of very careful tending by patient, meticulous devoted gardeners.

Once upon a time, the federal government had much more grandiose plans for farming the Matanuska Valley. In the 1930s, the United States suffered from both the Depression and a severe drought in the Midwest. In an attempt to expand the frontier in Alaska and to give drought-stricken farmers from the Lower 48 a second chance at living off the land, the Federal Emergency Relief Administration, egged on by local boosters in Anchorage, conceived a bold master plan.

The idea was to transplant 200 families to Alaska, give them enough government aid to get them started, and then allow them to develop into self-sufficient farmers, supplying Anchorage and surrounding areas with fresh,

jumped from the 3,500 counted in 1939 to over 11,000 in 1950.

Military spending formed the largest part of the Alaskan economy throughout the 1950s, and fishing and mining continued to support many workers. In 1954 a large pulp mill was built in Ketchikan, and in 1957, oil was discovered on the Kenai Peninsula.

Statehood

With a growing economy and a burgeoning population, the drive for statehood gained momentum. Tired of being considered "second-class citizens", Alaskans loathed dealing with what many perceived to be an uninterested

locally grown produce. However, like more than a few other government projects, things just never quite worked out according to plan.

In 1935, 200 families selected from farm regions in Wisconsin, Michigan, and Minnesota made the trip north. The colonists were met with enthusiasm in Seward and Anchorage where the local folks were convinced that the attention from the government and the attendant publicity boded well for Alaska's plans for the future. The families chose lots for the available farm tracts on May 23, and before the end of June, telegrams were being sent from the colony complaining about the conditions. By the end of June nine families were ready to leave. Not an auspicious beginning.

Most of the families chose to stay saving the plan, and by the end of December, housing for the remaining 164 families were completed. In the following years, more families dropped out of the project but additional residents were recruited to take their places. However, the harsh farming and living conditions, the lack of amenities, and the remoteness of the area slowly took their toll. The undertaking evolved from a "colony", a co-operative, idealistic showcase into a collection of independent farmers who just happened to be in Alaska. By the time the Second World War had come and gone, the original colony was no more, although some of the families and the improvements on the land remained behind.

The final legacy of the original Matanuska Colony is of a romantic, idealized notion that just never quite worked out.

and remote federal bureaucracy. Frustrated residents wanted all the rights and privileges granted to the 48 states, and a measure of local control over their resources and destiny.

As a way to show the people in Washington that they were serious about the issue, a constitutional convention was held in 1955. A state constitution was drafted and passed by a two-to-one ratio of the voters in 1956.

Partisan politics raised its ugly head in the national debate but to no one's surprise. With the Republicans holding the White House under President Eisenhower, Alaska's bid for statehood competed with Hawaii's similar quest. Hawaii was perceived to be a more Republican state, while Alaska was thought likely to elect Democrats, so a good deal of political deal-making took place. After going through the usual prolonged process of congressional shenanigans, statehood for Alaska was signed into law on January 3, 1959.

Alaska Native Claims Settlement Act

The discovery of an enormous oil field near Prudhoe Bay in 1968 triggered the next boom in the perennial boom-and-bust Alaskan economy. The effects of this development continue to this day, but few could have predicted its extensive consequences at the time. The impact on Alaska Natives was particularly profound, and quite unique.

The issue of native land rights had been under discussion for a number of years. Issues concerning which lands were owned by the federal government, which were owned by the state of Alaska, and which were owned by the Natives who had lived and subsisted on the land for centuries was a complex and emotional issue. Before the chance discovery

Foundation stone commemorating the first United States presidential visit.

of oil on the North Slope, there was little real impetus for a quick resolution of the problem. It was not until oil was found, and when title to the land between the oil fields and the port became a hotly debated issue, that an expeditious solution became critical.

Once the oil was discovered, the impending question of how to transport it to market arose. Since Prudhoe Bay is on the shores of the Arctic Ocean and very nearly as far north as you can go in Alaska, the transportation issue loomed as a huge technological challenge waiting to be solved. More so because the area was locked up by ice for most of the year, shipping oil from a Prudhoe Bay oil terminal was out of the question.

However, the seemingly simple solution of building a pipeline to the closest deep water, year-around port at Valdez was not as simple as it looked at first glance. Besides the technical difficulties of constructing a huge pipeline for nearly 800 miles (1,288 km) over permafrost, tundra, wetlands, and the considerable obstacle posed by the Brooks Range of mountains, there was also a question as to who, exactly, owned the land between Prudhoe and Valdez.

The decision arrived at by the government agencies, the oil companies, conservation groups, and Native representatives created 13 Native regional corporations under the Alaska Native Claims Settlement Act (ANCSA). Twelve of the corporations were established based on traditional Native land uses,

The Alaskan police force is fortunate enough to face one of the country's lowest crime rate.

and the thirteenth represented Natives who no longer resided in Alaska. These corporations received shares of a settlement totaling nearly a billion dollars and the rights to select lands from a pool of over 100 million acres. In exchange, the Natives had to relinquish title to the disputed areas. Every US citizen with at least one-fourth Alaska Native blood became a shareholder in one of the corporations, but restrictions on sale and transfer of the stocks were written into the law to guard against unscrupulous take-overs by non-Natives.

With the land claims settled, the oil fields at Prudhoe could be tapped and the oil delivered to markets in the lower 48 states, and Alaska's next economic boom got underway.

ANILCA

The Alaska Native Claims Settlement Act was neither a panacea for the Natives, the non-Native Alaskans, nor for the state and federal governments. Rather than solving all of the land use problems in the state, it merely created a whole new batch of them. When the Natives gave up title to much of their ancestral territory, a brand new problem arose, namely traditional hunting and fishing rights on the land that was signed over in the ANCSA agreement. Just because a Native corporation no longer "owned" a piece of land, did that mean that the local Native residents could no longer hunt and fish on these

Environmentalists & Economists

The Kenai National Wildlife Refuge, a triumph for the environmentalists.

Ever since the first commercially viable oil wells were drilled in the Swanson River oil fields on the Kenai Peninsula, conservationists have voiced concerns about the effects of oil development on local wildlife. The Kenai was and is prime moose habitat, although this has not always been the case. When the first settlers arrived on the Kenai, the dominant big game animal was the caribou. However, caribou are not very tolerant of the near presence of man and the inevitable habitat disturbances. After several widespread fires on the peninsula and meat hunting by the settlers, caribou were reduced to a remnant population. The homely but hardy moose thrived in the new environment, subsisting on newly emerging willow and birch shoots. Eventually the northwest corner of the peninsula was reserved as a refuge, and was christened the Kenai National Moose Range.

It was on this very Moose Range that oil was discovered in 1957. The decision by the federal government to allow drilling on a wildlife refuge was controversial. After all, the purpose of the Moose Range was to protect the moose from excessive human encroachments. However, development of the oil resource was considered critical to Alaska's economy, and for garnering attention for home rule and to bid for statehood. After stipulating certain environmental restrictions, work was allowed to commence. Effects on the local moose population were apparently minimal, statehood was secured two years later and in 1980 the refuge was renamed the Kenai National Wildlife Refuge and expanded to nearly 2 million acres.

The next major dispute arose with the discovery of the Prudhoe Bay oil field in 1968. Once the size of this enormous find was determined, concerns arose over how to get the oil out of the ground and safely deliver it over land and sea. The most direct route was an 800 mile-long pipeline to Valdez on Prince William Sound, where crude oil will be loaded onto tankers for shipment to west coast refineries. But environmentalists favored building a pipeline from the North Slope across Canada to the Lower 48, thus avoiding the potential dangers of shipping oil by sea. However the problems of securing land rights for the direct line to America proved insurmountable, and the Trans-Alaska Pipeline System (TAPS) from Prudhoe to Valdez was

lands as their ancestors had been doing for thousands of years?

In an attempt at solving the puzzle, President Carter signed the Alaska National Interest Lands Conservation Act (ANILCA) in 1980 to set aside over 100 million acres as expanded National Parks and National Wildlife Refuges. Under the terms of the new law, hunting was restricted to rural subsistence hunters, a move that angered a large number of urban hunters, a group not without political influence. This federal law was interpreted as being in direct conflict

eventually approved.

Environmentalists, however, tried to block construction of the pipeline, using a variety of legal strategies. Pipeline construction was in limbo for several years, until the OPEC oil embargo of 1973 provided Congress with an incentive to overrule the environmental obstacles to construction of the pipeline.

Environmentalists were able to secure major modifications in pipeline design and construction. In caribou migration areas, the pipe had to be raised far enough off the ground to allow the animals to pass underneath, and where the pipe was to be buried in permafrost regions, insulation and refrigeration were used to avoid melting the ground. Work got underway in 1974, and by the time the first oil flowed through the pipe in 1977, the final cost of construction came in at $8 billion. Although large portions of the money were spent on outside contractors and workers, a substantial amount stayed in Alaska, providing a windfall for the state and for local economies.

Oil drilling in the Arctic National Wildlife Refuge (ANWR), east of Prudhoe Bay has become the latest battleground of economy vs. environment. The oil industry is eager to explore the region more thoroughly after some preliminary studies, but concerns over environmental matters especially the disturbance to the calving grounds of the great Porcupine caribou herd have once again raised the thorny issue. Is the potential economic benefit worth the environmental risks?

The issue is far from being settled, and once again Congress will be pressured by the opposing sides, with final results determined by a combination of political, economic, judicial, and environmental factors.

with the Alaska State Constitution. While ANILCA gave preferential hunting and fishing privileges to rural residents, where a large proportion are Alaska Natives, the Alaska constitution actually forbids this sort of unequal treatment of Alaska citizens.

The issue is still in dispute, with the state legislature, the governor, the Department of Fish and Game, the US Fish and Wildlife Service, Alaska's Congressional delegation, the Native Corporations, the state and federal courts, and a number of environmental and sportsmen's organizations trying to disentangle all the conflicting claims, laws, constitutional provisions and emotions tied up in a very complex issue.

Another problem created by ANILCA surfaced when oil was discovered near the Arctic National Wildlife Refuge (ANWR). This refuge in the very northeast corner of the state was doubled in size by ANILCA, and is considered one of the most significant arctic wildlife ecosystems in the world. The secret results of a test well drilled on adjoining Native lands have led to much speculation about if and how much oil might be buried under ANWR, and has led to a direct conflict between preservationists and oil developers. One side sees the issue as the last chance to save a unique arctic wildlife system, while the other sees the chance for another oil boom to rival the Prudhoe Bay strike. The stakes are high in this struggle, and while the state is determined to develop the oil resources of this far north refuge, the issues posed by ANILCA and the general environmental mood of the Congress and the country seem to oppose development. The issue will play out in the political and judicial systems, with much input from the public relations arms of both sides.

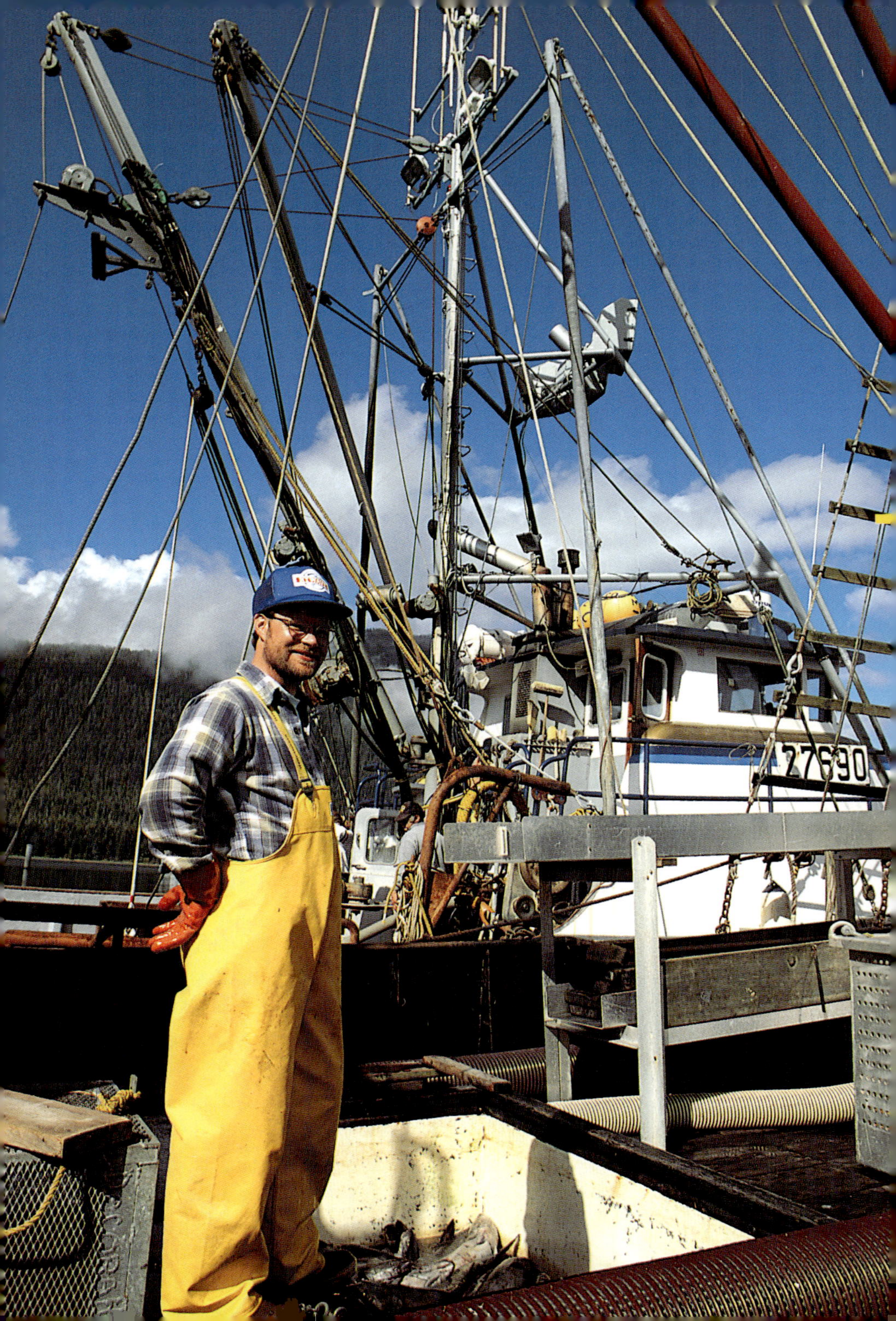
27690

JEWELS OF THE SNOW

Economy

The Alaska economy has gone through a series of up and downs ever since the first Russian fur traders happened upon the place in the middle of the 18th century. Fur, fish, gold, and military construction during and following the Second World War have all had their turn at bringing hopeful pioneers into the area. But by far the most significant discovery to date has been oil.

Petersburg known for fishing and its picturesque environment.

The presence of oil in Alaska was noted as early as 1882, but it took some seventy decades until the 1950s for local boosters to attract oil companies to try their hand at exploration here. Oil was already available in the less forbidding locations of Texas, Venezuela, and the Middle East. Bears, glaciers, and temperatures of -50°F (-46°C) were non-existent in those places, making them much more attractive to the highly speculative business of drilling holes in the ground and looking for an unseen liquid. However,

ECONOMY

36

Oil pipeline memorial at Valdez – a concrete reminder of the oil workers' struggles.

when political tensions increased in Iran and Egypt, Alaska began to look more attractive. A group of Anchorage businessmen tried to interest the major oil companies in Alaska's potential, but it was not until the small Richfield Oil Company of California took an interest in exploring the Kenai Peninsula that Alaska's oil boom got underway.

In July of 1957, Richfield struck oil near the Swanson River in the northern part of the Kenai National Moose Range, and the rush was on. Oil leases were bought, sold and traded in a frenzy of activity at the Anchorage office of the federal Bureau of Land Management. Swindlers and lawyers soon got into the act, leases were misrepresented to gullible outsiders, and lawsuits were filed contesting ownership of productive leases. Things settled down eventually and more wells were drilled in the area, several of which continue to produce to this day.

By the 1960s, oil companies had become firm believers in Alaska's oil potential. After the Kenai Peninsula finds, attention shifted to the arctic and the North Slope of the Brooks mountain range. Oil company geologists had targeted the area as being most likely to hold large oil reserves, and they were right, possibly beyond even their most optimistic expectations.

Part of the Alaska Statehood Agreement in 1959 had allowed the state to select 100 million acres of land formerly under federal control. One of the sites chosen by state officials was Prudhoe Bay on the coast of the Beaufort Sea. This move gave the state the right to sell oil leases there through competitive bids. Nearly every major oil company from the US and Europe expressed interest, but once again Richfield Oil won out and came away with the high bids on the most promising of the lease sites. Several other companies obtained leases on nearby sites, and the drilling began in earnest soon after. The North Slope oil fields hold tens of billions of barrels of oil, as well as trillions of cubic feet of natural gas. However access to the area, both for exploration and to transport the oil to market, was and still is a major and expensive problem.

When the oil companies working the North Slope decided to build a pipeline to transport crude oil to market, another construction boom was born. The pipeline was to run from Prudhoe Bay to Valdez on Prince William Sound, a distance of nearly 800 miles (1,288 km). The technical and environmental obstacles presented by the four-foot wide pipe were unprecedented, but by 1977 the project was completed, and on June 20, the first barrels of North Slope crude left Prudhoe Bay.

Once construction got underway, the impact of all that money rolling in affected nearly everyone and everything in the state. The OPEC oil embargo of the mid-70s made completion of the pipeline seem like a national security issue, and money to expedite the pipeline was plentiful. The oil companies spent money like sailors on shore leave,

Fur auction at Anchorage.

as did the workers when they hit town.

The pipeline construction boom hit Alaska hard in 1975, doubling the population of Fairbanks, adding 40 per cent to Anchorage, and putting an enormous strain on local facilities. Housing for the new residents was scarce, and real estate prices headed for the stratosphere. Other prices went up as well, as the law of supply and demand ruled the land and caused a temporary scramble.

While Fairbanks, the city closest to the construction area, flourished with pipeline construction and the influx of workers making more money than seemed reasonable, the effect on Anchorage was slightly different. The city fathers persuaded the oil companies to build their corporate offices there rather than in Fairbanks. High-rise office buildings soon dominated the Anchorage skyline, and housing for the people to work in those offices followed. The population increase in Anchorage has proven to be more permanent than that of Fairbanks, and today with a population of 230,000, over 40 per cent of Alaska's residents live in Anchorage.

Under the lease agreements negotiated between the state and the oil companies, the state of Alaska receives taxes and royalty payments on all oil pumped from beneath state lands. This money forms the backbone of the government's budget, accounting for 85 per cent of the money flowing into the state treasury yearly. This dependence on a single source of income continues to be a cause

Natural Resources of Alaska

The 800 mile-long Trans-Alaska Pipeline, Alaska's lifeline.

Alaska's natural resources are numerous, diverse, and valuable. Animal, vegetable, and mineral resources abound in the huge expanse of land. Getting to, extracting and processing these resources are Alaska's greatest source of income and employment.

First and foremost in dollar value is the oil and gas resource. The Prudhoe Bay oil field is the 18th largest oil field in the world, and the largest in North America. This field, along with several other North Slope oil fields, feeds oil into the four foot-wide, 800 mile-long Trans-Alaska Pipeline. It is pumped to Valdez, stored in tanks, then transferred to tankers for shipment to refineries in the lower 48. Taxes and royalties from this and other oil production in the state account for 85% of the annual state spending budget. However, the oil supply is finite, and production from Prudhoe is already declining. Eventually, other fields will have to be explored, drilled, and tapped. If not, then the state of Alaska will have to find other revenue sources, or undergo a drastic reduction in income, both to the state treasury and to the many households dependent on oil company paychecks.

Other mineral resources include precious and base metals, industrial minerals, coal and peat. Mines for these materials are scattered all over the state, and range from large industrial concerns such as the Red Dog Mine near Kotzebue to small gold mining operations.

The logging industry has been a mainstay of the southeast Alaska economy for years. The dense old growth forest of western hemlock and Sitka spruce trees provides logs for building materials and pulp, processed by mills in the area. However, in recent years, controversies over logging practices, forest subsidies, and pollution from mills have clouded the economic picture. While the world-wide demand for forest products remains high, political and environmental considerations continue to make for much economic uncertainty.

The fishing industry has also been beset by problems, even though the demand for fish on global markets is high. Fish stocks in abundance tend to attract large numbers of fishermen, and a variety of methods to limit catches have been employed. Closed seasons, expensive licenses, limitations on gear, etc., are used to prevent overfishing and the destruction of the resource. Measuring and evaluating the size and quality of wild fish populations is at best an inexact science, so there is a fair amount of trial and error in the process, and regulatory agencies have economic, political, and environmental pressures to contend with.

Adding to the natural problems inherent in extracting natural resources from a hostile environment are the fluctuating prices on world markets which cause uncertainty to the mix. If the price of zinc takes a dive, if Norwegian salmon producers sell pen-raised salmon cheaply, if Congress prohibits the export of raw logs from National Forests, or if the OPEC oil cartel over-produces and drops the price of oil, the repercussions are deeply felt in Alaska. All of the above things have happened in recent years, and other factors beyond anyone's ability to predict will come in to affect the natural resource industry in the future.

Valdez post, a fishing town and the end point of the Trans-Alaska Oil Pipeline.

of worry for state legislators and residents. Having one industry pay so many of the state's bills has kept taxation rates very low, to the extent that Alaska has no state income or sales taxes. However, oil is a non-renewable and finite resource, and production of North Slope crude oil has already begun to slow. Once Prudhoe Bay is drained, will another big find come along to allow life in Alaska to continue as it is, or will the bottom fall out of the state treasury, forcing everyone to confront life without the income from the big oil?

While oil production forms the backbone of the economy, it is by no means the only player in the game. Other forms of income help support large segments of the population, including fishing, tourism, mining, logging and the growing service industries.

Commercial Fishing

The fishing industry is one of Alaska's largest employers. Although the majority of the jobs are seasonal, the annual catch has a wholesale value of more than $1 billion. Besides the jobs for the people who actually catch and can the fish, the industry also provides jobs in the manufacturing, trade, services, and transportation sectors of the market.

The salmon harvest is the best known Alaskan fishery, and with an annual value of well over $300 million, makes up a substantial portion of the

An old fisherman and his crew after a good day's catch in Wrangell Narrows.

overall catch. Five species of Pacific salmon are harvested commercially, including king (chinook), red (sockeye), pink (humpback), silver (coho), and chum (dog) salmon. Red and pink salmon make up the majority of the catch, most of the pinks coming from the Southeast, and most of the red salmon from the Bristol Bay region of the Alaska Peninsula. More than 10,000 small-boat fishermen participate in salmon fishing every year.

Shellfish including shrimp, Alaska king crab, and tanner crab, (marketed as snow crab), are harvested from Alaskan waters, making up a sizable portion of the overall catch. In the 1970s and early '80s, king crab fishing took on gold rush proportions, with large catching and processing boats being built specifically for this relatively new and very lucrative fishery. Catch rates peaked in 1980 at 185 million lbs (83 million kg), then nose-dived to 15 million lbs (7 million kg) in 1985. Typical of Alaska's boom and bust cycles, some operators made a great deal of money, and some headed for financial ruin. The cause of plummeting crab stocks has never been definitively established, but fortunately catch rates are slowly heading back up.

Halibut fishing has also turned frenzied in recent years. In the 1970s, relatively few boats pursued these delectable deep-water fish, and the commercial season lasted for three months. However, as more and more boats saw the potential profits, and with no limits

Alaska's Fishing Industry

The natural taste of Alaska!

Commercial fishing in Alaska employs thousands of people, and the annual catch of more than $1 billion wholesale is the largest of any state in the Union. The commercial catch consists of both shellfish and fin fish, and a wide variety of boat and gear types are employed. The work is seasonal, and since a great deal of it takes place in the summer, entry level jobs are a great lure for students from the Lower 48 looking for big money and big adventure. Few if any of them ever get rich, but most do have experiences unlike anything to be found in their home towns.

There are state, federal and international regulatory bodies involved in Alaskan commercial fishing, and licenses and permits must be secured before a person is allowed to take fish in state waters. Laws concerning seasons, limits, gear and boundaries must be strictly obeyed, and failure to do so can result in fines, loss of the catch, or even impoundment of the boat. Enforcement of these laws in state waters is up to the Alaska Fish and Wildlife Protection office, and in federal waters by the National Marine Fisheries Service and the U.S. Coast Guard.

Shellfish

Shrimp and crab make up the bulk of Alaska's commercially caught shellfish. Most shrimp fishing is done by trawling, dragging a large net through the water, while crab is fished with pots baited and left on the sea bottom and then retrieved after they are allowed to "soak" for a while. Alaska king crab is famous the world over as a delicacy, and crab stocks have begun to rebound after a population crash of the early 1980s. When king crab became scarce, more fishermen began to pursue tanner crab, the two species of which are marketed as snow crab. A small fishery for Dungeness crab exists, as do even smaller catches of abalone, scallops, clams, sea urchins, geoduck, (pronounced gooey-duck), and large clam often sold in restaurants as king clam.

Salmon

Five species of Pacific salmon are fished commercially, and regulations for each locality determine which species of fish may be taken and with which types of gear. Most salmon are placed on the number of commercial boats allowed to fish halibut, the season got shorter and shorter. In recent years the season has been reduced to two 24-hour seasons, or openings, per year. Since the dates for these openings have to be established well in advance, weather becomes a risk, boats have to go out no matter how high the winds or how steep the seas happen to be. This

Another problem with such concentrated openings is that canneries are flooded with fish for a couple of weeks per year, and idle the rest of the time. Fish spoilage is a worry for boats and canneries, as is the ability to gear up sufficient employees and transportation for these twice-yearly gluts of halibut. A controversial system called Individual Fishing Quotas (IFQs) is currently under consideration to provide a more even flow of product to market and to reduce fish boat accident rates. As with any sort of change in a lucrative system, some operators see inequities in it, and are pursuing legal avenues to modify or kill off the proposal.

The groundfish, or bottom fish, market has also undergone rapid growth in recent years. Much of the product is sold to foreign markets overseas or transformed into surimi or "fake crab". Groundfish caught in Alaskan waters has grown from a $100 million market in the early '80s to nearly a half billion dollars in the '90s.

For the past few years, public concerns about overfishing and waste have arisen, and various legislative and legal bodies have focused attention on abuses of the resource and on potential solutions. Parallels between the current groundfish market and the king crab market of the 70s are becoming evident. The surimi market has fluctuated significantly in recent years, and shortened fishing seasons, huge harvests, and low prices have already resulted in seizures of fishing boats by creditors.

taken in nets of various kinds. Gillnets are strung in a line and the fish swim into the holes in the net, become entangled, and are picked when the net is hauled out. When gillnets are fished from a boat they are called driftnets, or they can be anchored on the beach and strung perpendicular to the shore, in which case they are called setnets. Some salmon fisheries employ nets called purse seines. The net is paid out from a boat and pulled by a smaller boat to encircle a school of fish. The larger boat then draws the net together with a "purse" line and winches the net full of fish aboard.

In Southeast, troll fishing is permitted for king, silver, and pink salmon. Individual lines and baits are pulled behind a slowly moving boat and hauled in as the fish strike the lures. Troll caught fish command the highest price on the market, since the fish are individually caught and handled, and do not have the often unsightly net marks found on many gillnetted salmon which are caught amass.

Halibut

Halibut are a bottom fish, caught by means of setlines 1,800 ft (549 m) long, to which baited hooks are attached. The line is baited and dropped onto the ocean floor, then retrieved after soaking. Since the seasons, or openings, for halibut in recent years have consisted of a series of two or three 24-hour periods per year, getting the lines, baited, dropped into position and picked back up before the 24 hours is over is quite a technical and mechanical challenge.

Other commercial fisheries in Alaska include groundfish, herring, and sablefish, or black cod. Groundfish in particular is an expanding fishery, with much of the product processed as surimi, a type of fish paste, and sold in Japan.

often results in disasters for the ill-prepared or the unlucky seaman, and bad weather coinciding with a halibut opening means around-the-clock shifts for the Alaska Coast Guard.

Pulp factory at Ketchikan.

Mining

Mineral production also provides employment and revenues to the state and residents. Besides gold, mines in Alaska also produce coal, zinc, platinum, copper, silver, lead, mercury, tin, tungsten, jade, soapstone, building stone, sand and gravel, and peat. In 1990, the mining industry in Alaska employed 3,600 people, and produced over a half-billion dollars in metals, minerals, coal and peat. Production costs are high due to the extremes of Alaskan weather and the high cost of access and transportation to remote sites. Also, the prices paid for the products depend on a sometimes highly volatile global market.

Logging

The timber industry has long been a staple of the Alaskan economy. Southeast and the Kenai Peninsula hold millions of potential board-feet of lumber, but whether or not this resource will be exploited depends on a variety of economic, environmental, and political considerations. For example, the market for raw logs in Asian markets is good, providing income for companies logging on private lands, but trees taken from the Tongass National Forest in Southeast are forbidden by law to be exported as raw logs. This closes the raw log market to timber from there, but provides jobs for sawmills in the area.

A Visitor Information Center, for all you need to know.

Pulp mills in Southeast have had problems meeting environmental standards and have had to contend with a weak pulp market in recent years.

Another major menace in Kenai is the forest pest, the spruce bark beetle. This insect bores underneath the bark of spruce trees, and evidence of its destructiveness is the presence of thousands of standing dead spruce. Driving on the Kenai, especially in the Cooper Landing area, these dead, brown trees are conspicuously interspersed with healthy green trees and in some areas, the dead trees predominate. Timber interests want to log the affected areas and salvage the trees while they still have some market value, while some conservation groups would rather let nature take its course.

Tourism

Second only to fishing in the numbers of Alaskans employed, tourism is a vital force in the economy. With more than 800,000 visitors to the state annually, this renewable resource industry employs over 10,000 Alaskans annually. Out of state visitors spend more than $1 billion here every year on food, air fares, packaged tours, and the increasingly popular adventure travel experiences.

Dependence on oil has brought prosperity to many Alaskans, and billions of dollars to state coffers, but eventually the oil will run out, and people who wish to remain here will have to face complex economic realities.

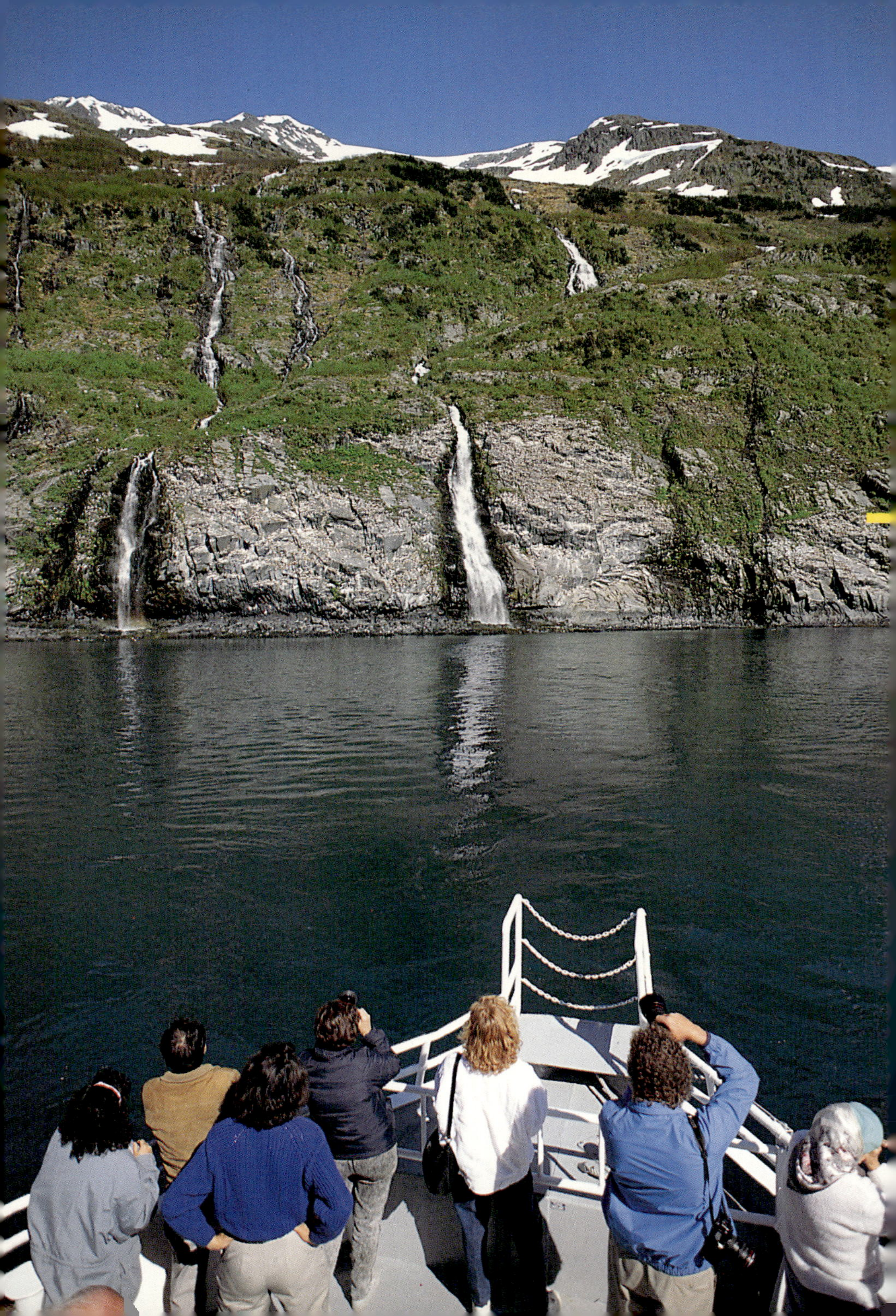

LAND OF EXTREMES

Geography & Climate

As might be expected of a state that measures roughly 1,400 by 2,400 miles (2,254 by 3,864 km) and which encompasses four time zones, there is a great variety in Alaska's physical make-up. The land rises from sea level to over 20,000 ft (6,100 m); some areas get more than 200 inches (508 cm) of rainfall annually while others manage less than 5 inches (12.7 cm); interior temperatures can test the limits of thermometers at -80° F (-62.2°C) in the winter, and the same areas often approach 100° F (37.7°C) in the summer; it is not uncommon in the winter to have the high temperature and the low temperature for the day differ by more than 100 degrees, with readings of over 50°F (10°C) in Southeast and less than -50°F (-46°C) in the Interior. To call Alaska a land of extremes is to indulge in an understatement.

The 500 mile (804.5 km) – long panhandle region of

Ice thaw in spring forms miniature cascades along Prince William Sound, a favorite cruising route.

Green mountains and valleys criss-cross at White Pass-Yukon Route.

southeastern Alaska, referred to by Alaskans as simply "Southeast", consists of towns and villages on islands and isolated portions of the mainland. No roads connect the communities with one another, or with the North American road system. Automobiles, commercial truck traffic, and passengers travel through the area on the state-owned ferry system, the Alaska Marine Highway has terminals in all of the larger communities and road connection in Bellingham, Washington, Prince Rupert, British Columbia, Haines and Skagway. Towns in Southeast include Ketchikan, Sitka, Petersburg, Wrangell, Haines, Skagway and Juneau.

The climate in Southeast is classified as maritime, characterized by small temperature variations, high humidity, high precipitation, and minimal instances of freezing weather, conditions very similar to the Pacific Northwest region of the Lower 48. Mean annual temperature is around 40° F (4.4°C), and annual precipitation in some localities approaches 200 inches (508 cm).

Southcentral Alaska is the state's population center, containing Anchorage, the Kenai peninsula and Prince William Sound. Temperature differences are greater than in Southeast, and annual precipitation ranges between 12–16 inches (30.5 cm – 40.6 cm) in the Anchorage area to over 180 inches (457 cm) in Prince William Sound.

Southwestern Alaska, like Southcentral, is in the transitional cli-

The awesome and alluring peaks of the Alaskan range sprawl between Fairbanks and Anchorage.

mate zone, characterized by more pronounced temperature variations throughout the day and year, less cloudiness, lower precipitation and humidities, and a mean annual temperature of 25–35° F (-3.9° – 1.7°C). The population is scattered among villages not connected to the road system, the largest being Bethel (population 4,400), and Dillingham, (population 2,200).

The continental climate zone, including Western Alaska, the Seward Peninsula and the vast interior region including Fairbanks, has high daily and annual temperature variations, low precipitation, and low cloudiness and humidity. The mean annual temperature of 15–25° F (-9° – -4°C) is misleading, as summertime highs can top 90°F (32.3°C), and winter lows test the lower limits of thermometers when they approach -80° F (-62.2°C), as in the record-setting winter of 1988-89.

The North Slope of the Brooks Range lies within the Arctic region, the Arctic Circle passing about 120 miles (193 km) north of Fairbanks. The mean annual temperature is 10–20° F (-12.2° – 6.7°C), annual precipitation is around ten centimeters, and strong winds are not uncommon. The low precipitation is accounted for by the fact that cold air does not hold as much moisture as does warm air. The city of Barrow and the beginning of the 800 mile-long trans-Alaska pipeline at the Prudhoe Bay oil field are found here.

Average temperatures and precipi-

AVERAGE TEMPERATURES (°F)

Climate zones = M (maritime) T (transitional) C (continental) A (arctic)

Temp = temperature

Town / Zone	Juneau (M)	Yakutat (M)	Kodiak (M)	Whittier (M)	Anchorage (M)	Fairbanks (C)	Prudhoe Bay (A)
JAN Temp.	+23.1	+24.8	+32.3	+25.5	+14.8	-10.3	-15.5
FEB Temp.	+28.2	+28.1	+30.5	+27.7	+18.5	-4.1	-24.1
MAR Temp.	+32.0	+30.4	+34.4	+29.3	+24.7	+10.0	-16.4
APR Temp.	+39.2	+35.9	+37.6	+36.3	+35.2	+30.0	-8.0
MAY Temp.	+46.7	+43.1	+43.6	+44.2	+46.5	+48.3	+19.5
JUN Temp.	+53.0	+49.5	+49.6	+52.0	+54.4	+59.5	+36.7
JUL Temp.	+55.9	+53.6	+54.5	+56.1	+58.1	+61.7	+44.9
AUG Temp.	+54.8	+53.1	+55.2	+54.8	+56.1	+56.3	+43.8
SEP Temp.	+49.3	+48.2	+50.2	+48.4	+48.0	+45.0	+36.0
OCT Temp.	+41.9	+40.9	+41.2	+38.2	+34.7	+25.2	+18.1
NOV Temp.	+32.8	+32.2	+35.0	+30.2	+21.8	+3.8	-5.3
DEC Temp.	+27.2	+27.0	+32.1	+26.9	+15.2	-8.1	-11.0
ANNUAL Temp.	+40.3	+38.9	+41.3	+39.2	+35.7	+26.5	+9.9

tation totals drop as you go north, with a couple of notable exceptions. Yakutat, at the northernmost point of Southeast, has temperatures very similar to Juneau, 85 miles (137 km) south. However, Yakutat receives twice the rainfall Juneau does. Whittier is on Prince William Sound and is only 50 miles (81 km) from Anchorage. Again, their temperature averages are quite close, but

In the cool shade of an iceberg.

because of the peculiarities of Whittier's location, the folks there get more than 12 times as much annual precipitation.

Within these zones, local conditions can vary considerably, especially in the mountains where weather conditions changes rapidly. Large mountains tend to create their own weather patterns. Temperatures, winds, and precipitation levels can differ depending on where you are in relation to mountains. This has made weather prediction a challenge over much of the state.

The Good Friday Earthquake

On March 27, 1964, a massive and destructive earthquake measuring 8.7 on the Richter scale devastated Southcentral Alaska. Striking suddenly at 5:36 PM local time on Good Friday, the quake did almost US$500 million dollars in total damage. It destroyed the community of Chenega in Prince William Sound and forced the relocation of the city of Valdez. At least 115 people were killed in this catastrophe which shocked the carefree Alaskans. The Good Friday Earthquake is recorded as one of the most powerful quake ever to hit North America, the tsunami generated by the quake killed coastal residents as far south as California. Signs of the massive earth movements can still be seen in the Anchorage area at Earthquake Park, and in Portage at the east

Avoiding Hypothermia

Hypothermia is a lowering of the body temperature. If your body loses heat faster than it is able to produce then, the body's core temperature begins to drop. Eventually, the hypothermic person becomes mentally disoriented, and unconsciousness and even death can result. This is to be avoided if you plan on having fun in the wide outdoors.

While most people associate it with extremely cold temperatures, most instances of hypothermia actually occur in relatively mild temperatures. That is because people who venture out into sub-zero conditions tend to be prepared for very cold weather, and on their guard against losing too much heat. A party going out on an overnight camping trip in mid-winter carries plenty of warm clothing, fire-making accessories, sleeping bags and other hiking necessities.

Most people get into trouble when the temperature is between 30° and 50° F (- 1° and 10°C), especially when rain and wind enter the picture. Water rapidly carries heat away from the body, and wet clothing pressed against the skin adds to the problem. Wind also accelerates cooling. A cool, windy, rainy day is a worst-case scenario to a person outdoors. These conditions are by no means unusual in Alaska, even in the summer, when temperatures in the mountains are much more cooler than at lower elevations, with considerable rainfall in some regions.

To avoid hypothermia, learn the basics of staying warm and dry. The weather here can turn from warm and sunny to cool and wet with amazing speed, especially in the mountains. Carry good rain gear, even on short day hikes. The latest high-tech rain wear such as Gore-Tex allows perspiration to escape, while keeping rain out. Wear and carry appropriate clothing. Polypropylene long underwear is lightweight, inexpensive, and keeps moisture away from the body, as does polyester fleece material. Wool is warm and retains most of its insulating properties even when wet.

The worst clothing in hypothermia country is cotton. While it is cool and comfortable in warm weather, it holds moisture next to the skin, and takes a very long time to dry out in cool weather. Wet cotton draws heat from the body very efficiently.

Of course, the best defense is to avoid the problem in the first place. Wear proper clothing, and put on your rain gear before you get wet, and put on warm clothing before you get cold. If you do not allow yourself to get wet and cold, you need not waste energy drying yourself up or re-warming yourself. Pay attention to the weather, keeping an eye out for changes that indicate rain or wind. Follow these simple rules, and hypothermia will be just another new word in your vocabulary, and not a threat to spoil your Alaskan adventure. Think ahead!

Signs on impending trouble include shivering, slurred speech, mental confusion, and physical coordination. If anyone in your group exhibits these symptoms in conditions conducive to hypothermia, immediately stop, get out of the wind and rain, warm the person up, and return to your base. You can warm up by vigorous exercise, and by eating and drinking. Carry snack foods high in carbohydrates such as bread, crackers, and eat before you get hungry. Also, stay well hydrated. Drink plenty of fluids, even if you do not feel thirsty. Your body needs fuel and water to produce heat, so carry enough for your party, and eat and drink as you go.

---

end of Turnagain Arm.

Mountains

Alaska contains altogether more than 30 mountain ranges, each with a characteristic of its own. Some like the Alaska Range stretches for hundreds of miles and dominates the landscape over a huge chunk of real estate. Others occupy little-known nooks and crannies, usually visited only by the most daring of climbers, and are almost lost in the

The twin peaks of Mt. McKinley.

great expanse like the tiny but engrossing Kiglapak Mountains near Goodnews Bay in Southwest Alaska, rising no more than 1,100 ft (335.5 m).

In Southeast, the Coast Range separates this panhandle region from Canada. Averaging only about 5,000 ft (1,525 m) above sea level and home to numerous glaciers and snowfields, this range parallels the coastline, its lower flanks covered with the coastal rainforests that typify the area. Deep fjords carved by glaciers cut into the land as steep mountainsides rise up out of the water, and scattered along the coastal waters are islands large and small.

Continuing north, the much higher St. Elias Range begins near Glacier Bay and stretches into Canada. Mount St. Elias at 18,008 ft (5,492 m) dominates this range, along with several other peaks over 14,000 ft (4,270 m).

Following the curve of the coast, the mountain ranges that parallel it include the Chugach Mountains, the Kenai Mountains, and the Kodiak Hills.

The next range to the west is the Alaska Range, majestically reposed between Anchorage and Fairbanks, and dominated by Mt. McKinley. At 20,320 ft (6,198 m), it's the tallest mountain in North America, and certainly one of the most spectacular. The twin peaks of Mt. McKinley – the North and South Peak – have lured many climbers since its first sighting in 1794. The Alaska Range parallels the coastline, tapering off on the Alaska Peninsula. From there the

Denali – true wilderness at its natural best, with the McKinley Range in the background.

Aleutian Range continues back out to sea. This semi-circle of mountains, from the Aleutians around to the Coast Range in Southeast, is geologically active, as evidenced by numerous volcanoes and frequent earthquakes.

Farther north, the Brooks Range, which like the Alaska Range runs generally east-to-west, separates the interior from the North Slope. A rugged, mostly treeless range, the Brooks is an extension of the Rocky Mountains, stretching from the Canadian border to the Chukchi Sea.

An enchanting rain forest trail at Glacier Bay Lodge.

Greens

The central and southeast portions of the state contain large expanses of primary forest. The enchanting Chugach National Forest in Southcentral Alaska extends from near Anchorage to include most of the Prince William Sound area, covering nearly 6 million acres of green plains. The predominant tree species are black and white spruce, birch, poplar, cottonwood, and aspen.

The Tongass National Forest in Southeast covers more than 16 million acres with mostly western hemlock, cedar, and Sitka spruce. These huge national forests make up only a portion of all the forested land in the state, with other large portions managed by the state, by Native corporations, and by other federal agencies.

The forests of Southeast truly qualify as rainforests. Annual rainfall in some parts of Southeast averages over 200 inches (508 cms). The ancient old-growth forests, dense, untouched and usually dripping with moisture, are home to the

The big thaw at Barrow, the northernmost point of Alaska, as summer returns.

Sitka blacktail deer, black and brown bears, several species of furbearers and other critters of the wild. Mountain goats live among the steepest, highest cliffs here, developing the agility to hop from cliff to cliff, and visible to the naked eye only as white dots.

Wetlands

Besides great mountain ranges, Alaska is also home to large expanses of flat wetlands, such as the Yukon-Kuskokwim Delta region in western Alaska. This area, dotted with lakes and streams too numerous to count, provides nesting and rearing habitat for millions of waterfowl. The ducks, geese, cranes, and shorebirds migrate from the Western US to breed in the fertile wetlands, the numerous mosquitoes and various other bugs providing feed for their hatchlings. The young birds have only a matter of months to grow large and strong enough to accompany their parents on the southward migration. Some birds begin the journey south as early as mid-August, so time is short.

The Aleutians

The Alaska peninsula juts out from the lower left corner of the state, its spine formed by the peaks of the Aleutian Range. As the peninsula tapers off to a point ending at False Pass, the Aleutian

Beauty of the Fjords

A life-supporting rock wall in the silent waters of Misty Fjords offers refuge to both land and marine life.

Not all of Alaska is tundra, taiga, and muskeg. Bordering the Gulf of Alaska from Southeast all the way around to the Kenai Peninsula, coastal rainforests, glaciers, and deep fjords form an ecosystem far different from that found elsewhere in the state. The climate, landforms, plant and animal communities are diverse and spectacular. If you so inclined, you could spend a lifetime exploring this area and never hope to see it all.

The enormous ice sheets that covered the area in Pleistocene times carved deep and steep fjords out of the mountains. Rock walls dive into the water, their sides covered with the largest trees in Alaska. The cliffs extend below the waterline down to depths of hundreds of feet, providing deep water habitats for marine life. Ice fields, remnants of ancient times, cover the highest elevations and send glaciers down to tidewater. Varieties of plants and animals have evolved to cope with this environment, and the watchful visitor can enjoy some amazing sights.

Tidewater glaciers come down to meet the sea, and enormous blocks of ice topple off their faces becoming icebergs. Ice and snow in higher elevations melt off causing the mountainsides to spout waterfalls that can drop for hundreds of feet. The thick forests support wildlife populations that include blacktail deer, brown and black bears, moose, and communities of smaller rodents and members of the weasel family including otters, weasels, and pine marten. Far above the forests, on cliffs too steep and too high for trees, mountain goats live out their lives clinging to the rocks and defying gravity.

In the waters, mammals and fish feed on various food sources, and on one another, in keeping the ecosystem alive. Marine mammals frequently encountered include humpback, Minke, gray and killer whales, seals, sea lions, sea otters, and porpoises. Under the water, shellfish, halibut, all five species of Pacific salmon, rockfish, and other rare marine denizens thrive.

Seabirds, waterfowl, and shorebirds abound, and bald eagles are everywhere. Look for the eagles on treetops along the shores, and on the shorelines at low tides. Their pure white heads contrast nicely with the dark green of the rainforests, and with a little practice, you will be able to spot them consistently.

The region is interlaced with islands of all sizes, from chunks of rock barely exposed at low tide up to the largest island in the region, Prince of Wales Island. The tide ranges along the fringes of the Gulf of Alaska are large, exceeding 15 ft (4.6 m) in most areas, and this large fluctuation between high and low water means that the currents in between the rocky islets can be very impressive. Currents of six or seven knots make for hazardous navigation by even large vessels, and the movements of small boats are often dictated almost entirely by the tides. You will often see several of them waiting for slack tide before entering some of the more challenging straits and narrows, discretion being the better part of valor where small boats, strong currents, and large rocks are involved.

GEOGRAPHY & CLIMATE

The towering Bear Glacier at Resurrection Bay.

Navigating Alaskan Roads & Highways

Magnificent backdrops rise to meet the solitary highway drivers.

For all of its vast size, Alaska has not been blessed with an abundance of highways. Percentage-wise, very little of the state is accessible by road, and what road there is tends to be two-lane highways. There are some sections of modern four-lane highways, mostly found within the larger cities, still, sizable sections of state highway remain unpaved, fortunately, in the more out-of-the-way areas.

Although the state highways carry names as well as official numbers, no one, but no one, uses the numbers. Ask an Alaskan how to get to Route 1, and he or she is likely to look at you like you have got two heads. Instead, ask for directions to the Seward Highway or the Richardson Highway, and you are back in business. For one thing, Alaska does not have many highways, so it is easy to simply memorize the names. It is also just about impossible to get lost or to take the wrong road to your destination, since in almost every case, there is only one road that goes to any one place. If you are in Anchorage and you want to go to Seward, just get on the Seward Highway and drive right to the end of the road and that will be Seward. Simple enough.

For quick roadside information on services and scenic views, every motorist should have a copy of *The Milepost*. This annually published book covers in great detail every driveable highway in Alaska, as well as the Alaska Highway through Canada with all the details you need to know. It details roadside businesses, scenic locations, camp sites, lodging, fishing holes, restrooms, in short, nearly everything the motorized tourist requires for a safe driving trip. It is available in just about any bookstore and roadside businesses in the state, or order directly from the publisher, Vernon Publications, at 800-726-4707.

Remember that services and rest areas are few and far between when you are on the long, lonely stretches of road far from the major cities. Therefore, advance planning and attention to details are essential before hitting the open road. Keep an eye on your gas gauge, and make sure the tank is full. Be especially careful when traveling in the off season as some roadside businesses close for quite awhile when most of the tourists go home.

Since most of the highways are two lane, it is best to pull over for sightseeing.

Watch out for wildlife, and not just because it is fun to see animals. Hitting a large mammal can be extremely unpleasant, expensive and dangerous. People have been killed in car-moose collisions. Scan the roadsides as you drive, keeping watch for the large dark shape of a moose. Slow down and be ready to stop if you spot an animal next to the road as they are amazingly quick and agile, and can dart out into the road at the blink of an eye. If you see an animal cross the road ahead of you, do not assume that it is safe to proceed at full speed. Often a cow moose will cross the road and then wait for accompanying calves to follow.

If you are driving a rented vehicle, check out the spare tire and jack before you leave the office, and have someone show you how to operate the jack before you hit the road.

Carry food, water, and some spare clothing. It is not as if you will be mounting a major expedition driving between cities, but it is comforting to know that you will at least be fed, watered and warm if you have an emergency while driving at the highway.

Island chain continues out to sea for another thousand miles, coming to an end at Attu Island. This island is so far west that it is almost east, positioned at a point nearly due north of Christchurch on the South Island of New Zealand. The Aleutian islands are windswept and remote, rich in marine life but nearly devoid of trees. The islands are merely the above-water portions of a submarine mountain range, many of the mountains still have active volcanoes. Volcanic eruptions in the area are quite common, although noticed mostly by seismologists, the few residents of Aleut villages, and the occasional passing fishing boat or trans-Pacific airliner.

Daylight (or lack thereof)

An often misunderstood part of the Alaska mystique is the notion that all over Alaska, it is dark all winter and light all summer.

Alaska is 1,400 miles (2,253 km) from north to south, stretching from Cape Muzon at 55 ° North Latitude on Dixon Entrance at the Canadian border to Point Barrow at 71° North Latitude. The length of days and nights differs dramatically between these two points. On December 21, the shortest day of the year in the northern hemisphere, Ketchikan has approximately $7^{1}/_{2}$ hours of daylight, and Anchorage has $5^{1}/_{2}$. This only counts the hours between sunrise and sunset, and does not take into account the hours of lingering light at either end of the day. On June 21, the longest day, Ketchikan has over 17 hours of light, and Anchorage, $19^{1}/_{2}$. Again, twilight extends these hours significantly. In Southcentral Alaska, it does not get truly dark in June and July, except for the wee hours of the morning on a heavily overcast day.

A close-up view of huge icebergs dominating Margerie Glacier.

The far north conditions are more stereotypical. The Arctic Circle of latitude at approximately 66 1/2° North is the point on the globe where on December 21 the sun does not rise above the horizon, and on June 21, the sun does not set. At Barrow, 325 miles (523 km) north of the Circle, the sun rises for good on May 10, and hovers at the horizon for another 84 days. In the winter, the sun sets for the season on November 18 until January 24. It is not quite the six months on and six months off, but that is as close as we can get in Alaska.

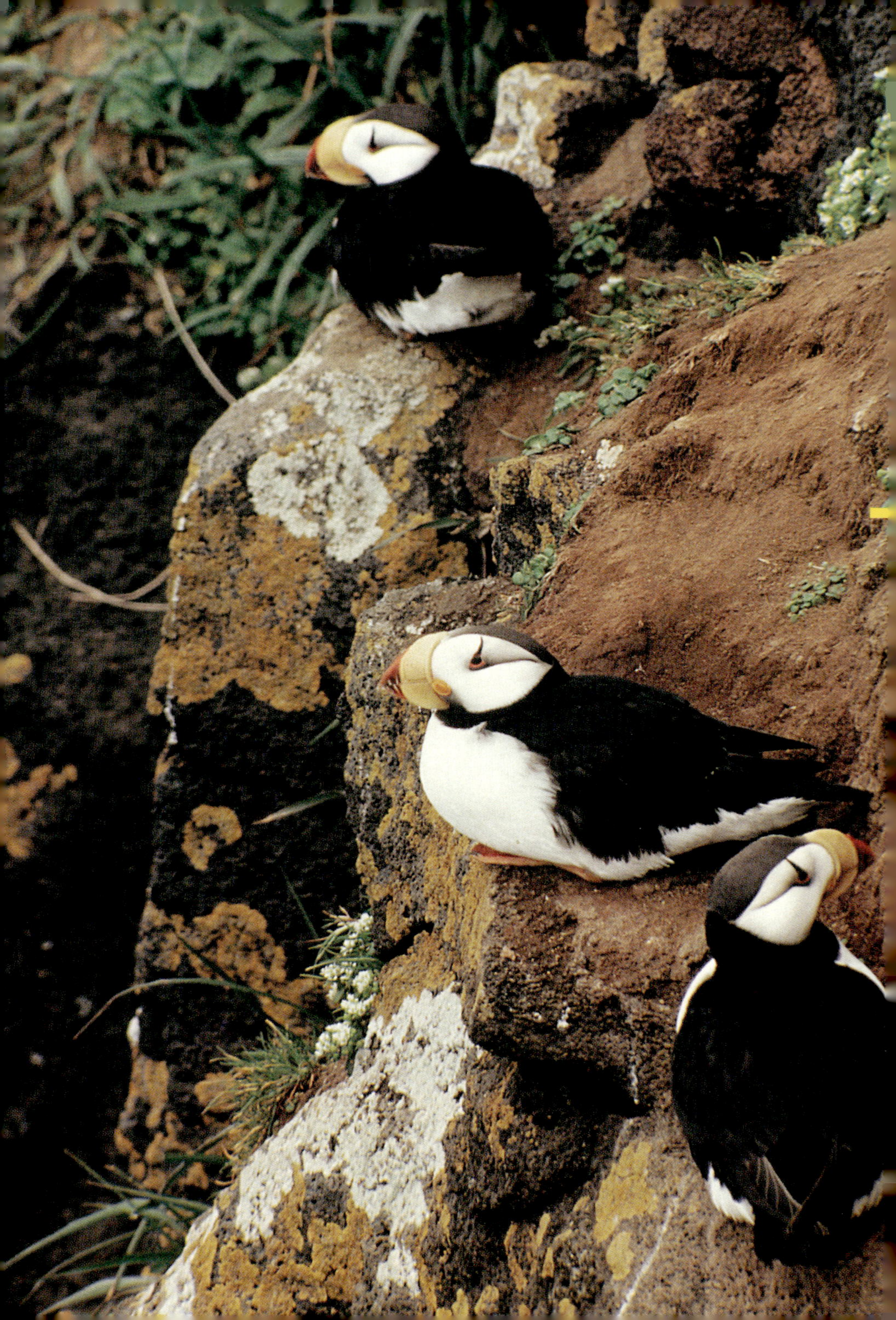

THE GREAT LAND'S UNTAMED

Flora & Fauna

Alaska is justifiably famous for the abundance and variety of wildlife. However, this gigantic quantity of animals is spread out over an equally gigantic chunk of real estate, so you will be disappointed should you expect to see a moose behind every tree and a grizzly bear in every open space. Finding and viewing Alaska's wildlife takes a bit of effort and knowledge, and sometimes more than a little luck. If you are willing to do a little homework, chances are that you will be richly rewarded for it.

It helps to know a bit about the life and habits of the animals you are looking for. If you know that Dall sheep live in the mountains and that grizzly bears prefer open tundra, you have got a better chance of finding those animals by looking where they live. Also, if you know what an animal's daily rou-

The docile and doll-like charm of Horned Puffins prevails, despite Alaska's harsh weather.

FLORA & FAUNA

The pint-sized Arctic Blue Fox, among the wildlife found on the Pribilof Islands.

tine is like and the kinds of food it prefers, you are that much more likely to be looking in the right place at the right times. This does not mean that you need a degree in biology in order to spot a moose, but a few general ideas about what to look for, where and when will help enormously.

Look for wildlife every chance you can get. If you are riding in a car, bus, train, boat, or airplane, stay alert for the possibilities of spotting animals. Be especially alert in the early morning or late evening, when animals tend to be more active. Edges of habitats are productive viewing spots, whether they are edges of forests, lakes or rivers. Binoculars or spotting scopes come in especially handy in viewing wildlife without getting too close and scaring away the animals.

Do not approach wild animals—Alaska is not a petting zoo. Human encroachment on an animal's "space" stresses the animal, and can provoke a flight, or even a

FLORA & FAUNA

Snug and replete, an Arctic Fox at Anchorage Zoo says it with a yawn!

charge at the offender! Do not push your luck – always watch and enjoy from a distance.

Marine Mammals

Marine mammals in Alaska include seals, sea lions, sea otters, polar bears, walruses, porpoises, and whales. Boat trips out of Southeast ports, especially to Glacier Bay National Park, and from Seward to Kenai Fjords National Park and Homer on the Kenai Peninsula provide the greatest opportunities for viewing most of these animals. Finding polar bears and walruses demands a greater commitment of time, effort, and money, since they live in the more re-

A bald eagle surveys the environs before going in for the hunt.

Bears & You

'Peekaboo'.

Of all the animals in Alaska, bears provoke more awe and more unnecessary fear than any other. Like all wild animals, bears should be treated with respect and caution. However, do not let unreasonable fear prevent you from exploring the backcountry.

Bear Rumours

Bear attacks get lots of media attention but the scare factor produced is out of proportion to the real risks. From 1900 to 1985, bears killed only 20 people in Alaska. By comparison, in a recent 10 year period, 19 Alaskans were killed by dogs. Realistically speaking, the most dangerous part of any trip is the drive to the trailhead. Bears have sharp hearing and an almost supernatural sense of smell – if you warn them of your presence by making noise or by hiking with the wind at your back, they will be more than happy to clear out. Trouble only starts when people make themselves attractive to bears through careless food handling, or by inadvertently sneaking up on them, triggering a violent defensive reaction.

While you are hiking, talk, sing, ring bells, do whatever it takes to give plenty of advance warning of your presence. Bears will do their best to avoid humans in almost all cases.

If you are camping, your cooking site, your tent, and your food storage site should all be separate areas, and at least 100 yards from each other. If you are camped near trees, put all your food and fragrant items such as toothpaste, insect repellent, soap in plastic bags and hang them from a branch, well out of a bear's reach and far enough from the trunk that a bear climbing the tree cannot reach them.

Do not cook in your tent – lingering food smells could prove irresistible to a curious bear.

When cooking, do not huddle over pots of steaming food, and do not wipe your hands on your clothing. If your clothes become permeated with food smells, store them with your food at night. Do not take food or fragrant items into your tent at night. Store all garbage with your food, and carry everything out. *Do not bury it*. Bears will quickly smell and uncover any food, scattering debris everywhere.

If you spot a bear, your subsequent actions depend on certain variables. If the bear is far away and traveling in a direction that would not bring him any closer, stay quiet, watch till he is out of sight, and then proceed.

mote sections of the Alaskan waters.

If you take a guided boat trip, most likely the skipper or an on-board naturalist will point out the animals to you, and give you some background on their habits. Keep your eyes focused, and if you spot something of interest, do alert your fellow passengers and the boat's crew – more folks watching the water means greater chances to spot some unique species.

The most common whales seen in

If the bear is heading towards you, you will either have to make your presence known, or vacate the area quietly. *NEVER RUN FROM A BEAR!* Grizzlies have been clocked at speeds near 40 miles (64 km) an hour over short distances, and there is no way you will ever approach that speed, no matter how much adrenalin you are pumping. Also, running from a bear is liable to trigger a chase response, much like dragging a ball of string in front of a cat, so you are likely to make a bad situation worse.

While most brown bear attacks are responses to perceived aggression, many black bear attacks are thought to be made by hungry bears. You want to appear non-threatening to a brown bear, but not easy pickings for a famished black bear. If an aggressive or curious black bear approaches, make lots of noise, throw things, and do your best to drive him off.

When confronted by a brown bear, however, your intention is to identify yourself as a human and to assure the bear that you present no threat. Circle slowly upwind to allow the animal to identify you by smell. The bear will probably assist you in this maneuver by circling downwind, and may stand on its hind legs. This is *not* an aggressive stance – the animal is only trying to see or smell you better. Raise your arms and wave them back and forth slowly, and talk to the bear in a low, calm and firm voice. Begin backing away slowly, and preferably at a slight angle so that it can better judge your intentions. *Do not run*! Once you are out of sight, leave the area quickly.

As an alternative to firearms, bear repellent sprays are available from several manufacturers. It has been tested on bears in controlled situations, and it has been used in the field in uncontrolled situations, indications are that it works as advertised, at least in some cases.

Alaskan waters are orcas, or killer whales, humpbacks, and grays. Beluga whales, unmistakable due to their white color, which stands out quite clearly, are frequently spotted in Cook Inlet and in Turnagain Arm near Anchorage.

Killer whales at Resurrection Bay.

The Great Land's Untamed

Terrestrial mammals present at least as great a variety as do marine mammals. They include Sitka blacktail deer, moose, caribou, elk, musk ox, bison, Dall sheep, mountain goats, brown/grizzly bears, black bears, wolf, coyote, wolverine, and foxes. And these are only the big animals! Smaller mammals include beaver, muskrat, porcupine, river otter, mink, weasels, lynx, along with the small rodents and squirrels.

The Ubiquitous Deer

Members of the deer family make up the

Birding In Alaska by Morten Strange

In Alaska all tourists are ecotourists. Even those who just fly into Anchorage for a business appointment are conscious that they have entered a great wilderness region, the last frontier as the term goes, and most visitors try to experience as much of the Alaskan scenery and wildlife as possible.

It has been said that among the 50 American states, Alaska is one of superlatives: the largest, the tallest, the richest, the coldest, the fewest people and so on. In many visitors' view it is also the best ... for watching wildlife of course! Moose, Caribou, Brown Bear, even Lynx and Wolf can be viewed here better than probably anywhere in the world. And spending a summer's day at one of the remote Bering Sea bird cliffs or in the tundra where thousands of arctic waterbirds breed is an adventure you will not forget for a long time to come.

Boreal Chikadee.

Parakeet Auklet.

The South and the Interior

There are basically 3 ways of entering Alaska. You can fly into the international airport of Anchorage, drive up through Canada to Fairbanks along the Alaska Highway or ... you can sail. Ferries will take you up along the Panhandle coast past Juneau and if you go this way make sure you pass by the Glacier Bay National Park. The scenery in this inlet where ice formations flow into the sea from the tall coastal mountain ranges all around is breath-taking and you will never forget what you see here. The bird life is particularly rich with many alcids on the water; alcids are members of the Alcidae family and includes Common Murre (Guillemot in Europe), Horned and Tufted Puffins, Kittlitz's and Marbled Murrelets among others. This area also supports many gulls and waterfowl and Bald Eagles should be a sure tick. The area around the park lodge is home to many northern arboreal birds and Blue Grouse.

Once you get to Anchorage, check out Westchester Lagoon near the city centre which is always good for Red-necked Grebe, Red-throated Loon, Arctic Tern and many ducks and shorebirds especially in late summer when congregations for migration start. Accessible from Anchorage, the Katmai National Monument on the Alaska Peninsular has now become a major ecotourism destination – but mostly because of the volcanic landscape and the many, many brown bears fishing for salmon there!

If you are mostly interested in birds try not to leave Alaska without seeing the alcids at their breeding grounds. There are huge breeding colonies on offshore islands in the southern and western parts of the state. Many can be seen on the Aleutian Islands but today, the Pribilof Islands 450 km from the mainland, is the place to go with tourist facilities available at St. Paul Island. Over one million birds breed on St Paul alone, and some of the best cliffs are just a 10 minute walk from the hotel! St. George Island 60 km southwest of St Paul has even more birds but fewer facilities. Parakeets, Crested and Least Auklets, Thick-billed Murre, Pigeon Guillemot, Red-faced Cormorant and Red-legged Kittiwake are some of the birds to look out for here. But there are many more resident species and also a good number of Asian stragglers otherwise rare in North America.

To the north in the Bering Sea, St. Lawrence Island is accessible from the town of Nome on

Buff-breasted Sandpiper seeking an early worm.

Golden Eagle atop a peak.

the mainland. On the south eastern coast there are cliffs dropping from 400 meters vertically into the sea, in June and July they are packed with birds, especially alcids, look out for the small Dovekie, it is not found anywhere else in Alaska, the rare Emperor Goose breeds on the lower parts of the island. These cliffs are a tough place to get to, the weather here is often windy and wet but seeing them is a once-in-a-lifetime experience that you will always treasure.

It is a quite different journey to the Mt. McKinley National Park. In fact you cannot help but notice the place when you drive from Anchorage to Fairbanks – the highest mountain in North America is just off to the left! In the summertime the weather is warm and pleasant, unless you try to scale the peak which has proved fatal to a few experienced climbers! The 2,995 sq miles (7,756 sq km) park surrounding the mountain is a great place to see large mammals and also many sub-arctic birds at their breeding grounds like the Arctic Warbler, White-crowned Sparrow, Boreal Chickadee, Wandering Tattler and many other shorebirds and ducks. The Gray Jay is so tame in this area that it will come and take food out of your hand.

Some high arctic species like Long-tailed Skua and Laland longspur also occur. Most of the birds are naturally migratory, but a few like the Willow Ptarmigan, the Raven and the Golden Eagle stay put all year round and stick out the dark, cold winter months when the park is devoid of most lifeforms, including people.

The Brooks Range and beyond

To the north of Fairbanks lies the Brooks Range which marks the boundary to arctic Alaska. You will never find a prettier range of low mountains anywhere, they are accessible by postal planes from Bettles into the native villages, and the now 20-year old Dalton Highway cuts through them as well. Spring in the Brooks Range is a special time when the sun gains strength, winter looses its grip, the icy rivers break up while the geese start flying overhead towards the North Slope unveiling the vibrance of spring.

You can experience the tundra of the North Slope by flying into the oil fields at Prudhoe Bay or better still by visiting the northern-most point in the U.S., Point Barrow. The point itself is nothing much except a deserted gravel pit but the tundra, south and east of the village, is a wonderful habitat for birds. You do not have to bring a raincoat – even in July precipitation here falls as snow! The coastal ice formations come right up to the beach. But the midnight sun thaws out the shallow surface waters above the frozen ground and during summer the tundra turns into a waterlogged marsh. There is not a tree in sight, not even a bush, the mountains to the south are not visible (they are visible from Prudhoe Bay to the south-east). Even then this barren and featureless landscape is full of life, it is packed with birds.

Two families especially dominate, the sandpipers Scolopacidae and the ducks and geese Anatidae. There is a wealth of shorebirds; high arctic species that can be found in few other places in Alaska are, of course, of particular interest, they include specialties like Black-bellied Plover, Bar-tailed Godwit and Western, Pectoral, Baird's and Buff-breasted Sandpipers.

FLORA & FAUNA

69

Birding in Alaska

Some of these can be seen during the winter season at migration locations in the "lower 48" and other countries but to encounter these birds in full breeding plumages at their remote home nesting grounds is nevertheless a sight to behold. Look out for another peculiar shorebird, the Red Phalarope which prefers to swim like a small, lighting quick duck on the tundra ponds. It is an exclusive high arctic species and actually you do not really have to look out for it at all, it is everywhere and remarkably tame too!

Among the ducks keep an eye out for high arctic specialties like Tundra Swan, Brant Goose and King, Spectacled and Steller's Eiders. The Sabine's Gull is the most common gull here and the Pomarine Jaeger which is otherwise not widely distributed is very numerous around Barrow in the North.

The tundra is funny in the sense that you can walk for hours in some places and see very few birds, then suddenly, you reach a small patch that looks just like the rest except birds are everywhere, and you have to walk carefully not to step on nests with eggs all over the grassy ground.

Apart from the waterbirds there is a good density of the amazing Snowy Owl here which is however, a bit difficult to approach closely. There are also many Snow Buntings in the tundra and around the Barrow village area. Otherwise perching birds in the order of Passerines are not well represented in this habitat – there are not many places for them to perch anyway!

More Information

There is a beautiful and informative book available on Alaskan birds and anybody visiting the state ought to get a copy. The 346 pages "Guide to the Birds of Alaska", by R.H. Armstrong covers 437 species in photographs with attractive color plates and includes a detailed description of status and habitat of each bird, the latest revised edition is from 1990.

Apart from that one most guide books to North American birds also cover Alaska. For identification "A Field Guide to the Birds of North America", 1987 by The National Geographic Society is preferred today by many travelling birders, and "Where the Birds Are", 1990 by J.O. Jones is a site guide to all American states including Alaska. Visitors to the population centre of Anchorage should consider acquiring "A Field Guide to Birding in Anchorage", 1989 by L. Roberts.

For the latest information on the best places to see good birds in the state there is a telephone hot-line service available to serve the avid bird-watchers, the number to call directly is (907) 248-2473.

Red Phalaropes in the marsh.

Shoals of sea lions basking at the Gulf of Alaska.

majority of big game animals, and most of them are caribou. The current caribou population is approximately 800,000. Unfortunately, the vast herds so often seen on TV nature shows are far removed from roads and people, to find and view this wildlife spectacle again takes both time and money. Nevertheless, there are possibilities for viewing smaller herds close to roads, and any opportunity to see these gorgeous creatures should be pursued.

Denali National Park contains a sizable caribou herd, and any trip into the park on a tour bus or park shuttle bus will most likely turn up a caribou. There are also herds occasionally seen romping along the Denali Highway between Paxson and Cantwell, and along the Richardson Highway between Glennallen and Tok. Caribou prefers open tundra, and they are highly migratory, so it is possible to spot them almost anywhere in the interior where open country exists. There is also a small resident herd near the Kenai airport, and lucky and observant hikers can find them on the Resurrection Pass Trail between Hope and Cooper Landing on the Kenai Peninsula.

Moose are the most frequently seen big game animals in Alaska. They coexist well with humans, and Anchorage has a large population of animals in town and around the fringes of the city. The Kenai Peninsula is considered the best moose habitat in the world, and the observant tourist will almost surely spot

A permanent feature of Alaskan wildlife, the homely moose, takes a quiet stroll within the confines of Denali Park.

several animals on a driving trip through the area. Drivers in moose grounds are cautioned against speeding.

Moose prefer mixed woodlands, willow thickets, and wetlands. The largest bulls weigh more than half a ton and carry antlers measuring more than six feet across. During the mating season or mid-September the bulls can be rather aggressive, as can cows accompanying calves at any time of the year. Keep your distance from moose, as from all wild animals, and do not chase or harass them in any way.

Elk have been transplanted onto islands near Kodiak and in Southeast, and are seldom seen. Sitka blacktail deer live in the forests of Southeast, on islands in Prince William Sound and on Kodiak Island.

Dall sheep populate most of the mountain ranges, and their snow white coats make them easy to spot during the summer. They are frequently seen from a distance in Denali Park, and there is a resident band of animals that cause frequent traffic jams along the Seward Highway just south of Anchorage. Near milepost 107 there are turnouts on the highway at a spot where the sheep frequently graze near the road. Look for them in the mountain cliffs on the Kenai, near the Sheep Mountain roadhouse on the Glenn Highway, near Eklutna Lake north of Anchorage, and from the Glen Alps area in Chugach State Park.

Mountain goats occupy the highest, steepest, and most treacherous ter-

A Dall mountain sheep and her kid rough it out on rocky cliffs, their natural habitat.

rain of all. They are seen on seaside cliffs in Southeast and on the Kenai, in Portage Valley south of Anchorage, and on the cliffs near the town of Hope. They are often mistaken for Dall sheep, and binoculars are usually necessary for positive identification.

Bison, introduced in 1928, live in herds near Delta Junction, spending lots of time in barley fields there. Scan the open fields there, near mile 242 of the Richardson Highway, and near the Taylor and Edgerton highways.

Wild musk and ox herds live in remote areas such as Nelson and Nunivak Islands in Western Alaska. Captive animals can be viewed at the University of Alaska, Fairbanks research farm, and at tourist sites in Palmer.

"Grizzly" and Cousins

Three species of bear live in Alaska: polar, black and brown/grizzly bears. Polar bears live on the pack ice along the arctic coast, far from the vast majority of tourists. Black bears live in most of the wooded areas in the state, from Southeast through Southcentral, the Interior, and Western Alaska. Shy and elusive, they are seldom spotted except by the very persistent and very lucky. They can sometimes be seen in open meadows on hillsides, especially in the warm season of spring.

In the past, coastal brown bears and the grizzly bears of interior regions were considered different species of bear.

Hazards of Oil Spills

The restored lucidity of Bligh Reef, site of the oil spill, belies the prolong damage done to wildlife.

When the oil tanker *Exxon Valdez* hit Bligh Reef in Prince William Sound, 11,000,000 gallons of oil gushed out of her holds. The spill was unprecedented in US waters, and the impact on the area's people and on the wildlife of the Sound was enormous.

Although it is a natural substance, oil is a hazard to wildlife. Besides being poisonous, it destroys the insulating qualities of fur and feathers. Many animals not killed outright or by ingesting oil while trying to clean themselves died of exposure, while others continued to consume oil present in the food chain with dire consequences for breeding.

The terrestrial animals fared best in the spill's aftermath. The brown and black bears and deer in the area were able to avoid the oil's worst effects. There was evidence of bears eating oiled bird carcasses that washed up onto beaches, but studies seemed to indicate little long term effects on bears. Deers that feed on kelp on the beaches would seem to have been at high risk, but again studies failed to document any significant impact to their population.

Sadly, river otters did not do as well as deer and bears. Since they live and feed in marine waters around the area, their food supply was diminished. The river otter population in oiled areas has suffered, as have individual animals.

Marine mammals did less well than land mammals, as might be expected. When the oil hit the area, land mammals could escape the threat by merely walking inland. No such easy option existed for sea creatures.

Orcas live in groups known as pods, and individual animals are easily identified by the configuration of their white "saddle patches." Mortality rates of resident whales were significantly higher than normal, and it is estimated that recovery of the Sound's killer whale population could take 15 years.

Approximately 200 harbor seals died from the spill, but the mammal most severely affected was the sea otter. Over 1,000 carcasses were recovered, with the total kill estimated at 3-5,000 animals. Sea otters live on the surface of the water, making them especially vulnerable. Oil coated their fur and destroyed the insulating qualities, and otters ingested oil as they tried to groom themselves. Long term effects are sig-

The current thinking is that they are really the same bear. Coastal browns have access to salmon streams, causing them to grow much larger than bears living in the interior. Those bears subsist mostly on vegetable matter, with protein supplements of rodents, carrion, or the occasional large mammal.

Brown bears grow to over 1,200 lbs (540 kg) on their rich diet, and are found in Southeast, Southcentral, Kodiak, the Alaska Peninsula, and coastal Western Alaska. Chugach State Park, bordering Anchorage, has a population of ap-

nificant, as mortality patterns indicate more prime-age animals dying than before the disaster. On the brighter side, birth rates appear to be high in the spill area.

It is also estimated that the spill killed between 300,000 and 645,000 birds. The highest numbers of dead birds were common murres, with losses estimated at 175,000 to 300,000. Besides the initial effects on local birds, long term effects on reproduction were severe, with expected breeding success at some nesting colonies reduced to zero in subsequent years. Other seabirds affected by the spill include harlequin ducks, black oyster-catchers, pigeon guillemots, arctic terns, tufted puffins, loons, grebes, murrelets, kittiwakes, and gulls. Some species seem to recover quickly even from major population losses, while the ultimate effects on others is still being evaluated.

Although bald eagles do not live on the surface of the water like seabirds, they scavenge from beaches. This behavior accounted for the loss of approximately 900 birds from a local population of 8,000. Reproduction rates in 1989 were down by 85 percent, but appear to have rebounded to normal levels.

Immediate reductions in fish numbers were low, but the effects on eggs were severe. Salmon egg mortality in some oiled streams increased by as much as 96 percent, and juvenile fish were also affected by slower growth rates and survival percentages drop.

Herring, trout and bottom fish in the area were affected as well, but the long term effects on the fish in the area are varied and still under study by ecologists. Management of commercial and sport fisheries will continue to be even more complicated than usual to ensure safety.

proximately 40 browns, and on occasion one of them finds his way into town. This invariably provides much excitement for all involved, but too often means the unfortunate demise of the bear.

Good viewing areas for brown bears include the Stan Price State Wildlife Sanctuary at Pack Creek on Admiralty Island in Southeast, the McNeil River State Game Sanctuary on the Alaska Peninsula, Brooks River at Katmai National Park on the Alaska Peninsula, and the Fraser River on Kodiak. None of these areas are road-accessible, and advance reservations or permits are required.

For grizzly bear viewing, Denali National Park is the place to go. Naturalist-led bus tours or the park shuttle buses will get you into the park and into grizzly country. It is possible to sight a bear in open tundra country away from the park, but not probable. Bears are hunted in most non-park areas of the interior, making them understandably suspicious and wary of humans.

Other Mammals

Finding any of the other mammals on the list is largely a matter of luck. Wolves live in most regions of the state, but seldom wander close to human habitations. Coyotes, foxes, and the furbearers are likewise shy and retiring types, and you will have to either spend a great deal of time surveying the geography with binoculars, or just get very lucky.

Flight of the Fair Birds

The variety of birds in the region is not as great as in tropical or even temperate climates, but numbers of some species

Brown bears fishing for salmons at a waterfall.

are quite high, especially in fertile marine environments. Boaters and beachcombers are likely to spot gulls, kittiwakes, and seabirds such as murres, puffins, shearwaters, guillemots, auklets, murrelets, and numerous shorebirds. Waterfowl includes a variety of species of ducks and geese, and sandhill cranes migrate up to spend summers here.

Bald and golden eagles reside here, and the world's largest concentration of bald eagles occurs near Haines in Southeast. The Chilkat Bald Eagle Preserve hosts thousands of these majestic birds, maximum numbers coinciding with a salmon run from October to December, peaking in November. Bald eagles are common in coastal Alaska, except in the farthest north regions. Golden eagles live in interior regions, especially in alpine and rocky areas. (See Birding Box for more information on birds of Alaska).

Hunting Seasons

Big game, small game, upland birds and waterfowl hunting seasons vary widely around the state, although most take place in the fall. Hunting is a popular and widespread form of recreation all over Alaska, and many residents especially the natives, depend on this form of food gathering to provide most if not all of their annual meat supply.

Hunting regulations vary by season and geographic boundaries, and are quite complex. Persons unfamiliar

FLORA & FAUNA

Marmott, a tiny critter of the vast Alaskan plains can barely reach a firewood.

with Alaska's challenging environments should consult a knowledgeable and reputable guide, on outfitting services, and the Department of Fish and Game before attempting a hunting trip. This is to minimise hunting accidents. Hunting regulations are available from the Alaska Department of Fish and Game, Public Communications Section, Juneau.

The Pristine Forest

The varied environments of Alaska support several distinct ecosystems. Some of the resident flora is quite widespread, while other species are very site specific, growing only in specialized niches where conditions are just right for it to flourish.

A gray jay perches gently on a wild stalk.

Forests of varying make-ups cover much of Southeast, Southcentral, and Interior Alaska. Many lowlands and much of Western Alaska is wetland of one type or another, and tundra covers the upper reaches of mountains and the northernmost portion of the land.

Southeast Alaska is the land of big trees and moist understory. Sitka spruce and western hemlock predominates, and in the dense, old-growth forest mosses cover most of the ground. Coastal forest in Prince William Sound, on the Kenai Peninsula, and Kodiak consists almost solely of Sitka spruce.

Interior boreal forests are referred to as taiga, and consist primarily of white spruce and paper birch trees. Other significant tree species are black spruce, poplars, quaking aspen and cottonwood. The trees of interior regions lack the imposing size of the forest giants of Southeast, and the farther north, the smaller the trees, until you reach the northern treeline. Just as mountains have lines above which trees cannot grow, the globe has a northernmost treeline. In Alaska, this line roughly approximates the crest of the Brooks Range, with numerous wiggles and swoops along the precipice.

Above treeline, both on the globe and on the mountains, the ground cover consists of tundra. Tundra is divided into wet, moist and alpine types and is made up of a variety of undergrowth including low shrubs, grasses, sedges and wild berries.

Arctic daisies speckle the shores of St. Paul Island.

Seabeach Senecio, a common-looking flower with an uncommon name.

Wildflowers

Flowers of an astonishing array and variety thrive in Alaska, much to the surprise of people who visualize the entire state as a frozen wasteland. There are more than 1,500 species of wildflower present here. As can be expected of such a large and variegated geographic area, blossoming times vary considerably by all of the factors that govern living things, such as time of year, moisture, sunshine, latitude, snow cover and altitude.

Wild Berries

Numerous edible berries are available for picking, most of them reaching maturity in late summer and fall. Depending on location and time, you might happen upon blueberries, bearberries, currants, wild raspberries, wild strawberries, huckleberries, cloudberries, crowberries, highbush or lowbush cranberries, lingonberries, salmonberries, or watermelon berries. There are also inedible and poisonous berries around, so make sure of plant identification before indulging. Also be aware that bears are every bit as fond of berries as we are, and in many interior areas, berries make up a substantial portion of the diets of local bears. Be especially wary in large patches, make plenty of noise, and do not become so preoccupied with food gathering that you lose caution.

Monkshood flower, delightfully purple.

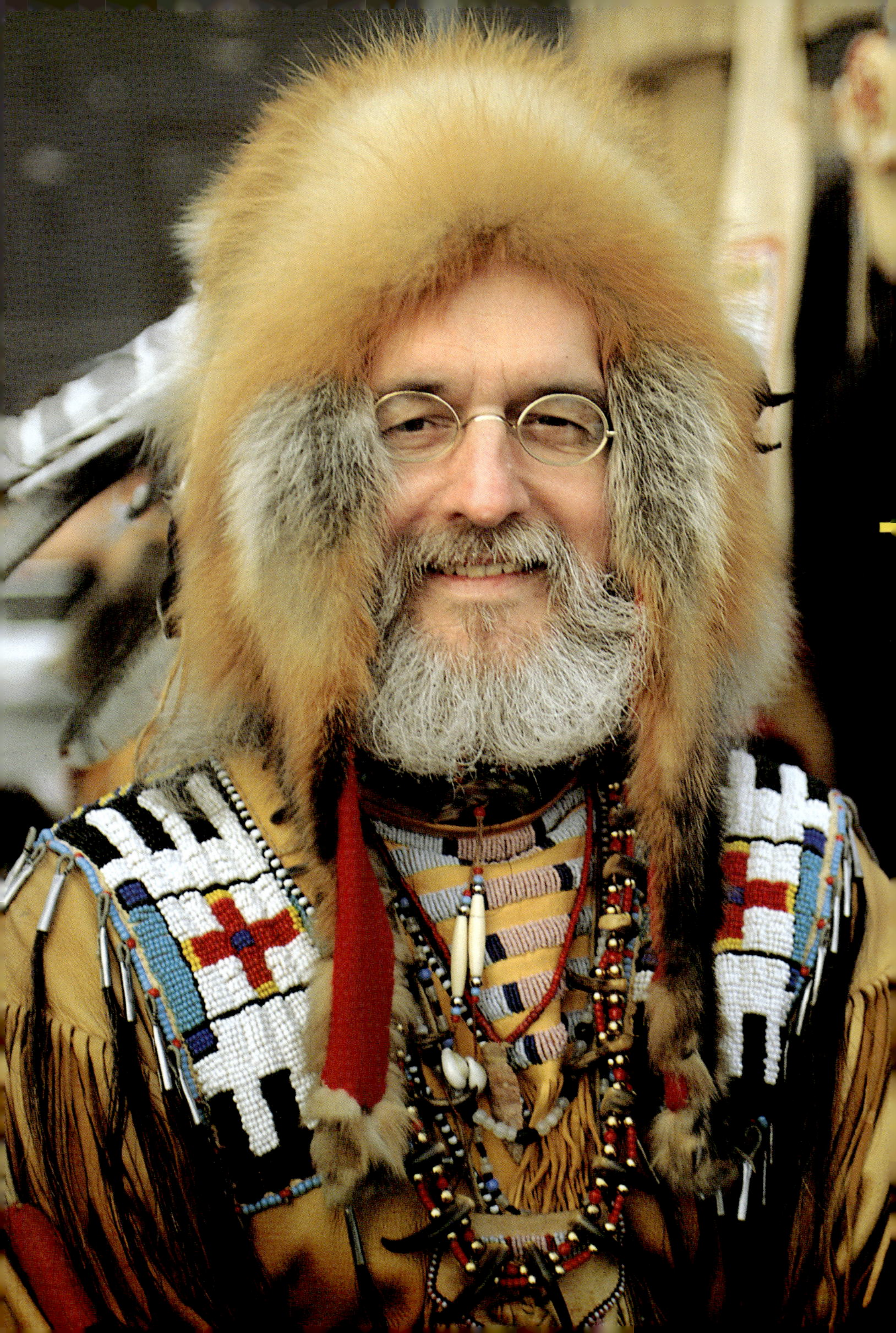

NATIVE PEOPLES

People

A land bridge that once connected North America to the Asian continent, during the Pleistocene era, had allowed for large scale migration across the Bering Strait. This "land bridge" was not, as the name might imply, a narrow path crossing a waterway. Rather, it formed a vast, dry, grassy plain supporting large groups of grazing animals such as the woolly mammoth, bison and horse. It is thought that this Beringian plain was exposed in three separate periods, providing access to North America for successive migrations of animals and people from Asia into the Great Land.

In time, these peoples migrated south and east, eventually populating North and South America. When white men first happened upon Alaska, a variety of peoples with their own unique lifestyles and cultural sysytems had already existed. There were coastal and interior Inupiat Eskimos, coastal and interior Yup'ik Eskimos, Aleuts, coastal and interior Athabascan Indians, and Tlingit and Haida Indians. Within these broad categories,

An Alaskan gentleman resplendently dressed for a winter festival.

A pair of Native Alaskan twins at the Fur Rondy, Anchorage.

sub-groupings based largely on language differences begun to flourished, as did further local divisions into communities and family groups.

The Inupiat Eskimos lived in coastal areas north of Norton Sound and in the interior north of the Brooks Range. The interior Inupiat depended largely on caribou for food and for clothing materials, and like the caribou, their existence was largely nomadic and migratory. The Inupiat living near the sea were luckier as they had a more readily accessible food source in marine mammals, and established larger and more permanent communities. At the time of the first contact with Europeans, the villages of Barrow and Pt. Hope were home to nearly 600 people.

The Yup'iks

Yup'ik Eskimos lived in coastal regions, on St. Lawrence Island in the Bering Sea and from the Yukon-Kuskokwim Delta on the Alaska Peninsula around to Prince William Sound and on Kodiak Island. Within this expanse of territory, their livelihood depended mostly on the marine environment, with some local uses of land mammals, salmon, waterfowl, greens and berries.

Eskimos speaking the Yup'ik language were made up of Pacific and Bering Sea groups, each with several smaller sub-groups. There were an estimated 30,000 Yup'iks living in Alaska then, making them the most numerous

A village mother and child within the shelters of a log cabin.

native people on the land.

The Aleut & Athabascans

The Aleut people of the Aleutian Chain, Koniag, Chugach and Eyak are closely related to the Eskimos. At one time numbering some 15,000 to 20,000 people, foreign diseases and aggression have greatly reduced the population to an estimated 4,000 by 1840, a minority in their own land today.

Not anymore fortunate are the Athabascan Indians who lived within the interior regions of Alaska, with the home ranges of several groups extending into Canada. Although the area covered by Athabascans is vast, their population at the time of contact with Europeans was estimated at no more than 11,000 people. Distribution of game in the interior is spotty, with local abundances of salmon and caribou offset by large segments of land where game is scarce or access is limited by geography.

The Tlingit & Haida

The Tlingit and Haida lived in the panhandle region of Southeast Alaska. Southeast is dotted with islands separated by deep, fast tidal waters with the mainland steep and heavily forested. Subsistence for Natives in the region depended on boats and access to the coastal waters. The Tlingit Indians

A fusion of tradition and skill makes a mighty totem pole carver at Totem Bight.

moved south to the area from mainland Alaska, and the Haidas moved north from the Queen Charlotte Island region of coastal British Columbia.

Subsistence Styles

The subsistence styles of coastal and interior Natives evolved differently, as interior residents stayed on the move in order to maintain contact with the herds of caribou. Coastal peoples established more permanent settlements and pursued whales, seal, and walruses from their riverside villages.

The coastal Eskimos, Aleuts and some Athabascans were highly skilled in ice-hunting techniques. An Eskimo is known to be able to hunt a 50 over ton whale with the aid of a simple jade-tipped harpoon and a skin kayak. These coastal hunters relied on boats of various sizes, the hulls made of animal skins. The multipurpose boats were used in hunting whales, seals, sea lions, and walruses, for tending salmon nets, and for travel, trade, and carrying large loads between villages. The larger boats, up to 40 ft (12 m) long, were called umiaks, the smaller, one-man boats called 'kayaks' or 'baidarkas'. Tlingits and Haidas built dugout canoes from cedar logs, while interior Athabascans built their canoes from birch bark.

Clothing was made of animal skins. Inner garments of caribou hide were usually made with the fur facing inside

Saxman village children at Ketchikan grow up with the sights and sounds of their heritage.

to catch the heat and keep the wearer snug and warm, whilst outer garments faced the fur outside. Coastal Eskimos are also deft in making waterproof outer garments with sea mammal intestines sewn together.

Trade between interior and coastal Eskimos centered around the animal products each group had access to and this became an important channel for exchange between the two groups. Coastal people traded seal oil and whale meat for caribou skins and other furs not easily gathered on the seacoasts.

A Chilkat dancer passes down the tradition to his young apprentice.

Housing

Houses for Eskimos, Aleuts, and some Athabascans were similar in their semi-subterranean configuration. Built into the ground for insulation, the roofs were constructed of sod laid over a framework of wood or whalebone. Entrances for Eskimo dwellings were tunnels, the passageway acting as a kind of arctic entry trapping the cold air below the level of the living area. The dome-shaped Aleut houses, called 'barabaras', had their entrances cut into the roof, with entry to the dwelling by means of a ladder. Indians who lived in areas where big timber was available used logs and planks for construction materials.

Inupiat and Yup'ik communities also had community houses used mostly by the men as common work areas and for dancing and feasting occasions. Yup'ik men's houses could also be converted to use as steambaths.

Social Organization

The roles of men and women in native societies were largely the sort of traditional roles one might expect. Men did the hunting and the tool making, and women took care of the home by sewing clothing, preparing food, and gathering berries, roots, bird eggs, and tide pool organisms. There were also rituals and taboos observed by women, often linked to the hunting success of the men. Men usually occupied the leadership positions in the community.

However, there were significant variations from this general theme. The Aleuts traced lines of descent and house ownership matrilineally, or through the female side of the family. Tlingit, Haida, Yup'ik, and many Athabascan societies were organized in similar fashion. Where tribes or clans existed, a child belonged to the same clan as his or her mother. Inupiat communities differed from this norm in using a bilateral kinship arrangement, with relationships to both mother's and father's sides of the family receiving equal consideration.

Social controls and relationships were manifested in a variety of ways. In some communities, boys were, from

The Utqiagvik Find

Archeologists had to trek through austere snow fields in Barrow to make their finds.

One of the factors that makes archeology such a difficult discipline is the very thing that makes it so interesting. The forces of nature take their toll on the objects and the remnants of the cultures under study, and the scientists have to rely on detective work to piece together the puzzles. When archeologists find a place where ancient peoples lived, worked, or played, they have only a few durable remnants of the civilization to work with. Everything else, the people, the animals, their food, and many of their building materials are gone, buried and disintegrated by time.

In studying Native cultures of the far north, archeologists have to work under very difficult conditions. The harshness of the environment degrades the artifacts on the site, and it is also hard on the scientists doing the work. The season for actually unearthing and studying archeological sites gets shorter and shorter as you move farther north.

When you get as far north as the Point Barrow area, you are dealing with a very short season indeed. The time available for excavating makes every find all that more valuable, so when a well-preserved home site at the ancient village of Utqiagvik near Barrow was discovered in 1982, archeologists were excited as it promised to yield some very interesting results.

What they found when they uncovered the site exceeded their expectations. Sometime between 250 to 500 years ago, a massive chunk of sea ice, what the Inupiat call *ivu*, crashed down onto a sod house, killing the five people inside. Three of the bodies consisted of skeletal remains, but the other two bodies were frozen and preserved. These bodies of two women were flown to Fairbanks and underwent autopsies.

The chance to examine tissue remains from an ancient culture was very unusual, and the autopsies revealed some interesting glimpses into the lives of coastal Eskimos.

Both of the women suffered from black lung disease. Normally associated with coal miners in the Lower 48, black lung was the result of breathing the fumes from seal oil lamps in the confines of the sod house.

The older woman, her age estimated at 42 years, suffered from hardening of the arteries, and had survived pneumonia, kidney disease, and bronchitis. The other frozen body was of a woman in her 20s, and she showed signs of black lung as well. Both women suffered from osteoporosis from lack of vitamin D in the diet, both women had recently given birth; it was also discovered that the older woman was nursing at the time of her death, and they both showed signs of seasonal malnutrition.

Archeologists were able to infer many other things from the site as well, including the fact that the older woman was probably the mother of the younger one, and the men of the household were not present when the tragedy occurred. There were tool kits in the house that belonged to two men, their kits distinguished by property marks.

After gathering all the data possible from this unique discovery, the bodies were returned to the area, and the Inupiat elders reburied them in a traditional ceremony.

Reenacting the gold rush days of wine and women.

young days turned over to the mother's brother for training in the ways of men, with the boy's father playing a supporting role. Other forms of adoption were also used to forge bonds between families. Among Tlingit and Haida Indians, a person was born into one of two clans in the community, and could not marry a member of his own clan.

Social disputes in Eskimo and Aleut communities were frequently solved verbally, but Tlingit and Haidas often resorted to warfare in the form of raids and ambushes to capture slaves and property, and as a way to avenge perceived wrongs. Many Athabascans used the potlatch, a ceremony of feasting and gift giving, to settle disputes and make peace.

First Contact with Europeans

When explorers from the European world made contact with Alaska Native societies, the changes wrought by these interlopers were profound. However, this change was neither immediate nor uniform in its character or its effects.

The Aleuts were the first to be affected by newcomers, and the Russian fur traders were neither benevolent nor gracious. They decimated the populations of both the Aleut people and the sea otters, then moved on.

The Tlingits and Haidas were caught in between the English and Americans moving up the coast and the Russians moving east from the Aleutians prospecting for more furs. They were embroiled into international affairs when the British and Americans gave firearms to the coastal Indians for use against the Russians. The Russians managed to establish a garrison at Sitka, the only toehold that they were able to secure in Southeast.

As Europeans extended their explorations to the north coast in search of whales, and into the interior on quests for gold and other minerals, they met up with Eskimos and Athabascans, the last of the native groups to have contact with the newcomers.

The effects of the mingling of Native and European cultures were almost universally negative for the natives. The explorers brought diseases for which

Young Alaskan-Americans enjoying a parade at Homer.

natives had no natural immunities, in many cases decimating local populations. The colluding Europeans and Americans wiped out indigenous wildlife populations as well, and often forced native hunters to help them in these depredations by kidnapping the hunters or their families, or by using murder as a form of coercion. Alcohol was also introduced, the scourges of which continue to plague many native communities today.

Another by-product of contact with the white man was the imposition of political boundaries having no meaning to native peoples. The most notable of these artificial lines was drawn between Big Diomede and Little Diomede Islands. Lying a mere 2.5 miles (4 km) apart in the Bering Strait, Russia claims ownership of Big Diomede, while the United States claims Little Diomede. When the Cold War gathered steam, the Soviet Union converted Big Diomede into a military installation, and all the resident natives were removed to the mainland. Little Diomede residents who strayed across the line into Soviet territory were taken prisoner and detained. With the recent thaw in U.S.-Russian relations, native families are trying to re-establish contacts after generations of foreign interference.

Of course, the most significant example of colonialist behaviour took place when the Russians, having established a handful of trading outposts in the Aleutians and in Southeast, sim-

Evolving Hunting Lores

Eskimo hunting lore comprises a vast amount of knowledge, accumulated over generations and reaching back to the times before things were written down. This body of traditional information, often crucial to survival, was passed along, from father to son, mother to daughter, uncle to nephew, grandparent to grandchild. Children had to learn and remember if they were to survive the harsh realities of the Arctic and prosper in their world. This sum of knowledge covered every aspect of life. Eskimos had to know how and where to build their houses, how to find and catch fish, sea mammals, caribou, birds; how to prepare these animals as food, and how to preserve them in times of scarcity. As Natives have acquired modern tools and equipment, the manner of gathering and preserving food from the wild has continued to evolve. The relationship between the people and the animals they depend upon has remained constant with those village Natives who have managed to stay in touch with the natural world. Synthetic materials for nets, outboard motors, guns, and snow machines have played a part in modifying the traditional methods of gathering wild food, making it more efficient. However, the need to know how to locate animals, when to expect them to appear in certain places, and how to preserve them for storage has remained relatively unchanged.

Fishing has always been an important food resource for interior Eskimos, and knowing when and where to catch each kind of fish as well as how to preserve the catch is vital. Traditionally, fish were taken by using hand-made nets and fish traps. Some fish could also be taken by the use of long-handled gaff hooks. Salmon schooling up in freshwater streams are vulnerable to gaff-hook fishing, as are burbot. Fishermen today can use flashlights to spot burbot at night as they lie in wait for smaller fishes. The gaff, a hook with an eight foot-long handle, is eased into the water and used to snag the fish.

Waterfowl hunting has been changed dramatically by the introduction of shotguns. Before guns were available, waterfowl could be taken during a period each summer called the molt when adult ducks and geese lose their flight feathers and grow new ones. During this transition period they are flightless and vulnerable to capture by hand. The young geese that have not yet learned to fly are also large enough by this time to be worth taking, so the Eskimos would round up flightless adults and juveniles for the larder. One method of catching flightless geese in the rivers was to herd them with boats to steep cutbanks where they could not climb out of the stream. Another adaptation to modern hunting has been to employ the use of dead geese as decoys by propping up the bodies of

ply sold Alaska in its entirety to the United States in 1867. At the time, these practices of conquest and establishment of land ownership were accepted and seldom if ever questioned, especially by members of the dominant society.

Who Owns the Land?

In the years after Alaska became part of the US, the influence of American society began to seep into the native communities. Missionaries from various churches traveled among native villages, bringing the advantages and the disadvantages of modernisation. Natives whose traditional home ranges happened to lie within areas deemed desirable by the American intruders felt these impacts sooner and more dramatically than those whose homes were more remote. Eventually, however, the lives of all native Alaskans would be significantly affected by western society.

Over the years, from the time of the

geese with sticks, making them look lifelike and as if they are feeding. The hunters then call passing flocks into shotgun range by imitating their calls.

Moose hunting has also undergone a significant change with the advent of modern tools. Traditionally, some Athabascan Indians of the interior used snares made of babiche, a kind of raw hide. A noose was suspended over a moose trail, and secured to a tree. The unlucky moose who happened to come by would ensnare himself in the noose, and be quickly strangled. Today when an Athabascan makes a moose snare, he uses steel cable instead of the traditional babiche. Today, the rifle has made moose hunting more efficient than snaring.

Hunters use their tracking skills, along with knowledge of moose behavior, to get within rifle range of a moose. These huge animals provided a plentiful supply of meat and relatively few hunters are needed to provide enough meat for a village's annual use. Even though the hunters contribute equally to the costs of the hunt, the meat is distributed according to need in the village. Larger families receive more meat than small ones. In times of scarcity, food sharing is actually more common than when supplies are plentiful, the opposite behavior from what one would expect in a more self-centered and "capitalistic" community.

Sweet sixteens.

sale of Alaska up through the granting of statehood, the ownership of the land was in a continual state of uncertainty. Ownership of land was an alien concept brought upon the native population. Attempts were made to establish reservations for the natives similar to the Indian reservations of the Lower 48, but this concept did not translate well in Alaska. The granting of homesteads to natives, and the granting of the ownership of small amounts of land surrounding native villages was proposed as well, but rejected as unconventional and impractical for Alaska Natives.

The issue languished for years, its lack of resolution perhaps aided by disorganization within the native community. Long-standing and deep-seated mistrust among the native communities had kept agreements to a minimum and delayed solutions to the issue.

In 1967, the Alaska Federation of Natives was formed, largely as a response to the land claims problem. With an organized group pushing for a settlement, negotiations among the natives and the state and federal governments gathered steam. Proposals and counter proposals were raised, with input from the native groups, sportsmen, miners, the U.S. Department of the Interior, the

An old Eskimo couple at Nome in traditional winter clothing.

U.S. Forest Service, the oil and gas industry, the U.S. Senate Interior Committee, and various other sundry private citizens. But what really forced a final settlement was the Prudhoe Bay oil find.

To get the crude oil from the North Slope of the Brooks Range to the oil terminal in Valdez, a pipeline had to be built over an 800 mile-long corridor. And before work could begin on this project, ownership of the land along the way had to be established. The natives held a trump card in the form of a court order forbidding construction work before land claims were settled. With that kind of incentive hanging over the project, a solution was worked out.

The Alaska Native Claims Settlement Act (ANCSA) was signed into law in December of 1971 and provided for the establishment of 12 Native Regional Corporations, another corporation for natives not resident in Alaska, and some 200 village corporations. Every qualifying native received corporation shares, and the final deal involved land distribution to the various corporations and a total cash settlement amounting to a figure of US$1 billion.

As the Native Corporations invested their cash in business ventures in Alaska and outside, the results were variable. Some corporations made money, some lost, and some underwent management difficulties and changes. Today they are a potent economic force in Alaska, with business interests touching every corner of the state.

ANCSA, however, could not solve all the native problems or the issue of land ownership. While Indian tribes in the Lower 48 commonly have the right to manage fish and game on their land and to levy taxes, the state government here interpreted the ANCSA agreement to mean that Alaska Natives had relinquished those rights. Native sovereignty – the ability of Natives to govern themselves and their lands according to their own traditions – has become an issue in recent years. In 1993, the federal government granted tribal status to Alaska Natives for the first time, opening the door to a new round of court decisions concerning self-determination.

Today, generalizations about how or where Alaska Natives live are impossible. While some members of the na-

A father and daughter enjoy the sea breeze at Juneau harbour.

tive communities have assimilated into the dominant western culture by going to schools and colleges in Alaska and outside, others live in a way not much different from their ancestors.

There are native villages where the signs of twentieth century civilization are few and far between, and where the people live soul-bound to their land and traditional cultures. Most villages and communities are somewhere in between the two extremes, maintaining the simplicity of a subsistence culture with the often conflicting characteristics of the American cash economy. Each individual can pick and choose between the features of the two worlds, combining the old with the new to try and form a comfortable blend.

Alaskan Natives, living in two worlds.

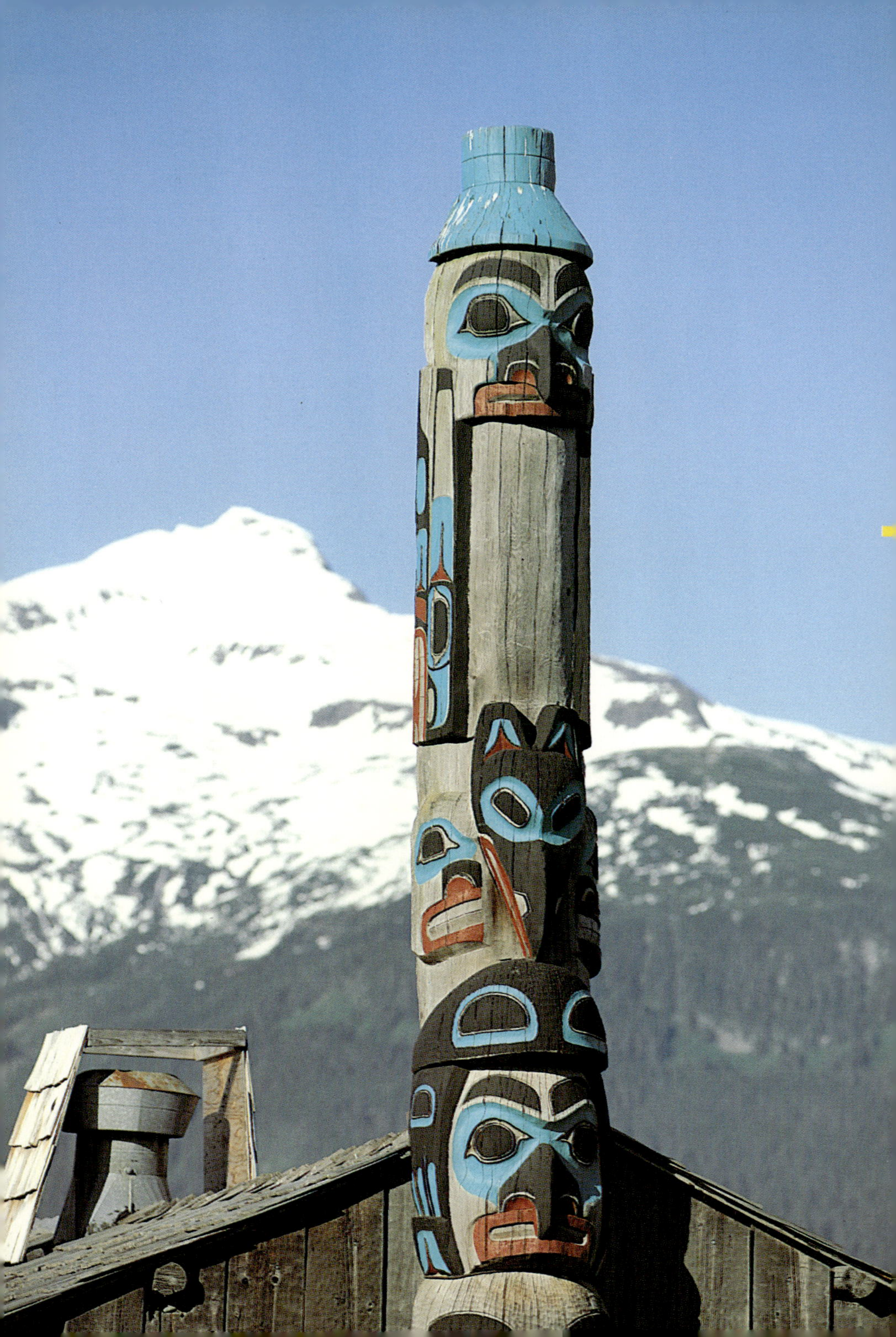

RITUALS & REVERENCE

Religion

When Russian and American missionaries came to Alaska, they found a native population that was in some ways predisposed to accept the teachings of western religions. All the native groups already had a belief system encompassing the concept of a spiritual life, most believed in the idea of a creator, and they also understood the idea of an afterlife. Adapting these beliefs to fit the white man's religion, was still a formidable task. The sheer size of the country to be covered, and the physical hardships that they had to endure made the proselytizing and conversion of the Natives a test for even the most dedicated of missionaries.

Totems, the native bedrock.

Russian Orthodoxy

The first Russians to visit the Aleutians were fur traders, or *promyshlennini*, eager to exploit the sea otter populations. A variety of ways were used to bring the Aleutian hunters into their fold. They used

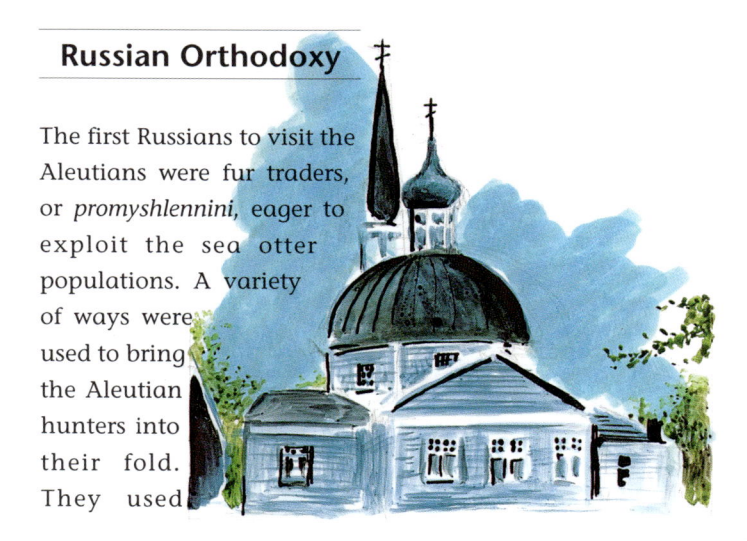

Russian church spires at Sitka.

threats of violence, murder, and the holding hostage of families as powerful inducements to co-operation. The fur traders also used baptism as a way of acquiring natives as workers and hunters, both to assist them in their pursuit of furs, and to keep other traders from using them.

'The Three Saints'

The religious influence of the Russians was made official in 1794 when a Russian ship, *The Three Saints*, arrived on Kodiak bearing Russian Orthodox monks and novices. The clerics sought to "enlighten the heathen" natives, and minister to the needs of the Russians. The Shelikov-Golikov Company, the precursor to the Russian-American Company, paid the expenses of the clergy. With the passing of time and with the arrival of more Russian workers, the brutality of these company men toward the natives soon became a constant source of recurring conflict between the missionaries and employees. As the Orthodox missionar-

A medieval enchantment awaits visitors of St. Peter and Paul Church, St. Paul Island.

ies began their work among the Natives, they found that the Koniag Yup'iks on Kodiak, were in a way predisposed to accept the teachings of Christianity in that their belief system recognized the existence of both a good and an evil spirit, and the concept of an afterlife.

Mission Schools and Hospitals

The Russians put together the means for writing and preserving the Aleut language by devising both an alphabet

Native Religions

Totem Heritage Center, Ketchikan.

Native religions have much in common with one another, as well as significant differences from one culture to the next. One of the universal similarities was a belief in an active and thriving spirit world. This world was inhabited by both human and animal spirits. Natives communed with the spirits of the animals and tried to influence their behavior by following certain rituals during hunting seasons.

Aleuts believed in a powerful creator, responsible for success in hunting and in the reincarnation of the spirits of humans. This deity was also responsible for making the volcanoes erupt, for causing the sun, moon, and stars to shine, and for providing the natural bounty necessary for the Aleut well-being. There were also good and evil spirits to contend with, and animal spirits to consider when hunting. Amulets and charms were worn by the men to ensure good luck afield, and wooden masks were worn as part of dance ceremonies to communicate with the spirit world.

As a means of prolonging the presence of the recently deceased, a practise of ancient tribes, Aleuts sometimes removed the internal organs from the body, stuffed it with grass, and kept it in the 'barabara', sometimes for months. Unique among Native Alaskans, Aleuts sometimes mummified their dead, a practice apparently reserved for honored whaling captains.

The Inupiat Eskimos believed in reincarnation and a recycling of both human and animal spirits. Newborn infants were frequently named after recently deceased people, and animals killed for food were treated with respect to ensure that the animal's spirit could leave the body to inhabit another. If the spirits were not properly released, or if parts of the animal were wasted, the animals would not return to offer themselves again as food.

Inupiat culture made use of shamans, people who had a special relationship with the spirit world. Shamans presided over certain ceremonies, and could forecast the weather and the return of animals. Whaling cultures prayed to Allingnuk, Dweller of the Moon, for the return

and a dictionary. In line with official church policy, they translated some materials and songs into Native languages, providing texts in Aleut, Tlingit, and Yup'ik. They organized schools and orphanages along with the missions, and provided medical care as well.

As the fur hunters killed off the otters in the regions bordering the Gulf of Alaska, the Russian-American Company began to explore western Alaska and the interior. The church missionaries followed and established churches at St. Michael on Norton Sound, St. Paul and St. George Islands in the Pribilofs, at Russian Mission and Little Russian Mis-

of the whales and that the whaling captains would be successful in their hunts.

The Yup'ik Eskimos also believed in the cyclical nature of the human spirit, and that it was brought back to earth and passed from one person to another. There was both a good spirit and an evil spirit that was a part of their lives. The good spirit, known as Sky's Child, lived above the earth and was able to look down and to oversee the lives of the people.

The Yup'ik engaged in ritual activities and ceremonies and avoided taboo behaviors in order to stay in the good graces of the animal spirits. A lack of respect to these spirits would result in a lack of hunting success. The Yup'ik people depended on a shaman to predict hunting success and to interpret the spirit world.

The Athabascans believed that in the past, the spirits of men and the spirits of animals talked to one another. However, these ancient relationships were transformed by the deceit of the mythical Raven, the trickster of many Native legends and tales. The Athabascan shaman practiced medical cures and pointed the hunters towards game populations when game was scarce and the tribe famished.

Tlingit and Haida cultures used myths and legends to explain their place in the world and their relationships with the animal world. The raven as trickster occupies a prominent place in their myths, along with the wolf, eagle, and bear. Spirits of humans were believed to be reincarnated, and these Indian peoples also used the services of shamans to intercede in the spirit world, and to do battle with the shamans of other clans or tribes. As such, Shamans held a high placing in their society.

sion in the Yukon-Kuskokwim delta region, and at Kenai. To keep up with the expansion of mission territory, and to help in keeping up with native populations that were sometimes quite mobile, the missionaries trained natives for the priesthood.

When Alaska was sold to the US in

Looking out from a chapel by the lake at Juneau.

1867, the Russian-American Company left, as did most of the clergy. Missions were left in Kodiak, Sitka and Unalaska. The terms of the treaty allowed the church to keep its property in Alaska and to continue to pursue its mission under the guarantee of freedom of religion. The missions continued to receive financial support from the state until the Bolshevik Revolution of 1917.

Influx of Protestantism

In 1880, the representatives of the various Protestant denominations got together and divided up Alaska into spheres of influence. They reserved Kodiak and the Cook Inlet area for the

Kiana Friends Church, a place of prayers for Quakers.

Baptists, the Yukon region for the Episcopalians, the Aleutians and the nearby Shumagin Islands for the Methodists, the Kuskokwim and Nushagak river areas for the Moravians, the Cape Prince of Wales area of the Seward Peninsula for the Congregationalists. The Presbyterians kept their established missions in Southeast, and agreed to provide for the Point Barrow region as well.

In addition to these Protestant sects, the Friends Church, or Quakers, also sent missionaries to Alaska, and gained a foothold in several Eskimo communities, spreading their unique form of prayers to the locals.

Some of the Protestant denominations were not as accepting of existing native beliefs and practices as were the Russians. Falsely believing that the ceremonies involving shamans to be the worship of evil spirits, the missionaries forbade the natives to practice their traditional rituals. And whereby the Orthodox clerics learned the Native languages and translated texts for their use, other religions found it easier to compel the Indians to learn English, and to stamp out the Native languages. They also forbade the traditional dances and potlatches in the process of converting them to Christianity. These actions jeopardized the very survival of native culture and tradition.

A more positive influence however, was asserted by the missionaries in trying to counteract the taints of white culture on the natives. They saw the

The holy abode of a Russian bishop's house at Sitka.

brutal treatment of many of the American miners and traders, and especially the horrible consequences of the introduction of alcohol. The missionaries lobbied against the sale of alcohol to natives, and some tried to outlaw all alcohol sales in Alaska.

Reverend Sheldon Jackson

A leader in this movement was Sheldon Jackson, a Presbyterian minister. Reverend Jackson began visiting Alaska in 1877, and soon saw the need for protection of the native population from the exploitation by the whites. The Reverend Jackson was appointed as the agent for education in Alaska, and soon clashed with the civil authorities over the issues of alcohol and education facilities for native children. He also foresaw problems with the economic status of the local Indians with the coming of the Europeans, and saw the importation and herding of reindeer as the answer. This enterprise prospered, and provided employment and income for some of the reindeer herders.

The Roman Catholics sent Jesuit priests to Alaska as missionaries, and the first Catholic parish was established at Fort Wrangell in 1879, and a resident priest was sent to Juneau in 1885. The first Catholic diocese was established in Juneau in 1951, followed by Fairbanks in 1962, and the Archdiocese of Anchorage in 1966. As dioceses were estab-

Totem Poles

Totem poles carved by Indian tribes of the Pacific Northwest, from Washington state up to Southeast Alaska are a distinctive and unique art form. Tribal differences exist between poles, their symbolism, and carving details. For the most part, certain generalizations about the poles, their histories, and their uses can be made. The earliest types of carvings made by the coastal Indians were house poles and mortuary poles. House poles were the main upright structural members supporting the main beams in the large wooden houses inhabited by the Indians. These poles were often decorated with elaborate carvings as symbols of status in the houses. Mortuary poles were erected at Indian graveyards. Carved poles were used as gravesite markers, and as receptacles to hold the ashes of the deceased. The first carvings on house and mortuary poles were done with relatively crude tools of stone and jadeite. Details were later carved with finer tools made of shell and beaver teeth. Only after white men brought iron and steel tools to the region did the carving of elaborate poles sometimes topping 60 ft (18 m) high became practical.

Totem poles served two functions – to tell tribal myths, and to show a family's lineage and status. The carved figures represented animals or mythic beings. The topmost animal signified the crest of the family that owned the pole. Human figures were represented as well, and mythic figures were created that combined features of humans and animals. Familiarity with the symbols used, and the significance of their placement on the pole and their relationships with one another is necessary for interpretation. As totem poles evolved into more impressive and larger specimens, a class of skilled artisans evolved as well. These men traveled from village to village, accepting commissions. They would listen to the story that the pole was meant to represent, then design an appropriate arrangement of symbols. These artists often directed workers in the rough stages of the

The intertwining fate of hunters and the hunted as depicted on totems.

lished, parish priests gradually took over from the missionaries.

The Nuns

The Catholics also sent nuns to Alaska. The Sisters of Saint Ann arrived in Juneau in 1886 and established a school and hospital there. They worked with the Jesuits in building a mission on the Yukon River. The Ursuline Nuns and the Sisters of Providence, the Sisters of St. Joseph of Peace and the Grey Nuns of the Sacred Heart followed, providing schools and hospitals.

carving, leaving the fine detail work for themselves. They were highly paid and enjoyed the respect of the members of the tribes. The coming of the white man and his iron tools meant that totem pole carving could reach new levels of skill and sophistication. The ability of tribal chiefs to trade furs for other goods also meant increased prosperity for the upper classes of Tlingit and Haida society.

However, other changes were not so advantageous. The first Christian missionaries saw the traditional beliefs and ceremonies as detrimental to the spiritual well-being of the new potential converts. Potlatches and other tribal ceremonies were eventually forbidden, as was the carving of totems, which the missionaries interpreted as idolatry. After a while, the craft of totem carving died out, and the art form was nearly lost.

However, in the late 1930s the Civilian Conservation Corps undertook a project to refurbish, repair, and replace the totem poles in Southeast Alaska. Poles that had been left to rot were salvaged and moved to collection points. There the old poles were repaired when possible, or new poles were commissioned to replace those beyond saving. A few old craftsmen were found who remembered bits and pieces of the traditions, and a new generation of carvers was trained. Today, totem pole carving lives on, and the process can be viewed at workshops in Haines, Sitka, and at Saxman Totem Park in Ketchikan. Outstanding examples of poles are available for viewing at Klawock and Hydaburg on Prince of Wales Island, and at the totem parks of Ketchikan.

A highlight for Alaskan Catholics came in 1981. Pope John Paul II, in traveling between Tokyo and Rome, stopped in Anchorage to visit the faithful. During his brief stop, the Pope celebrated an outdoor Mass on a specially built altar, gave a sermon to thousands of attendees, and even had time for a

Orthodox churches tell of the past links with Russians.

quick ride on a dog sled.

Today's Alaska: Flourishing Faiths

Today, numerous religions flourish in Alaska and have added the Jewish and Asian faiths to the mix of Christianity. The Russian Orthodox religion continues to prosper, and several Russian communities of "Old Believers" have retained their heritage and traditions intact over the years. Many natives have held onto their "new" religions through successive generations, while others have returned to more traditional ways, reviving the ceremonies and rituals that were at one time suppressed.

RELIGION

104

The ample surroundings of the Russian bishop's house at Sitka, amidst a forest and lake.

RELIGION

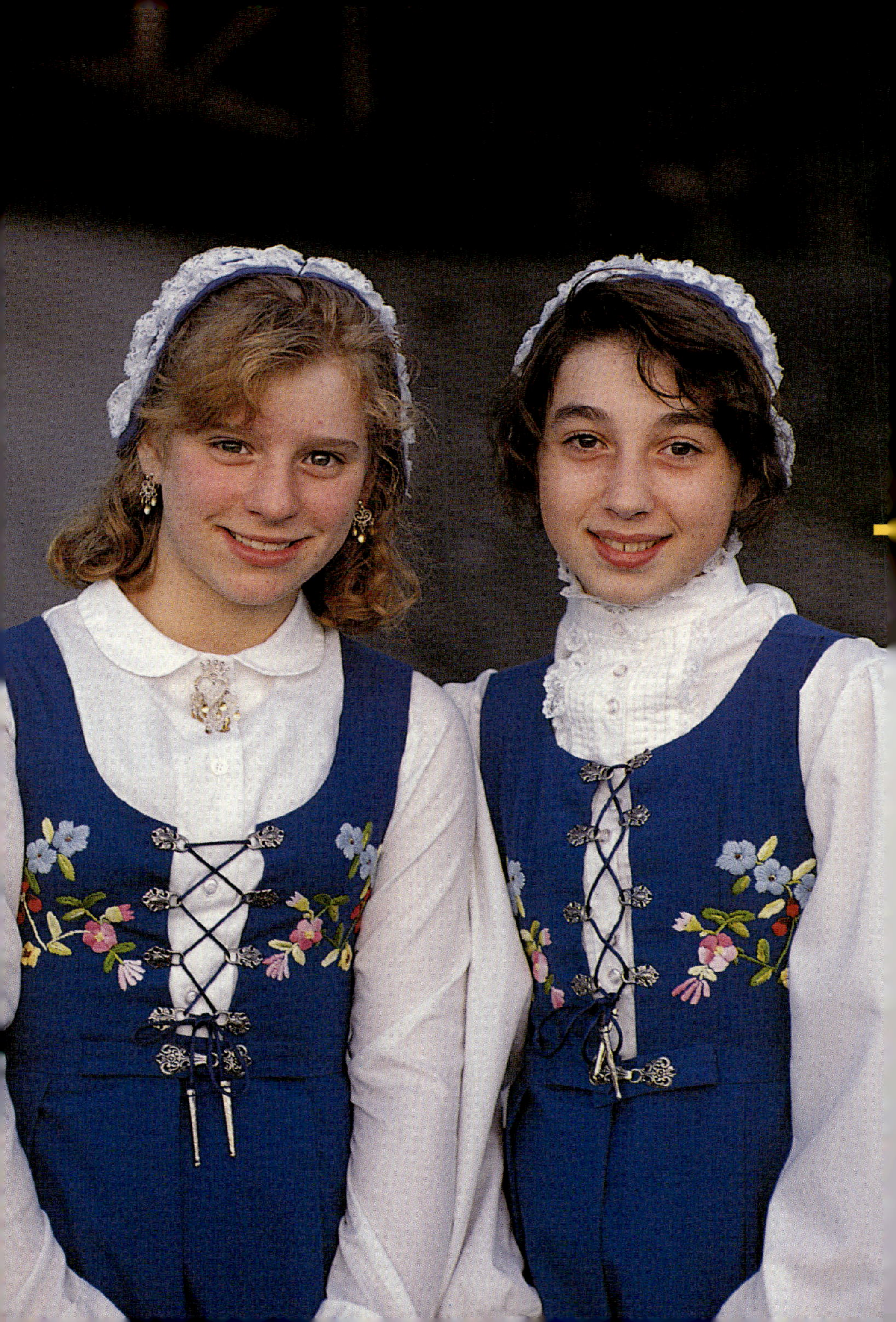

THE HEAT OF WINTERFEST

Culture & Festivals

When it comes to festivals and other related excuses for having a good time, it is hard to match Alaska in variety and exuberance. Celebrating everything from the longest day of the year to the ice breaking up on the rivers and the infamous Talkeetna Moose Dropping Festival, there is a celebration going on just about anytime the whole year round somewhere in the state.

Some folks might think that winter time in Alaska is a time of bitter cold and darkness, when sensible people would go all out to avoid the outdoors and gatherings. Well, that might be what most sensible people do, but lots of Alaskans think that winter is the perfect time to stage a bash of some sort, if for no other reason than to fight off the effects of cabin fever during long winter.

Young Norwegian dancers celebrate Norwegian Independence day at Petersburg.

Winter Festivals

Kicking off the winter festivities is the Talkeetna Wilderness

An eskimo band playing at Nome, King Island.

Women's Contest and Bachelor Society Ball. The town of Talkeetna lies about 100 miles (161 km) north of Anchorage, and is a favorite jumping off point for climbers heading for Mt. McKinley. In December, the local bachelors crawl out of the Bush, get cleaned up, shaved and auction themselves off to presumably fun-loving females, while at the same time the Wilderness Women's contest shows off the skills of prospective backcountry brides in such essential skills as wood chopping, water carrying, and fetching beer for the men.

In Nome, the first Saturday in December is the time for the Fireman's Carnival, held by the Nome Fire Department. Games of chance, concession stands, and raffles help to break up the winter monotony.

In January, Seward celebrates with the Polar Bear Festival, which culminates with brave or foolhardy souls jumping into the icy waters of Resurrection Bay to raise funds for charity. This foolhardy event is always a real crowd pleaser. Sitka and Kodiak reflect their Russian heritage by celebrating Russian Christmas, and a masquerade

'Fur Rondy' is the most widely participated winter festival in Alaska.

ball is held in Kodiak to celebrate Russian New Year.

February sees Winterfest in King Salmon, the Iceworm Festival in Cordova, Chistochina Fun Days in that community near Glennallen, the Festival of Native Arts at the University of Alaska, Fairbanks, and the Nenana Ice Classic week-end festival.

The Nenana Ice Classic is the Alaska version of a state lottery. Alaskans buy US$2.00 tickets, and indicate the date and time they think the ice will go out on the Tanana River. A tripod is set out on the frozen river, attached to a timing device on the shore. When the ice breaks up and the tripod moves downstream, it trips the mechanism, indicating the time. Whoever is lucky enough to guess the closest time wins the pot, usually in excess of US$70,000.00.

The largest and most popular winter carnival in the state is the Anchorage Fur Rendezvous. Held in February, "Fur Rondy" commemorates the days when trappers would come into town to sell their year's catch of furs, and get together for their annual dose of city entertainment. Over 150 events every year include North American Championship sled dog racing, auto racing, masquerade balls, craft and ice sculpture competitions, midway rides, fireworks, parades and other fun and festive. Extending over two week-ends and the week-days in between, it draws party-goers from well outside the confines of Anchorage.

In March, spring is just around the

Fur Rondy's traditional blanket toss, a definite crowd-puller.

corner and the ice begins to thaw, but it is still cold enough to hold the last of the winter festivals. The Copper Valley Winter Carnival is held near Glennallen, and North Pole and Fairbanks hold winter carnivals as well.

In Nome, the end point for the 1,100 mile (1,770 km) long Iditarod Trail Sled Dog Race, the town's population swells with race officials, friends, families, helpers for the racing mushers (mushers are the 'commanders' of a team of sled dogs), and other assorted folks who happen to think that being in Nome in March might be fun. There is always a large crowd on hand to welcome the mushers as they cross the finish line on Front Street, no matter what time of day or night it happens. Other festivities in town include dart, racquetball, volleyball, bowling, and basketball tournaments, a snowshoe softball game, art exhibits, Native dancing, movies and slide shows, to name a few. The Iditarod Awards Banquet is held 72 hours after the race winner arrives, and subsequent banquets are held as more mushers finish the race.

'Frostbite footracers' at Fur Rondy compete against time, cold winds and of course, frost bites.

Spring Festivals

As spring gathers steam, the nature of the festivals changes from enduring winter to celebrating the arrival of springtime. In Cordova, Copper Day on the second Saturday in April honors Cordova's mining and railroad history. The Homer Spring Arts Festival in April and May features guest performers and local artists in theater, dance, and visual arts, and in May the Kachemak Bay Shorebird Festival greets the returning

A magnificent night scene at the Fur Rondy carnival.

migratory birds. In Juneau, the Alaska Folk Festival is held in April, and the Juneau Jazz and Classics Festival in May. In Petersburg, the Little Norway Festival commemorates Norwegian Independence Day in May.

Summer Festivals

June is the beginning of summer, and the long days, gorgeous weather augurs the return of the tourist crowd with more festivities and outdoor excitement. Starting of the season is the Sitka Summer Music Festival which draws international chamber musicians to the area for 3 weeks every June. In Fairbanks, the Great Tanana River Raft Classic Race ends 80 miles (129 km) downstream in Nenana, where Nenana River Days means races, games, a street dance, and a parade.

The summer solstice, the longest day of the year, carries special significance for people who have weathered yet another long, cold, and dark winter. The people in Fairbanks play a midnight baseball game without the necessity of artificial lighting, and in Nome the Midnight Sun Festival features a midnight parade, a raft race, softball tournament, games, food, etc. There is also a midnight sun marathon and solstice celebration in Anchorage, and a solstice picnic in Skagway. Sleep is deferred until autumn.

July sees the Talkeetna Moose Dropping Festival. (Don't worry, they don't

Forget-me-nots flower baskets add to the festive mood in Anchorage.

Anchorage's Fur Rendezvous

The winter festival parade at Homer.

Every February, the folks in Anchorage throw a huge 10 day-long party, and everyone is invited. A medley of over 140 events, varying from the serious to the frivolous, it is just the sort of celebration needed to break up the long monotony of winter and step into the heartening pace of springtime.

During the time when fur production was one of Alaska's major industries, trappers looked forward to the end of winter for a couple of reasons. The hardships of the long, cold, dark time of year were drawing to a close, and a chance to visit with fur buyers and the other trappers meant a break in their isolation. Moreover, selling the year's furs put money into their pockets, and 'Fur Rondy', as it is fondly called, gave them a chance to mingle, drink, dance, and have a great time.

Anchorage began to honor this old tradition in the 1930s, and except for a short break during the war, has kept up with the celebration every year since. And each year, the party gets bigger and bigger, with events included according to the whims of creative organizers.

Today the Fur Rondy begins with a fireworks display on a Friday night, and runs through the following weekend. There is something for everybody young and old, including dances, contests, sled dog races, food, rides, shows, films, music, and games.

Events held outside include a Grand Prix auto race, and the World Championship Sled Dog Race. There are also championship sled dog races for juniors and women, skijoring contests and the World Championship Dog Weight Pull (Alaskans love any contest involving dogs!). There is also an internationally-sanctioned snow sculpture contest, where contestants carve some truly amazing objects out of blocks of packed snow. Some of the more whimsical outdoor events include snowshoe softball games, outhouse races, and an ice bowling contest that promise fun for all.

Indoor activities abound as well. Arts and crafts shows give people a chance to choose from the varied offerings of local artisans. Tournaments in basketball, pool, chess, and wrist wrestling offer quite a variety of tests of skill for both the energetic and the thinkers.

Another tradition of the Rondy is the Wild Game Barbecue. Since the law does not allow game meat to be sold, this free barbecue is one of the few chances that visitors have to taste Alaskan wild game. The variety of food includes moose, elk, caribou, seal, muktuk, bison and just about everything edible that wanders around in Alaska, and cook in a variety of ways that will make anyone's mouth water.

So if you find yourself contemplating a winter trip to Alaska, by all means, time it to coincide with this annual event. Your friends might think you are crazy for visiting Anchorage in February, but put on your fur-lined party hat and give Rondy a shot.

Alaska's championship sled dog race begins in Anchorage.

drop the moose from anywhere). The festival centers around a contest whereby the participants throw moose droppings. In King Salmon, the "Fishtival" is a two day event featuring a survival suit race, a salmon filleting contest, and a parade. The Deltana Fair in Delta Junction features local handicrafts, a horse and livestock show, and agricultural exhibits. Fairbanks celebrates Golden Days, commemorating the town's founding, and holds a two week Summer Arts Festival, where workshops and concerts, from jazz to the classics come on show.

Fourth of July celebrations are held statewide, with noteworthy events in Delta, Haines, Homer, Seldovia, Tok, Nome, and North Pole. In Seward, the annual run to the top of Mt. Marathon and back attracts participants from all over the state eager to test their stamina. The Ahtna Arts and Crafts Fair is held in Copper Center, near Glennallen.

August is the month for state fairs, and Alaska has no fewer than five of them. Because of the size and travel requirements, the state fairs are held more or less regionally, with a big one in Southcentral Alaska.

The Southeast Alaska State Fair is held in Haines, and it coincides with the Bald Eagle Music Festival. The Kenai Peninsula State Fair is celebrated over a week-end, and the Tanana Valley State Fair goes on for a week in Fairbanks. In Kodiak, they put on a state fair and rodeo over a week-end.

The "real" state fair is held in Palmer

The New Archangel Dancers entertain audiences at Sitka.

on the last week of August and the first week of September. Games, agricultural exhibits and contests, food, midway rides, concerts, everything you would associate with county and state fairs in the Lower 48 is there.

Autumn Festivals

As the summer winds down, the festival schedule too thins out. September has the Seldovia Blueberry Festival, and October's offerings are pretty much limited to the Taste of Homer, a food festival featuring local seafood specialties, and an Oktoberfest in Anchorage. Autumn turns into winter, and soon enough it's time for the cycle to start again.

The Arts

Artistic and cultural pursuits other than festivals can also be found, although they tend to be less numerous. In Haines, the Chilkat Dancers perform Indian ceremonial dances, giving regular performances all summer. The local Lynn Canal Community Players also present a melodrama, "Smell of the Yukon", and masked story telling, "Chilkoot Legends", at Dalton City. Located on the fair grounds, Dalton City was re-created from the movie set of "White Fang", and also features Tlingit carvers, the Alaska Natural Resources Museum, and Gold Rush memorabilia.

Homer features a thriving artist's

CULTURE & FESTIVALS

116

The impressive Museum of History and Art located in the heart of Anchorage.

colony with numerous art galleries. There is a Concert on the Lawn in August, and during the summer, the Pier One Theatre on the Homer Spit features local talent in live theater, presented in a come-as-you-are warehouse on weekends with some weekday events.

Anchorage is home to the Performing Arts Center, offering year-round activities. Touring companies of Broadway shows, nationally known entertainers, as well as locally produced events in several theaters keep the place humming continually.

Museums

Museums are scattered around the state, offering glimpses into the past for the curious visitor. In Anchorage, the Museum of History and Art offers art exhibits and cultural artifacts, with an emphasis on northern items from the prehistoric to the contemporary. There is a large permanent art display, and more than 30 new shows and exhibits every year for the art enthusiasts.

Other museums in Anchorage include the Alaska Heritage Library and a Museum housing Native art, the Oscar Anderson House Museum. The Alaska Aviation Heritage Museum near Lake Hood commemorates Alaska's ongoing love affair with flying machines.

In Fairbanks, the University of Alaska Museum on the grounds at UAF is one of the most popular tourist spots in the state. The permanent and rotat-

The Wonder of Alaskan Story Telling

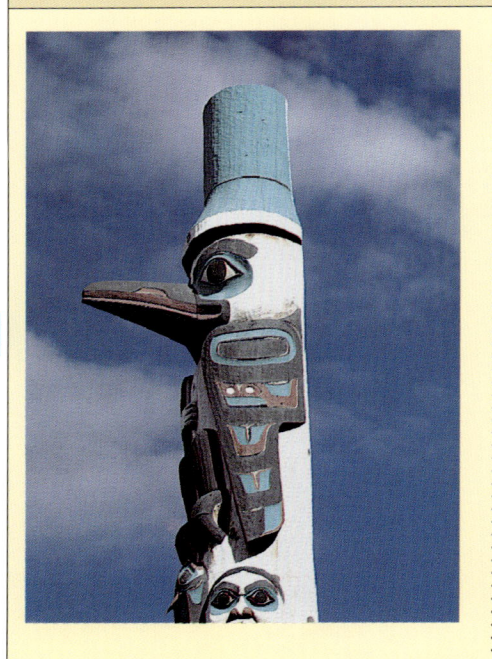

The spellbinding 'Raven' plays the lead in many a Indian tale.

The wisdom of elder Alaskan Natives were passed to the young by story telling as they had no written language. The Elders explained the natural world to children through the use of legends and fables, and told of the people's origin. They explained the behaviors of animals, and told how they came to have so many different shapes and sizes. They also reinforced group bonds with stories on moral codes and cautioned against transgressions.

The Inupiat Eskimos told tales about a man from long ago, Ekeuhnick, who learned about the world from the prophet Aungayoukuksuk. The prophet taught Ekeuhnick about the natural world, and how to count and name the months of the year and how to predict the weather. In the time of the prophet, the land was warm and the people lived an easy life. However, he taught the young man that one day, an earthquake would come, followed by the eruption of a volcano and an eclipse of the sun. This would result in snow and ice covering the land and Ekeuhnick would have to teach the people how to survive. He learned about warm clothing and fire, and by watching the animals he learned to live in the cold. He taught the rest of the people these lessons, and they too learned to adapt to the cold.

Respect for animals and cautions against breaking taboos were passed on through fables. One Eskimo tale tells of two boys who trapped a ptarmigan, then cruelly poked out its eyes to see if it could still see where it was going. Then they plucked off all its feathers to see if it could fly. After that, they left the bird to die. That night the boys became very sick, and the shaman could do nothing to help them. They died in pain and agony as they had shown disrespect for the ptarmigan.

The Tlingit and Haida Indians told many tales about Raven, the trickster. Raven was involved in many aspects of Indian life, and had the reputation as the giver of life, the maker of land, and the bringer of fire to the people and the bringer of water in the time of drought. He also played tricks on the other animals and on the people, and not always in a humorous manner. This complex creature embodied good and bad qualities, and could be responsible for planting all the trees in the world in one tale, and in another be the reason why the cormorant has no tongue, because Raven pulled it out long ago.

Athabascan believed that Raven created the world and brought light. Raven was very powerful, and even though he was mischievous, he was essential to the people. One day a chief grew tired of Raven's tricks, so he tricked the trickster, and captured him in a bag. He climbed a mountain, and threw the bag over the side. It crashed on the rocks below, killing Raven and scattering his feathers everywhere.

Soon after, all the water began to disappear. The Shaman explained that it was because Raven had been killed. So the chief had to gather up all the pieces and feathers from Raven, and put him back together again. Then Raven came back to life, and the water returned. That is why Natives do not harm Raven today as they fear reprisals.

Saxman village youngsters learn their cultural dance at an early age.

ing exhibits feature the state's natural and cultural history.

Juneau is home to the Alaska State Museum, featuring historical, cultural, and natural history exhibits. The Juneau Douglas City Museum is devoted to the area's colorful gold mining past where a visitor can travel back in time to the gold rush days that made Alaska.

The Resurrection Bay Historical Society operates the Seward Museum, with exhibits on Native art and culture, historical documents pertinent to the town, and an exhibit detailing the effects of the 1964 earthquake.

Other noteworthy museums around the state include the Talkeetna Historical Society Museum, the Dorothy G. Page Museum and the Museum of Alaska Transportation and Industry in Wasilla. Locally and professionally run museums includes Cordova, Copper Center, Ketchikan, Valdez, Homer, Nome, Haines, Skagway, Dillingham, Wales, and Wrangell. In fact, just about every town that caters to the visitor has a museum of one sort or another, all of them adding pieces to Alaska's wide and diverse historical puzzle.

Visitors interested in investigating Alaska's culture and history in greater detail can contact local travel agencies. They can put you in touch with tour companies specializing in historical, natural history, and cultural subjects. The possibilities are interesting and endless, the only limitations are your time and your budget.

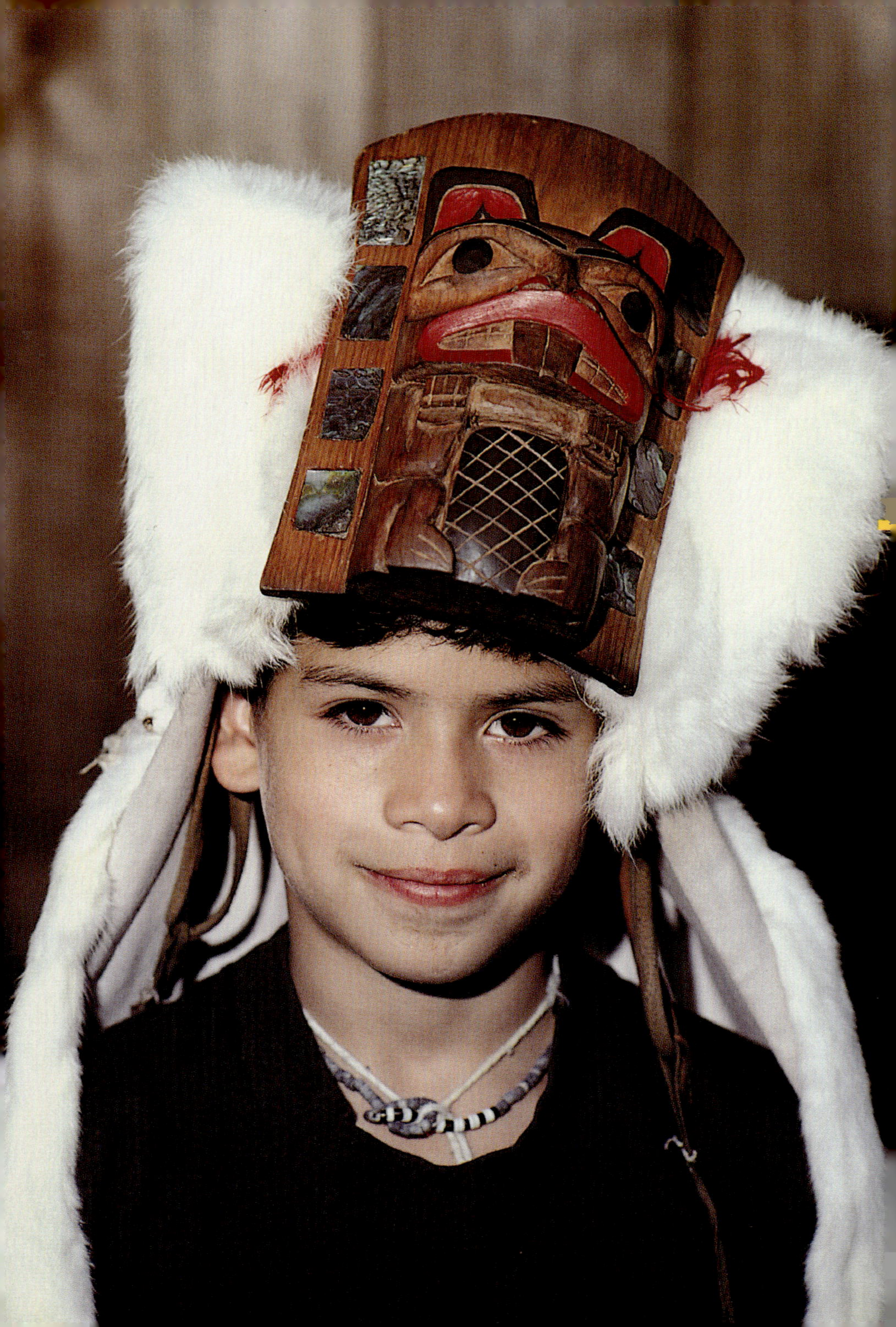

NATIVE INSPIRATIONS

Handicrafts

The marketing and trading of handicrafts as souvenirs can be thought of in two very different ways. On the one hand, the practice can be viewed as degrading to the art of indigenous people, taking useful or sacred objects and displaying them as mere curiosities. On the other hand, the artisans are perpetuating parts of their culture, spreading it to a wider audience for their appreciation, while honing their traditional craft skills and with it, cash and a measure of independence into their lives.

Native girl adorning a ceremonial headdress.

Some of the items sold as craft pieces today often began as inventions to allow the native people to better adapt in their environment and have through the years of making, evolved into stylized works of art. Baskets of woven grasses and birch bark, kitchen utensils such as wooden bowls, knives and spoons fall into this category of artwork.

Other pieces were traditionally used in religious or spiritual ceremonies. Native peoples lived in a world inhabited by the spirits of animals and the spirits of their ancestors, and

Modern tools bring speed and precision to native workmanship.

in some cases the worlds were divided by a very thin line. Art works such as masks and representations of animals often functioned as ways to exercise some control over the environment by communicating with spirits. Totem poles and decorations on ornamented hats, boxes, kitchen utensils, often described stories about the object's owners.

Art objects were produced according to specific rules of the culture. Today, much of the artwork is produced not for use in native ceremonies, but for sale to collectors and tourists. The qual-

duced carvings of ivory from walrus tusks and from whalebone, Aleuts wove baskets from local grasses, and Indians produced elaborate wood carvings designs for masks and other functional and symbolic objects. However, trade between groups also allowed artists to acquire exotic materials that enabled them to expand their artistic horizons and make new creations.

Some of the materials used by Alaska Natives are reserved for their use by the Marine Mammal Protection Act. Non-natives may not possess unworked walrus ivory or other parts of marine mammals. However, once the material has been transformed into artwork or clothing, it may be sold to and possessed by anyone.

Eskimo Carvings and Clothes

Local ivory carvings from the times before contact with white men were mostly functional or ceremonial in intent. All men knew how to carve, and they made charms and amulets to assist in hunting success, as well as animal pieces to adorn household items. The bow drill, the tool used to make many of the pieces, was often elaborately decorated.

In the latter part of the 19th century, when gold miners and whalers reached western and northern Alaska, the types of art produced showed a distinct change. In these earliest forms of market art, the natives began to pro-

ity of these objects varies considerably, and falls into the categories of collectible art and souvenir art. Those things produced for sale rather than for use by native artisans are usually referred to as market art.

The types of art objects produced depend for the most part on the materials available to the artists. Eskimos pro-

HANDICRAFTS

124

A native American in dance costume poses before her traditional home, 'barabara'.

Caribou masks of varied expressions are used by Eskimos to communicate with spirits.

duce daily tools such as dice, paperweights, and cribbage boards, used in keeping score of card games.

Traditional ivory carvings vary in style from village to village, and from artist to artist. In the past, much of the work was unsigned, but today, with greater acknowledgement, most of the larger pieces and many of the smaller ones as well carry the names of the native artists.

While carving has traditionally been done exclusively by men, the sewing of clothing has been done solely by women. Clothing has evolved from the purely functional to the elaborate and decorative. Parkas, hats, mukluks, were traditionally made from the skins and furs of locally available animals. Elaborate pieces, especially parkas, were made to show the skill and creativity of the artisan. Made from the skins of seal, caribou, and polar bear, they are often ornamented with bird and fish skins, and the hides of wolf, wolverine, and ermine, and with beadwork trim.

The women of Nunivak and Nelson Islands in Southwest Alaska make garments and accessories from qiviut, the fine underfur of the musk ox. This material is extremely fine and very warm for its light weight and is good to take on travel trips.

The skills used in making fur garments were used in making dolls as well. The dolls, outfitted in detailed and elaborate fur outfits, were made for children to play with, but also had some spiritual

Eskimo Ivory Carving

Bold and original, Alaskan motifs carved in ivory in both modern and traditional styles.

Since the passage of the Marine Mammal Protection Act in 1972, only Natives are allowed to possess unworked fresh walrus ivory. Once the ivory is turned into artwork, non-Natives are allowed to possess the artwork.

For at least 2,000 years, Eskimo artisans have been carving artworks and practical items from ivory. The souvenir pieces as well as the serious art items bought and sold today came down to us through a long tradition of carving.

The ivory comes from several sources. Walrus tusks and teeth are the major source of the fresh ivory used in artwork, while the fossilized ivory of walrus, mammoth and mastodon tusks can also be used. Old tusks are often found on river banks, beaches, or inadvertently dug up during excavation work.

The fossilized material differs quite a bit from fresh ivory. It has a distinctively different color from fresh ivory, and is often used in specialized pieces that take advantage of its unusual color. Also, its physical properties are different from fresh walrus ivory, which somehow limits its use in carving.

Walrus are a protected species under the Marine Mammal act, but they are not endangered. The natives take walrus for food and uses the other parts of the animal for clothing as well as for handicrafts.

Walrus ivory is highly prized by carvers because of its marvelous physical properties. It is possible for an expert carver to work out extremely fine detail in ivory due to its density, grain structure, and elasticity that make for an ideal carving medium. It takes to carving extraordinarily well, without flaking or chipping. It has a smooth, uniform surface that tools seem to love, and the finished products acquire a patina and glow that only ivory possesses.

The earliest ivory objects consisted of small amulets and charms, apparently produced as good luck pieces, to aid hunters in their efforts. Eskimo hunters carried these carvings of sea significance to the tribe. Doll making has also evolved into a branch of market art and is a hit with both local and tourist collectors.

The women made baskets as well as clothing. The baskets were made of finely coiled grasses or from the bark of birch trees. The grass baskets, complete with tightly fitted tops, were made for storage and carrying of household goods, and were ornamented with symbolic and decorative motifs. Natural dyes were used to color the grasses, into shades of red, blue and green, allowing for distinctive decorations to suit the occasions. Today the beautifully decorated baskets rival ivory carvings for popularity with collectors and art lovers.

otters and other animals with them as they pursued their prey, to guide them towards the animals and to ensure good luck.

They also made practical items out of ivory, including harpoon rests, ulu handles, and arrow straighteners, which were usually decorated with carving and engraving. The primary tool used by ivory carvers was the bow drill, and the handles of the drills were often elaborately decorated. Each man (for up until contemporary times, all the ivory carvers were men) engraved his drill handle with depictions of animals or events in his life.

Once contact was established with Europeans, the nature of ivory carving changed, and the idea of market art took hold. Gold rush prospectors, especially in the Nome area, bought ivory carvings from native artisans, and suggested items they wanted made. Whalers brought scrimshaw art – realistic scenes engraved on the teeth of sperm whales. Alaska artists copied the idea, adding their own variations. Native artists also produced cribbage boards, ship models, pipes, and other carved items to meet the demands of the souvenir market for the tourist.

Today, ivory carving as an art and a craft survives, with some artists producing traditional and souvenir items. At the same time, there is a movement towards "serious" art among some artists. These men and women are creating contemporary art pieces that show a dedication to self-expression and creativity that goes beyond the duplication of figurines for the tourist trade.

Aleutians Basket-weaving

The basketmakers of the Aleutians brought along with them, generations of experience and are considered by many to be among the finest in the world. Using the native rye grasses, carefully gathered and prepared, Aleutian

Tlingit Indian artwork.

women weave baskets of extremely fine quality, some achieving a fiber count approaching 2,500 per square inch, and decorated with feathers, caribou fur, and baleen. While some of the traditional art forms of Aleutian men have vanished, Aleut women continue to produce grass baskets both for family use and as marketable art.

Like the Yup'ik and Inupiat Eskimos, the Aleuts made masks for their traditional ceremonies. Many of them were destroyed by the shamans after use, and few examples remain to this day for posterity.

Hats made of driftwood were functional for the Aleut hunters, and provided a means of artistic expression. They shaded the eyes of hunters at sea,

Making Utensils for the Home

The Ulu knife has been around as long as the Eskimos. It is seen here cutting whale blubber.

While Native artisans made beautiful decorative art objects from the materials at hand, on a more practical level, they also excelled at adapting the products of their environment for use in their day-to-day tasks. Some of these items have passed from daily use due to the onslaught of civilization, while others still subsisted with more modern tools. The birchbark baskets crafted by interior Athabascans and Inupiat Eskimos served several functions, including storage of household items and use in berry gathering. They were also used as cooking vessels. Temporary cooking containers were fashioned with the brown side of the bark turned outside, filled with water and food, hung over a fire and tended very carefully. The other cooking method involved burying a watertight container in the ground, adding the water and food, and then dropping very hot rocks into it. New rocks were added to keep the water boiling, and these containers were reusable.

Baskets made from willow roots and grasses were used for storage, for carrying bird eggs and fish, and for trade with other people. Waterproof containers fashioned from seal skins were also used. In areas where Dall sheep lived, the horns, especially those of large rams, were made into ladles and spoons. One exceptionally beautiful example of a spoon was collected from Southeast, the handle was an intricately carved goat horn, combining function with form. Wood was carved into bowls, ladles, spoons, and storage boxes. The Tlingit and Haidas of Southeast had plenty of local wood available, and the coastal Eskimos used driftwood gathered from beaches.

The one household item that has stood the test of time better than all others, and which has evolved into a modern tool that is also made and sold as a form of market art is the ulu. This traditional "woman's knife" was first made of a piece of slate, polished and sharpened for cutting and fleshing tasks. As time progressed, the design was improved, and comfortable handles were added. The next step in ulu evolution was the crafting of elaborate and decorative handles, turning a purely functional tool into an object of art.

The final step was the introduction of metal by white explorers. With this new material, blades were fashioned from saw blades and the ulu became truly universal. Today, many Natives continue to make their ulus in this manner. While common knife blades have bevels on both sides of the cutting edge, ulus use a unique single bevel design. They are used for gutting and cleaning fish, seals, and caribou, for fleshing the hides in preparation for tanning, in the kitchen for chopping and slicing tasks, and in place of scissors for working with fabrics.

The ulu has also become one of the most popular Alaska souvenirs, with highly polished and engraved blades and handles made of carved ivory, wood, and antler. They are often sold in cases intended for display. There are even signs in many Alaska airports, cautioning returning visitors to pack their ulus in checked baggage rather than attempting to carry them on board- decorative or not – they are still big, sharp knives!

Many urban Alaskans have discovered the utility of this traditional knife, and they are often seen in kitchens as useful, practical knives.

Athabascan beadwork are made from carved willow wood, seeds, shells, porcupine quills and claws.

providing protection from sun, wind and spray. They were also used as indications of status and prowess, and the wearer decorated them extensively with paints and ivory carvings, often in designs partial to the native's experiences and sensitivities.

'Status Symbols' of Coast Indians

The Tlingit and Haida Indians had a flourishing art community. Indian artisans working with local wood, ornate spruce root weavings, bone, horn and fabrics, enjoyed high status among their fellows. As status was important to the coastal Indians, artwork served as a display of material wealth.

One of the consequences of contact with Europeans and with Christian missionaries was the destruction of much native art work. The missionaries, believing the shamans to be practicing idolatry, forbade the performance of traditional ceremonies and destroyed large quantities of art work. Recently, however, there has been a revival of interest in the native art forms, and many of the old ways are being rescued from obscurity.

Besides the elaborate totem poles visible in many villages, Tlingit and Haida art works took the form of carved and decorated storage chests, blankets and garments elaborately decorated for ceremonial purposes. Baskets and hats

Indigenous hats are often an indicator of status and prowess.

were woven of spruce roots and cedar bark, and hats and masks were carved from wood.

A unique status symbol of the coast Indians were large plaques formed of beaten copper made from ore. These 40 pound plaques were engraved with crests and decorations, and were highly prized as status symbols and for trade with other tribes. Handicrafts had served to promote trade between different tribes.

Chilkat dancing blankets were made from yarn spun from the wool of mountain goats. The colorful blankets are detailed with symbolic designs, the blankets were worn by chiefs to indicate their high status, and also conferred status upon the weaver for her skill and traditional knowledge.

Athabascan Accessories

Athabascan Indians are known for their work with animal skins and for their beadwork. Using the hides of moose and caribou, the creative Athabascan women made functional and decorative clothing and accessories. The beads were made from carved willow wood and seeds, and porcupine quills as well as shells. Animal claws and beaks were used for additional ornamentation, to add a touch of the Alaskan to the crafts.

The Athabascans also produced handy baskets, using birch bark and the split roots of willows. The birch baskets were often used as water vessels, and birch was also used to make spoons and

Eskimo winter shoes – designs and sizes to suit any feet.

cups. The baskets were reinforced with wood, and lashed tightly together with the split roots of the white spruce.

Among the more practical items made by Athabascans were fish nets, traps and snowshoes. Nets were made of twine fashioned from willow bark, with wooden floats at the top and weights of stone or antler to hold the bottom down. Whitefish, sheefish, pike and salmon were caught in the rivers, for human consumption and for dog food. Nets were often made specifically for certain eddies in the stream, the net's length and depth matching the size of the eddy.

Fishtraps were long, funnel-like devices made of strips of spruce wood lashed together with strips of bark. They placed the traps in the water, anchored to the bottom and secured with posts, and guided the fish into the traps with fences.

Snowshoes were fashioned from birch wood, bent around a frame. The webbing was made from "babiche", strips of untanned caribou hide, and the foot harness from moose hide.

The craft and art work of Alaska Natives served many functions. As art pieces, they expressed the individuality and creativity of the individual. As craft items, they enabled the people to adapt to their environment, to secure food for their families and to ease their progress through life. And as items used in ceremonies, they helped the people to communicate with the spirits of their ancestors, and to exert some control over the vagaries of nature.

Pevek
An'ujsk
Usi-Chaun
Ostrov Vrangel'a
Kr'ukovo
Arctic Oce
Mys Shmidta
Wainv
USSR
Cape Lisburn
Jeropol
Khrebet Pekul'ney
Ust'-Belaya
Point
Markovo
Paren
Penzhino
Mys Serdtse Kamer
Kivali
Nushagak
Konergino
Uel'Kal'
Strait
Kotzebue
Anadyr
Anadyrskiy Zaliv
Ueien
Wales
Seward
Teller
Pachaca
Providenya
Bering
Kavaca
Keniut
Nome
Gambell
Mys ol' Utorskij
St. Lawrence Island
Norton Soun
Alakanuk
Mount Villag
Hooper Bay
Chevak
International Date Line
Nunivak Islands
Kwigamiut
Dilling
Bering Sea
Pribilof Islands
Attu
Dutch Harbor
Fox Islands
Rat Island
Aleutian Islands
Atka
Andreanof Islands

Alaska

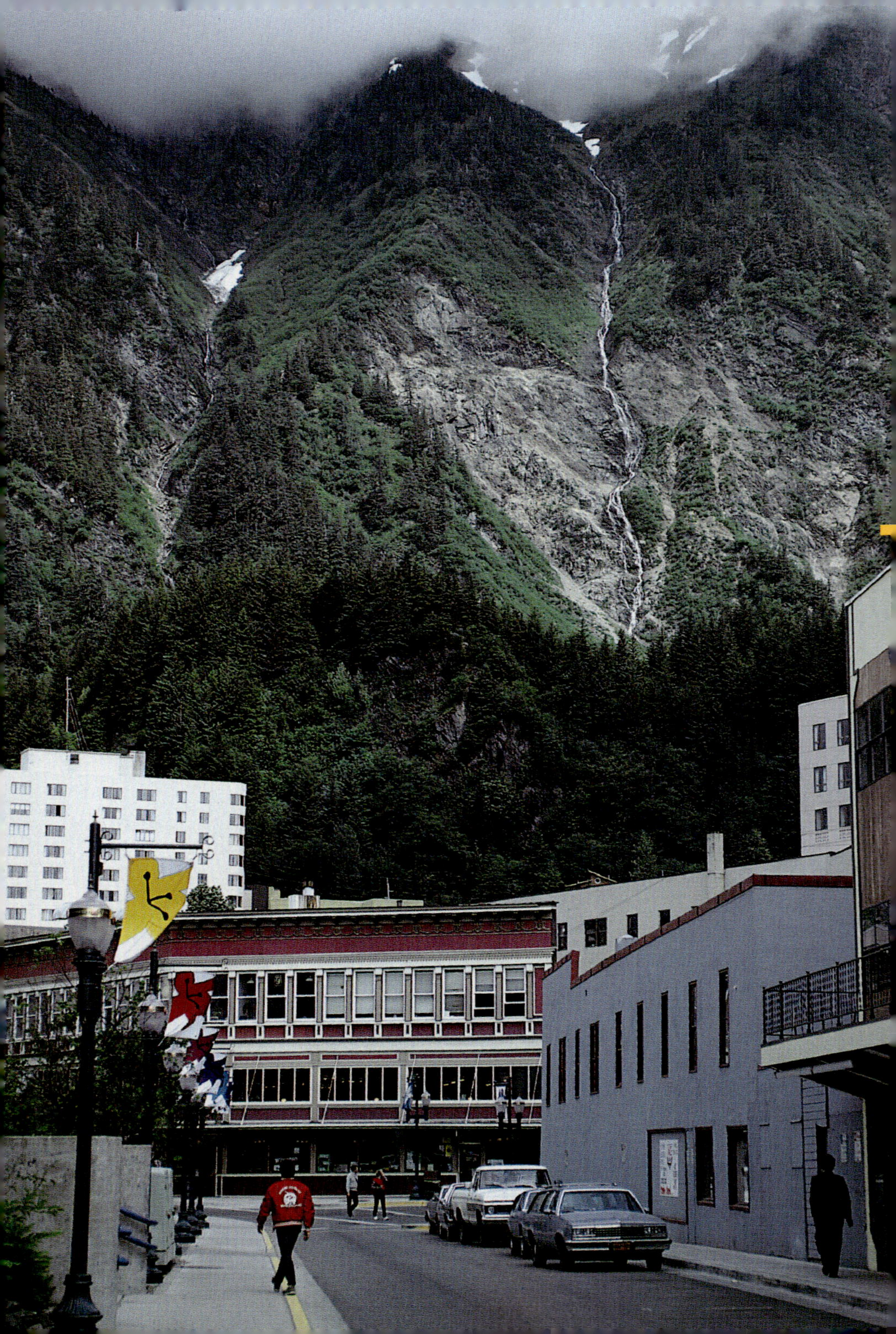

CAPITAL CITY

Juneau & Environs

In 1880, two prospectors – Joe Juneau and Richard Harris – struck gold in Southeast Alaska at a place called **Gold Creek basin**. News of the find drew an exodus from nearby **Sitka** town. Prospectors set up a tent city on the beach and a town soon grew from these humble beginnings. The town was first named Harrisburgh but was later changed to Juneau. Within six years, **Juneau** had overshadowed Sitka, the then territorial capital, as migration of the people and economic influence continued. The people later decided to move the capital – lock, stock and barrel – from Sitka to Juneau, and Juneau has been Alaska's capital ever since that fateful turn of events.

The **Alaska-Juneau** and **Alaska-Gastineau mines** on the **mainland**, and **Douglas Island** across the **Gastineau channel** soon developed into a major boom area for gold mining and ore-processing. Douglas

Morning has broken at Juneau, the Alaskan capitol.

The sound of horse carriages coaxes visitors in Juneau to enter an era of its own.

137

The Alaska Marine Highway

A marine highway ferry at Wrangell, Alaska.

The Alaska Marine Highway is the state-run ferry system, serving 32 ports in Alaska, British Columbia, and Washington. It is a popular and relatively inexpensive means of transporting people, vehicles, and cargo from the Lower 48 to Alaska, and between coastal towns in the state. The southern terminus of the system is at Bellingham, Washington, offering travelers a chance to drive their vehicles aboard and relax for the trip north. There is a lot in it to recommend as an alternative to driving to Alaska via the Alaska Highway- it is more relaxing, easier on the vehicle, and it allows travelers a chance to see a part of Alaska that highway travelers cannot get to. Visitors from the lower 48 often use the ferries in one direction, and drive the highway the other way, allowing them to see different scenery and visit different places on the journey.

There are two distinct branches of the system, the Southeast and the Southcentral/Southwest. The Southeast segment connects Bellingham, Washington, Prince Rupert, B.C., and the towns of Southeast. The northern point of the system at Haines and Skagway reconnects with the North American Highway system. The Southcentral/Southwest branch connects the towns of Prince William Sound with the Kenai Peninsula towns of Seward and Homer, with Kodiak Island and on to the Aleutians. The two branches do not meet- you cannot take a ferry from Bellingham to Prince William Sound or Kodiak and the Aleutians. Also, the ships serving Bellingham do not stop at Prince Rupert. Besides the large ferries running on the main line connecting Bellingham with Ketchikan, Wrangell, Petersburg, Juneau, Haines and Skagway, there are smaller boats that operate shuttle trips linking virtually all of the communities in Southeast with one another. The ferries are not cruise ships. You will not find discos, swimming pools, and huge buffets of food. However, they are clean and comfortable ships, carrying all the necessities of life for the trip. Restaurants and bars are available, and some ships show movies. During the summer many runs feature artists and musicians, and wildlife experts from the Department of Fish and Game, the Forest Service, or U.S. Fish and Wildlife

---

Island became a protoypical company facilitated with housing, stores and schools. Most in the Douglas community worked for the first mining company, Treadwell.

However, Treadwell's dominance of the **Douglas** community came to a sudden end in 1977. The years of tunnelling beneath the ground adjacent to **Gastineau Channel** eventually weakened the dividing line between land and sea, and on an April morning, the

provide environmental education along the route. The cheapest way to travel is as a deck passenger. The ships provide a covered area on deck where you can roll out a sleeping bag or put up a free-standing tent. The atmosphere is usually very convivial, although sleep can be difficult if your group consists of a few serious partiers. Staterooms with two, three, or four berths are available at extra cost if you desire convenience and privacy. There is no room service available, but the rooms are clean and secure, and fresh linens are available on request. Taking your vehicle aboard is possible with rates based on the size of the vehicle. Large vehicles, campers, and trailers can be accommodated- it just takes more money.

The Southeast system serves more communities more frequently and has much more passenger and vehicle traffic than the South west/Southcentral route. The ferries are used for commercial traffic along with the tourist trade, and the towns of Southeast get most of their supplies by ferry. The big blue boats are truly a lifeline to these communities.

The Southcentral/Southwest route goes to Valdez, Cordova, and Whittier in Prince William Sound, Seward, Seldovia, and Homer on the Kenai, Port Lions and Kodiak in the Kodiak Islands, and seven ports in the Aleutians. Service to these ports is not as frequent as in Southeast, but the ferry offers the chance to do some open ocean travel, and to visit towns seldom seen by tourists. The ferry routes are very busy in the summer. If you want to travel aboard the Marine Highway, make your reservations as soon as possible, especially if you desire a stateroom or will be transporting a vehicle. For reservations and information, call 1-800-642-0066.

ground collapsed. Sea water flooded the shafts as the tide rose, and although no one was killed in the cave-in, it was a catastrophe for the community, and the mighty Treadwell was no more.

On the mainland, the A-J (**Alaska-Juneau**) mine system took over local dominance, and along with several other smaller mines, established **Juneau** as the larger of the two communities. Today, the bridge across **Gastineau Channel** connects Juneau with **Douglas**, with the previously dominant town of Douglas relegated to suburb status. Mining is attempting a comeback in Juneau, with mixed results. Some local backers of the project see mining as a way to bolster the local economy, especially in the face of the recurring issue of relocating the state capital to **Southcentral**. Other folks see the trade-off as being a case of jobs gained versus degradation of the local environment, an issue that many Juneauites feel very strongly about.

With a population of 29,000, Juneau is at once a small town and the capital of the largest state in the union. It depends on the government for a large portion of its vitality, but there are other engines running the local economy as well. Tourism is a growing factor, with more and more cruise ships stopping over every year. Currently more than a quarter million cruise ship passengers visit the city every summer, bringing in money from all over the world. Tourists also arrive by plane and on smaller sightseeing boats as well as on numerous small private vessels that travel the **Inside Passage** every year. Fishing, both sport and commercial, is also important, and the state maintains hatcheries in the area to supplement the natural salmon runs that remain. The local halibut fishery, at one time seemingly

The town's favorite landmark at Red Dog Saloon.

on the decline, is apparently gaining in strength and popularity.

The threat to move the capital out of **Juneau** never seems to go away. The idea of having the state legislature seemingly sequestered in Juneau every year with lobbyists, special interest groups and miscellaneous government groupies riles the folks in the rest of the state. They imagine a cozy set-up where the fixers have access to the politicians, with regular citizens shut out by geography and the price of air fares.

The capital move idea came to a head in 1974, when the majority of citizens actually voted to move the capital to the town of **Willow**, between **Anchorage** and **Fairbanks**. This location was a compromise, given the rivalry between the two towns. No Anchorage politician who wanted to keep his job was about to approve a bill to relocate the capital to Fairbanks, and vice versa. However, even with the state treasury brimming with profits from **North Slope** oil, the projected price tag for the relocation was a bit too much.

In 1982, the issue was again placed before voters with the price tag pegged at US$2.8 billion, and once again, when it came to actually spending money to realize the idea of a capital near the population centers, the voters decided to leave things as they were. The most recent plan to move the capital came about with petitions circulating in 1993, and voted on in '94. The idea of moving the capital holds an appeal to a lot of

A skiplane taking off at Juneau harbor for a fly-in fishing trip.

Alaskans, it is just the paying for it that is the stumbling block.

Visiting Juneau

The city of **Juneau** sits on **Gastineau Channel**, at the bases of **Mt. Roberts** and **Mt. Juneau**. The downtown area is compact and easily covered by walking. Parking is hard to come by, but if, like the majority of visitors to Juneau you arrive by cruise ship or airplane, this is largely a moot point. Before setting out to tour the town, make sure you are prepared for the weather. Juneau-ites get a bit defensive about characterizations of their town as a dreary place where it rains all the time but it does rain quite often although the place has got enough days when the sun shines and shows the area off to its best advantage. The precipitation usually takes the form of light drizzles rather than fog-strangling cloudbursts, so a lightweight raincoat and water resistant footwear

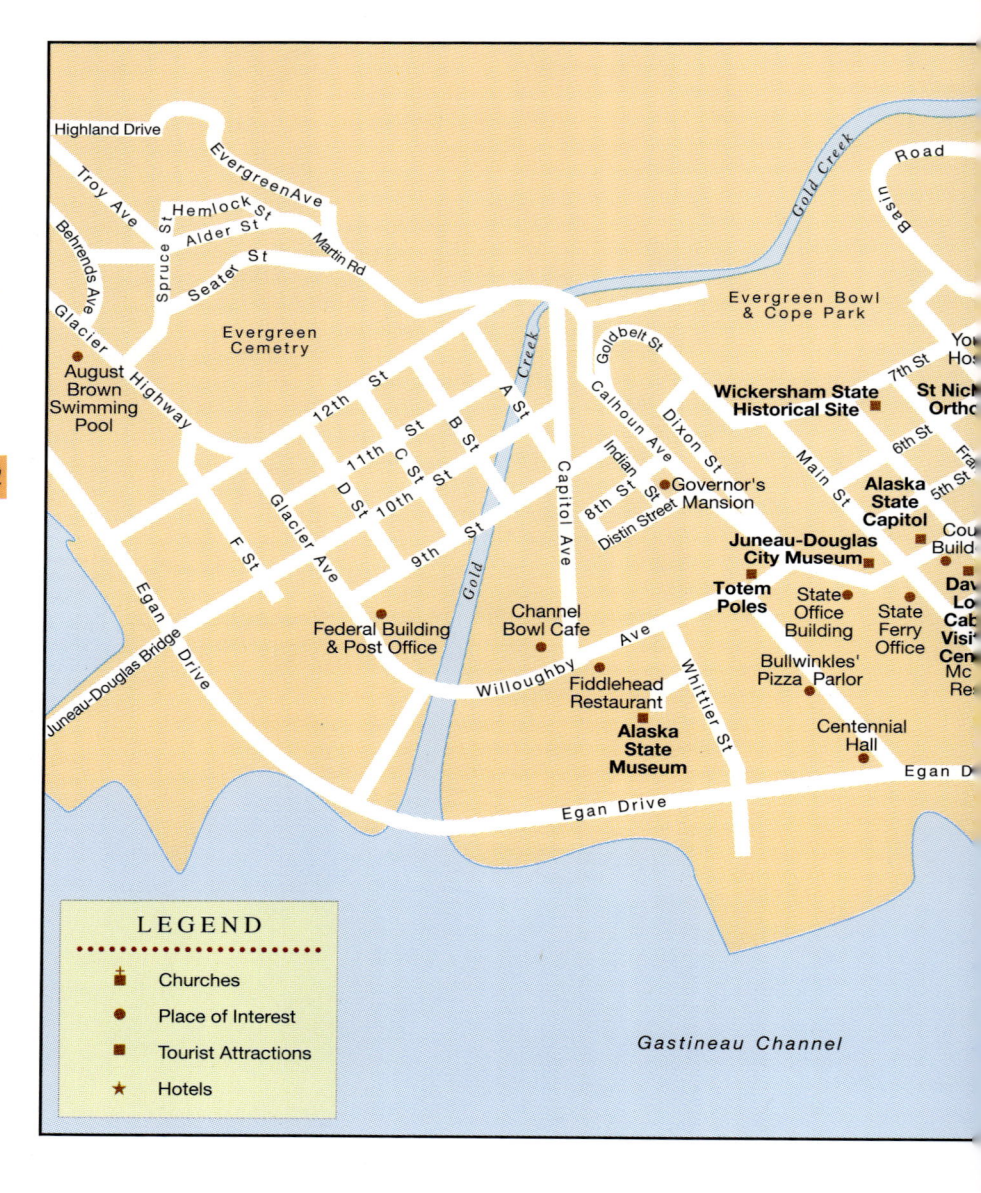

Juneau

Marine Park on a crowded Sunday afternoon.

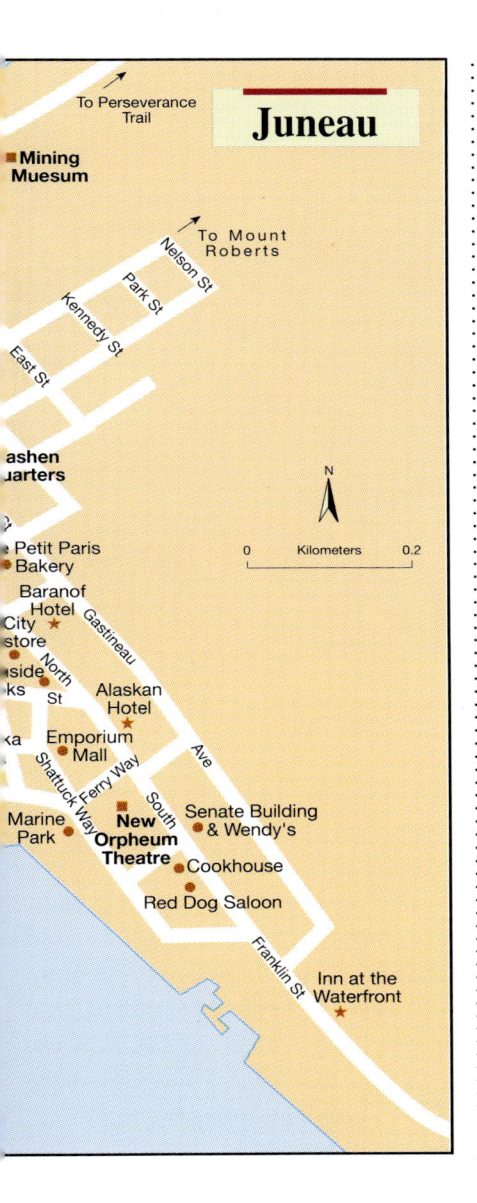

will usually suffice.

If you are starting out from the cruise ship docks, turn left on **Franklin St.**, and stop at the **Juneau library**, atop the parking garage at South Franklin and **Admiralty Way**. On a clear day, the panoramic view from the library windows is spectacular. After that, staying on the waterfront, visit the **Marine Park** along Admiralty Way. There is a visitor's kiosk and picnic area there, and during the summer, Friday evening concerts as well. Cross Admiralty Way and take Ferry St. over to **Franklin**. Turn left, follow Franklin to Front and bear left. Follow Front for about a block, and then turn right on Seward. Head uphill and visit the **Davis Log Cabin** (586-2284) at the corner of **Seward**. The **Visitor Information Center** there can supply you with plenty of local information, including walking tour maps, and brochures on local attractions,.

One block uphill would be the **Capitol Building**, and one block further is

Visitors cruise towards Margerie Glacier.

the **State Office Building**. Other attractions in the immediate neighborhood are **St. Nicholas Orthodox Church** at Fifth and Gold street and the **Juneau-Douglas City Museum** (586-3572) at Fourth and Main. The museum has a guide and walking tour map to local public art and totem poles. If you feel like climbing, head straight up Seward St., and get on the staircase at Fifth St. Continue climbing for two blocks and visit the historic **Wickersham House** at 213 Seventh St. Take one of the tours given during the summer. The effort in making the climb rewards you with a scenic view of Juneau harbour and out across to **Gastineau Channel**.

If you are still feeling energetic, take the stairs down to Sixth St., and turn left, continuing up Sixth St. until you reach another flight of stairs. Climb up again, and follow the **Mt. Roberts. Trail** to more elevated and exhaustive viewpoints along the way.

To reach the **Last Chance Basin** and the **Gold Creek Salmon Bake**, head uphill on East St. from the Sixth St. intersection. East turns into Basin Rd., and its about a mile and

Mural depicting old native legends.

a half walk to the basin. Enjoy dinner at the salmon bake, explore the gold mining artifacts, try your hand at gold panning, and if you do not feel like walking back to town, the salmon bake outfit provides a bus to shuttle you down.

One of Juneau's must-see spots is the **Alaska State Museum** at 395 Whittier (465-2901). It has the largest collection of Alaska historical objects in the state, featuring displays on Native culture and the histories of mining and fishing, as well as traveling exhibits.

If you have got the time and the inclination, visit the **Gastineau Salmon Hatchery** (463-5114), three miles north down town along the waterfront. The hatchery offers tours explaining hatchery operations, and a small aquarium of local sea creatures. For more information on hiking trails and outdoor opportunities in the area, visit the **Forest Service Information Center**, (586-8751) at **Egan Drive** and **Willoughby**.

Along the waterfront, you can stop by at the small boat harbors and inspect the amazing variety of watercraft used by locals and visitors to explore the nearby waters. Everything from kayaks, dinghies, and outboard boats up to and including some very impressive yachts.

If beer is to your liking, visit the **Alaskan Brewing Company** (780-5866) at 5429 Shaune Rd. in the **Lemon Creek** area, just about six miles north of downtown Juneau.

Getting out of town will enable you to sample Juneau's surroundings. Un-

The Forest Information Center at Centennial Hall.

less you brought your own vehicle in on the ferry, you will have to make arrangements for getting out and about. There are two major cab companies in Juneau, **Capital Cab**, (586- 2772) and **Taku Glacier Cab Co.**, (586-2121). In addition to standard taxi service, both outfits offer personalized tours as well. If you prefer bus tours, contact Gray Line of Alaska (586-3773) for sightseeing and charter services, Princess Tours (463-3900), or Mendenhall Glacier Transport (789-5460) will do.

Cruising

If you are itching to get out onto the local waters, there are several companies from which to choose. **Alaska Sightseeing/Cruise West** offers small ship cruises to **Glacier Bay** and **Tracy Arm**, as well as service to **Ketchikan** and **Seattle**. **Gentle Giant Journeys** (789-8251) conducts whale watching trips into the wilderness. Taku Cruises (586-6444) will take you on a 3-hour glacier and wildlife cruise, and Tracy Arm Reservations Center (463-5510 or 1-800-451-5952), offers full and half day cruises with a fly/cruise option as well.

Fly away

If getting off the ground appeals to your sense of adventure, you can choose between helicopters and fixed wing air-

JUNEAU & ENVIRONS

147

A majestic range at Inside Passage awes spectators.

Mendenhall Glacier

A natural ice cave at Mendenhall Glacier.

One of the most popular visitor attractions in the Juneau area is the Mendenhall Glacier Visitor Center, the first national forest visitor center in the U.S. Drive north out of Juneau on the Glacier Highway; just turn right at Mendenhall Loop Rd. at mile post 9.4 and go straight for (3 1/2 miles) six kilometers to the parking lot. From the visitor center, you can view maps and displays on the glacier and the surrounding environment, take photos from prominent points, or follow one of the area's hiking trails. There are telescopes available for viewing the glacier, and you can scan the area for wildlife. Mountain goats are often visible on Bullard Mountain- look for clusters of white dots, or small moving patches of "snow". Trails around the visitor center provide possibilities for a short, half-mile stroll on a self-guided nature walk or a 1.5 mile (2 km) Moraine Ecology Loop Trail walk. A bit more challenging is the 3.5 mile (5.6 km) East Glacier Loop Trail or the 3.4 mile (6 km) West Glacier Trail, a steeper climb to an all-encompassing viewpoint.

From Juneau, the local flight services offer helicopter and fixed-wing aircraft tours of the glacier, and the helos will set down on a safe area of the glacier, giving you the opportunity to walk on safe areas of the upper glacier. Rafting companies in Juneau offer trips down the 4 mile (6 km) Mendenhall River as it meanders down to tidewater. These are leisurely, non-whitewater experiences open to people of all levels of physical fitness. The Mendenhall and 37 other glaciers originate in the 1,500 sq-mile (3,900 sq-km) Juneau Icefield. There, snow accumulates year after year, forming a thick, highly compressed sea of ice. The weight of this immense icefield pushes the glaciers down hill via the paths of least resistance. Along the way these tongues of ice, hundreds of feet thick, move slowly but inexorably towards sea level. They push aside everything in their paths, displacing everything down

craft. The helicopters offer the chance to land on a glacier and walk around for a bit, while the others offer airplanes equipped with either floats or wheels. For helicopter tours, contact **ERA Aviation** at 586-2030, **Coastal Helicopters** at 586-5600, or **Temsco Helicopters** at 789-9501. Flight services include **Alaska Coastal Airlines**, (789-7818), **Wings of Alaska** (789-9863) or **Alaska Fly 'N Fish Charters** (790-2120).

Hit the Road

Car rental is available through nine agencies in **Juneau**, but reservations should be made well in advance if you are visiting in the summer. If you are exploring by car, do not worry about

to bedrock, carving out U-shaped valleys as they go. Valley glaciers like the Mendenhall usually end in lakes, where the higher temperatures of the lower elevations take over. The ice melts, forming a lake, and the wall of ice meets its inevitable end there. Tidewater glaciers occur when the wall of ice ends at the sea. As chunks of ice break off, or calve, into the sea, icebergs are born. If the water is deep enough, tidal action carries the icebergs out to sea where they function as resting areas for seals and are ominous hazards to navigation.

Glaciers either advance or recede at their terminal points depending on the ambient temperatures there. The Mendenhall glacier is currently receding, with the terminus moving slowly up the valley, even though it is still being forced down from the top by the weight of the icefield. As the glacier recedes, the exposed bedrock begins to sprout signs of life. Plant progression follows a regular and predictable pattern, with mosses and lichens making the first appearance on the minute amounts of dirt that accumulates on the rock. Larger and larger plants move in and take over as conditions become more hospitable, and eventually a mature forest of old growth trees exists where less than 200 years before only moss and bed rock existed.

As nature evolves, animal communities follow plant progression, with small rodents and birds taking up residence in the beginnings of plant habitat, culminating in populations of large mammals such as deer and bears in mature stands of forest.

The big thaw at Mendenhall Glacier.

racking up lots of miles. The farthest you can drive is about 40 miles (64 km) north of town on the **Veterans' Memorial Highway**. You can drive about five miles (8 km) south of town on Thane Rd., or drive over to **Douglas Island**, and you will get to the end of that road in about 12 miles (19 km). As a side trip if time is willing, you can head up **Fish Creek Road** to **Eaglecrest Ski Area**.

If you are looking for a more physically demanding sort of adventure, get in touch with **Alaska Discovery Expeditions** at 586-1911. They can arrange kayak rentals and trips as well as other types of wilderness expeditions.

Juneau is also the gateway into **Admiralty Island National Monument**, which is a bear's haven. It is also a beautiful and interesting town that just oozes with history and things of old. Visitors are appreciated and catered to, and the blend of colorful local shops and restaurants, official state functions, artworks and museums, and the astonishingly beautiful surroundings of the old and new, make it well worthwhile as a stopping point or as a destination during your Alaska visit.

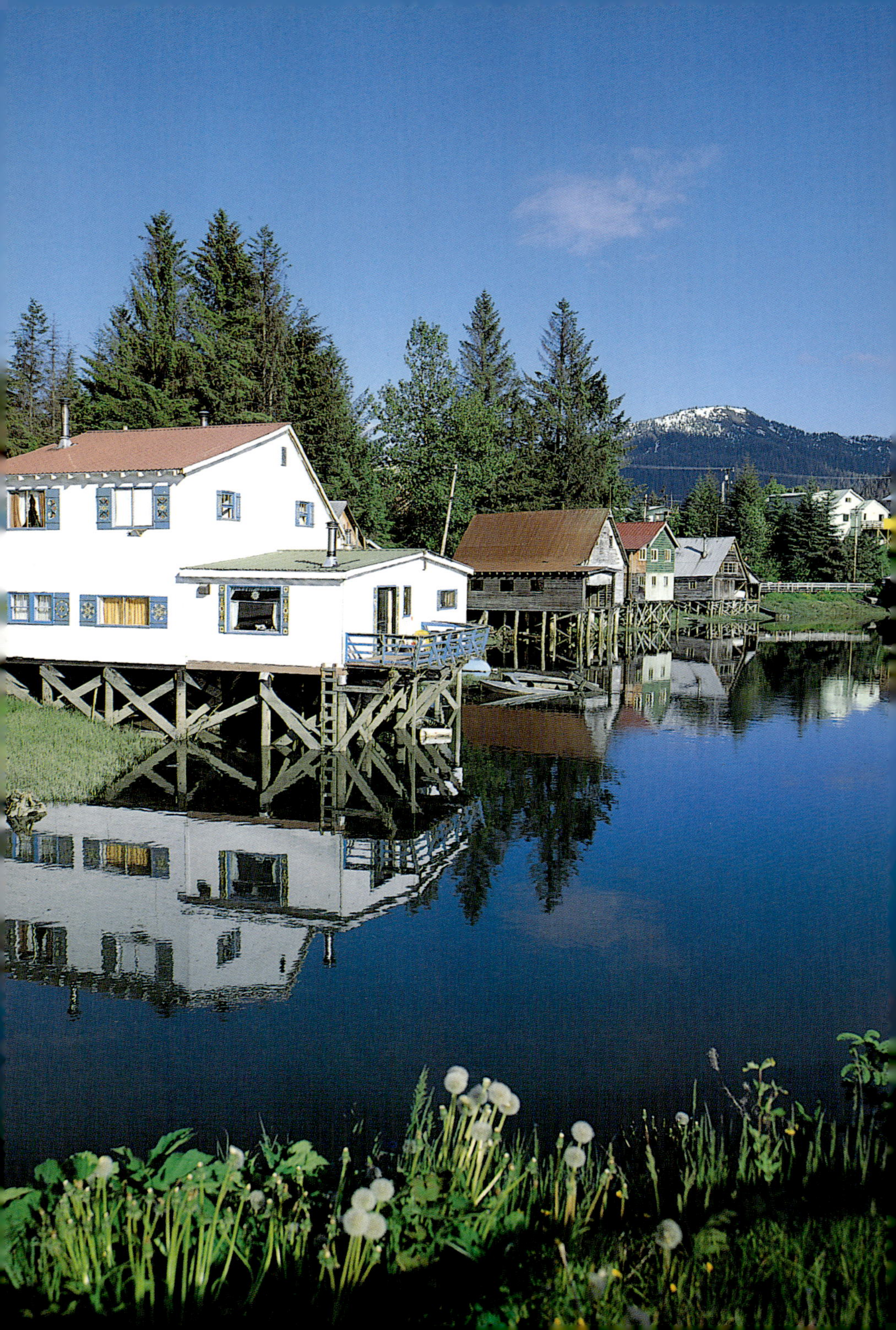

PANHANDLE COUNTRY

Southeast Alaska

In many ways, **Southeast Alaska** has more in common with the Pacific Northwest than with the rest of Alaska. The marine environment, high precipitation levels, and big trees certainly suggest western Washington or coastal British Columbia as opposed to stereotypical Alaska, land of frozen tundra and stunted spruce forests. This geographically separate region of the state has attractions and charms of its own. The narrow channels between islands filled with tidal flows, steep mountainsides covered with Sitka spruce trees and tidewater glaciers combines to create a beautiful and interesting area to explore. Southeast extends for over 500 miles (805 km) from **Icy Bay** at the northern end down to **Dixon Entrance**, separating Alaska from the Queen Charlotte Islands and Canada. In between lie innumerable islands and chunks of rock of varying sizes, and more territory than you could explore in a lifetime. If you are visiting Southeast on a state ferry or a cruise ship, you would not have a car available, but in

A picturesque lakeside scene at Petersburg.

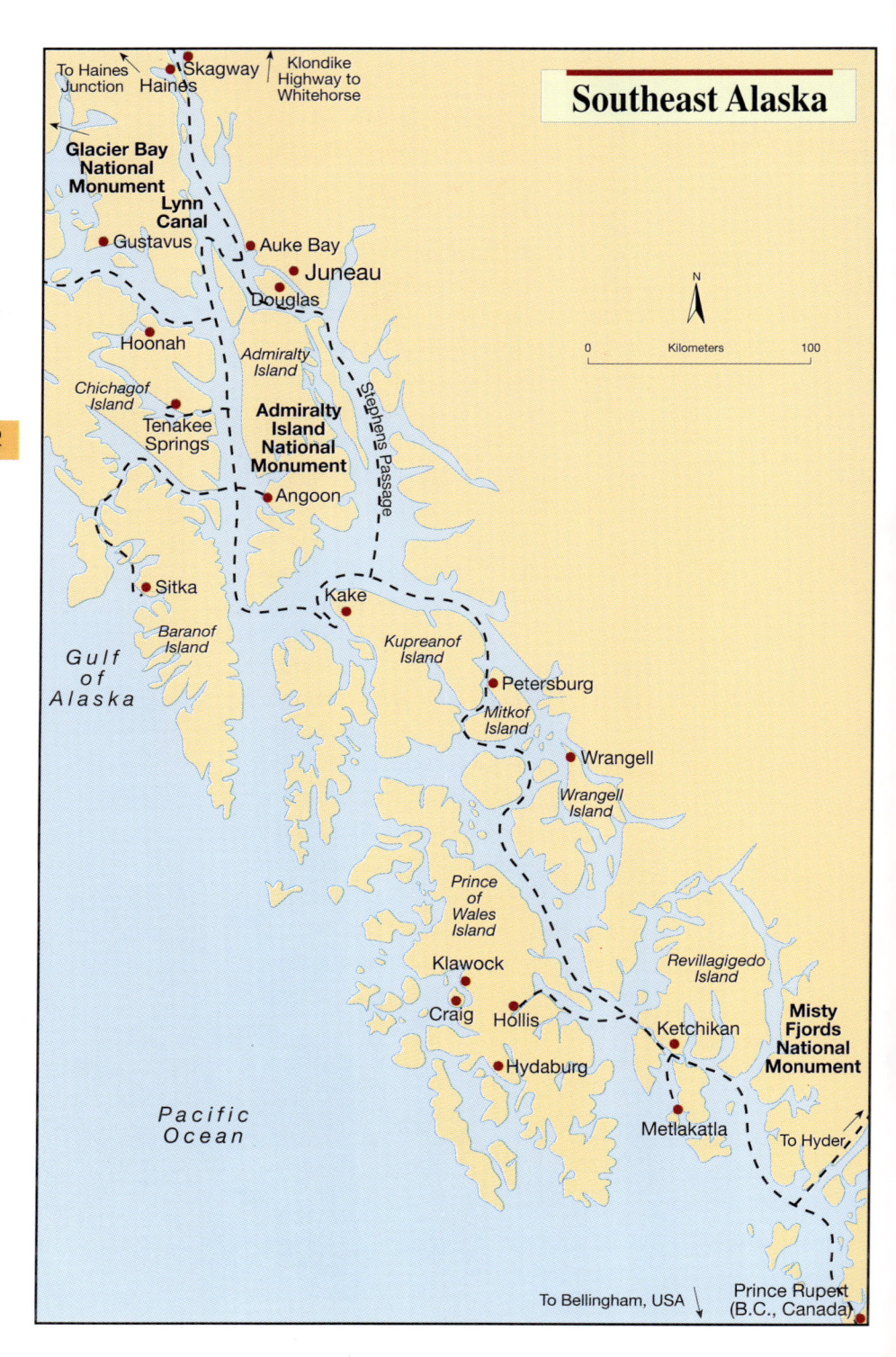

Southeast Alaska

Totem Bight State Park at Ketchikan.

most cases, you would not need one. The towns are small and compact, and foot travel is a good way to stretch your legs after being on board ship for any length of time.

The local businesses go out of their way to accommodate tourists, and the service-oriented businesses usually can arrange to pick up and deliver their customers from convenient locations. Some of the businesses will even arrange their hours around docking times, and tours are frequently scheduled to coincide with the times that the ships and ferries are in port.

As cruise ships and ferries head up the **Inside Passage**, the first stop is usually **Ketchikan**. This small fishing community sits, as do most of the towns in the region, scrunched between the cliffs and forests on one side and the water on the other. Visitors to Ketchikan can stroll along the streets and board walks, or charter a fishing boat to try for halibut or salmon.

There are three good totem pole exhibits in the area for those who desire to investigate the cultural artifacts of the local **Tlingit** and **Haida Indians**. **Totem Bight State Park** is eight miles (13 km) north of town, and **Saxman village** (225-8687) is about $2^{1}/_{2}$ miles (4 km) south. The third is within walking distance of downtown, the **Totem Heritage Center** (225-5900) at 601 Deermount St. Admission is US$2.00, and exhibitions and demonstrations are given regularly during the season.

Misty Fjords

Ketchikan is the jumping off point for **Misty Fjords National Monument**, a place beautifully sculptured by the natural forces of time. This 2.3 million acre park offers views of deep fjords and typical Southeast Alaska rain forest habitat. Wildlife on land includes Sitka blacktail deer, mountain goats, brown and black bears, and wolves. Seals, sea lions, porpoises and whales abound in the water, and there are plenty of bald eagles over head. From Ketchikan, you can visit Misty Fjords by boat, or flightsee by plane. Call **Outdoor Alaska** at 225-6044, **Alaska Sightseeing/Cruise West** at 800-426-7702, or **Ketchikan Char-**

A glimpse of dusk at Ketchikan fly-in fishing stopover.

ter Boats at 225-7291 to arrange boat tours. For flightseeing tours, call **Pro-Mech Air** at 225-3845 or **Ketchikan Air** at 225-6608. West of Ketchikan sits **Prince of Wales Island**, 130 miles (209 km) long from north to south. Prince of Wales Island is a bit off the beaten track, and the island is more attuned to logging than to the tourist trade.

There is a ferry from Ketchikan, but space can be a problem, so reservations to transport a car over are highly recommended. Once you have got a vehicle onto the island, there are plenty of logging roads to explore, and the towns of **Craig**, **Klawock**, **Thorne Bay**, and **Hydaburg** offer some services. There are notable totem displays in Hydaburg and Klawock as well.

Columbine, a flower of the Southeast.

Cruisers enjoy an endless view of icefields at LeConte Glacier.

Wrangell

Traveling north, the next stop on the ferry system is Wrangell. This town of fewer than 3,000 residents is not usually on the itinerary of the larger cruise ships, so if you visit on a ferry run, you are not likely to have to share the place with a band of fellow travelers. During its colorful past, Wrangell was governed by the **Stikine Tlingits**, the **Russians**, and the **British** before finally settling down under **American** rule. Lying near the mouth of the Stikine River, Wrangell held a strategic position for early military purposes, and for access upstream by fur trappers and gold seekers. Today, Wrangell's economy is based on logging, fishing, tourism, and as a jumping off point for recreationists visiting the **Stikine-LeConte Wilderness Area**.

The small downtown area contains shops and restaurants. Visit the public library on Church St., and the **Wrangell Museum** next door. Follow Front St. to Shakes St., and take the bridge out to Shakes Island to visit the totem park and Shakes House, a replica of a Tlingit community house. Ask at the visitors center at Outer Dr. and Breuger for directions to the petroglyph beach north of town, where you can make rubbings of Indian rock carvings. If you will be in town for a while, you can arrange a boat trip up the **Stikine River**, visit **LeConte Glacier**, or watch brown and black bears feeding on salmon at the **Anan Bear**

Gold Panning

A 'gold panning' mannequin at Skagway.

Entrepreneurs have come up with a novel idea, cashing in on the flow of tourist, by allowing enthusiastic visitors to try their hand at gold panning. It gives them a taste of what made the state so attractive to many people in the past and experience a slice of that historical era. A lot of Alaskans who get bitten by the gold bug usually wind up investing money in machineries such as dredges and sluice boxes, even staking claims with the government on sections of stream where gold mining is allowed. For many what had started out as a casual interest to get outdoors and look for a bit of "color" in a local stream quickly turns into an obsession with striking it rich.

A casual prospector simply requires a gold pan, a shovel and a pair of boots to get started in the game. Commercial establishments that cater to tourists generally have all these stuff on hand, so what you would need to supply is the enthusiasm. However, rather than just hand you your equipment and point you towards the creek, the better establishments do supply some training. They will give you a bag of dirt guaranteed to hold a few flakes of gold and then provide a quick run-down on the panning process. Basically, you fill the pan with dirt, add water, and shake.

The motion causes the gold, which is heavier than the sand and gravel, to sink to the bottom. As the prospector gradually swish out the excess dirt, any gold flakes will soon be visible at the bottom of the pan. Repeat the process about a million times, and if you are real lucky, you may have enough gold to pay for your own pan and shovel!

If you want to get away from the tourist traffic at the private concessions, you can pack up your shovel, your gold pan, and your boots and head for the hills. There are opportunities for recreational gold panners to try their luck on public lands at several locations.

Prospective prospectors must first establish that the land they are going to enter is open to recreationists as some are forbidden to outsiders. Land ownership is complex and constantly changing, so it is important that you first establish the legality of your efforts.

The federal government, the state government, Native corporations, and private owners all have differing policies concerning gold panning. Native corporations and private owners require you to obtain permission before gaining access to their reserved property.

The government owned land presents a more complicated situation. Some lands are closed to all mining, even recreational panning, some land is open only to persons who have staked and filed legal mining claims, and some lands are open to all.

In Southcentral, there are streams open to recreational gold seekers in Chugach State Park, the state parks on the Kenai Peninsula, at Independence Mine State Park at Hatcher Pass, and in Chugach National Forest. For details on specific locations, contact the Chugach State Park rangers at 345-5014, the Kenai park rangers at 262-5581, the Independence Mine Visitor Center at 745-2827, or the Chugach National Forest at 271-2500.

An Alaskan couple enjoy by their pleasure boat at Petersburg.

Observatory. Get in touch with **TH Charters** at 874-2085, **Tyee Travel** at 874-3383 or 1-800-942-9741, or call **Sunrise Aviation** at 874-2319 to arrange a flightseeing trip. Traveling north, you will go through **Wrangell Narrows** on the way to **Petersburg**. This winding, narrow passage provides for some fascinating exhibitions of seamanship, as skippers of vessels of all sizes and types try to make it through the many twists and turns without doing any damage or straying outside the channel and running aground. If you are awake when your boat is going through the Narrows, get outside and watch the show, even if it is after dark. The larger cruise ships will not attempt this route, so this is one section of Southeast the Love Boat folks do not get to see.

Petersburg

Petersburg is the most beautiful town in Alaska. Founded by Norwegian fishermen, this fishing village consists of a nicely laid out town plan, freshly painted storefronts, and immaculately kept houses with real live lawns (most unusual anywhere in Alaska) and a complete absence of junked cars and snowmachines inside yards. The ferry terminal is a mile from town, and if you do not have the time or inclination to hoof it to town, call **City Cab** at 772-3003. Once you are downtown, stop at the visitors center at First and Fram streets for a visitor's guide, and check out the small boat harbor, the shops and restaurants in the compact little business district, and the **Clausen Museum** at 203 Fram St. If you are fortunate enough to be in the area on the third weekend in May, Petersburg holds a **Little Norway Festival**, complete with dances, con-

All equipped with setnets and just in time for the fish runs.

Fish net buoys greeting the morning sun at Petersburg.

tests, and plenty of food. If you want to visit outlying areas by boat, to visit **LeConte Glacier** or just to sightsee local waters, call **Alaska Passages** at 772-3967, **Alaskan Scenic Waterways** at 772-3777, or **Sights Southeast** at 772-4503. For flightseeing trips, call **Kupreanof Flying Service** at 772-3396, or **Pacific Wing** at 772-4258.

Sitka

Ninety miles west of Petersburg on the west coast of **Baranof Island** lies the town of **Sitka**. Alaska's first capital, Sitka prides itself on its history both as a **Russian** outpost and as the territorial seat of government. The local economy is based on logging, fishing, and tourism, and the townspeople make an effort to cultivate the fine arts. There is an annual writer's symposium, a fine arts camp, and a summer music festival that attracts chamber musicians from around the world. Points of interest in Sitka include the **Sheldon Jackson Museum** (747-8981), which contains Native artifacts from all around the state. In the **Centennial Building** you will find the visitor's center and the **Isabel Miller Museum**, (747-6455) containing local artifacts. **St. Michael's Cathedral** holds many Russian treasures, and the **Russian Bishop's House** has been restored to 1850s style. The **Sitka National Historical Park** has a collection of totem poles, as well as an active native

A fishing tugboat is a regular sight in Alaskan waters.

An inviting crystal clear rivulet at Sitka.

arts program. The **Alaska Raptor Rehabilitation Center** (747-8662) cares for injured birds of prey, and makes an effort to return the birds to the wild if possible. **Baranof Tours** (747-1016) and **Sitka Tours** (747-8443) conduct tours of the local historical sites, timed to coincide with ship and ferry visits. Or call **Jane Eidler** at 747-5354 for a $1^1/_2$ hour walking tour.

If you would like a Sitka tour with a Native perspective, call **Sitka Tribal Tours** at 747-3207. They offer the opportunity to share **Tlingit** lore, see Native dancers, and the chance to sample some traditional native foods. For sightseeing, fishing or whale watching tours, contact **Triton Charters** at 747-5419, or **Allen Marine Tours** at 747-8100.

Roads and bridges are an engineering feat in Alaska's rugged landscape.

Glacier Bay

Glacier Bay National Park is one of the most popular spots for visitors to Southeast, and for good reason. This 3.28 million acre park and preserve is the summer home of humpback whales, as well as numerous other spectacular land and sea critters. The setting, among snow covered peaks and numerous tide water glaciers, is arguably the most gorgeous in **Southeast**, and many tourists consider a trip to Glacier Bay the highlight of their Alaska experience. Tours of Glacier Bay can be arranged out of **Juneau**, or from **Gustavus**, a tiny community sitting at the Bay's doorstep. There is no ferry service to Gustavus, but there is a daily jet service with **Alaska Airlines**, and scheduled flights with **Glacier Bay Airways** (697-2249) and **L.A.B. Flying Service** (766-2222) connect Gustavus with most Southeast cities. Marine tours from Gustavus include **Glacier Bay Puffin Charters** (697-2260), **Gusto Charters**, (697-2416), or try your hand at sea kayaking with **Glacier Bay Sea Kayaks** (697-2257) or **Spirit Walker Expeditions**, (697-2266). From Juneau, lots of tours to Glacier Bay are available from **Alaska Discovery Expeditions** at 586-1911, or **Glacier Bay Tours** and **Cruises** at 463-5510 or 1-800-451-5952.

At the northern end of the **Inside Passage**, the towns of **Haines** and **Skagway** provide connections to the

Pack Creek – Meeting Bears in the Wild

Enter the bear country.

The Stan Price State Wildlife Sanctuary at Pack Creek provides excellent brown bear viewing for visitors to Southeast. Located on the east side of Admiralty Island (30 miles) 48 km southwest of Juneau, the sanctuary is dedicated to the memory of its former resident, Stan Price. For 40 years, Stan Price lived on the island among the bears, tolerating them as they tolerated him. He walked the island paths unarmed except for a stick, which he would occasionally use to tap an over-curious bruin on the nose if it came too close for comfort.

The northern end of Admiralty Island is preserved as a National Monument, and the bear density of one animal per square mile represents the highest concentration of brown bears in the world. When the runs of salmon ascend Pack Creek in July and August, the bears are drawn even closer together. They scramble for fish in their rush to put on as much fat as possible for the coming winter. Ordinarily, brown bears are not at all tolerant of one another's presence. Males seek out females during the mating season and cubs accompany their mothers for two to three years after they are born, but other than that, the animals prefer to live alone. Boars encountering other boars will defend territory, often engaging in fierce battles. Adult boars will also attempt to kill cubs when they can. Even though the boars often outweigh the sows by a factor of two to one, getting past a protective mother is no easy task. So as you can see, these are not exactly sociable animals. However, when it comes to situations like a flood of salmon in a stream, the normal rules are suspended, and brown bears will tolerate others of their kind in close proximity. Their personal space requirements shrink to fit the occasion. During the rest of the year, big boars would not tolerate other males within hundreds of yards while in the salmon hunt they are standing nearly shoulder to shoulder, catching fish. The reasons for this behavior are assumed to be adaptive as it is to the advantage of these bears to concentrate on acquiring lots of fat and protein in a short period of time.

With all the bears attracted to the salmon streams, no one bear could possibly defend a large section of stream against all other competitors. Since there are plenty of salmon to go

highway system. Most ferry passengers continuing on by car get off at **Haines**, since it is closer to the Alaska Highway, and the ferries stop there before continuing on to Skagway. Haines is justifiably famous for eagles. In the fall, the world's largest gathering of eagles congregates at the **Chilkat Bald Eagle Preserve**. A late run of spawning salmon draws these magnificent birds from untold distances to cash in on the easy pickings, and the ice-free **Chilkat River**

around, the most efficient use of each bear's time and effort would be to eat as much fish as he or she can possibly catch, while minimizing the efforts and risks involved in a fight. However, this studied avoidance of one another does not mean that all is sweetness and light on the banks of the creek.

There is a definite hierarchy among these animals and the biggest and most aggressive bears will, of course, get to claim the best fishing spots. Some fishing spots are just plain better than others and the biggest bears will latch onto and defend these spots with ferocity against any competitors. The best spots are those where a bear can catch the most fish using the least amount of effort. This equation of large intake against little energy expended translates into more fat on the animal's body to sustain him through the winter.

Fights between bears usually take place between animals of similar size. When a small bear sees a big bear coming to take over his fishing spot, he will meekly move away, using displays of body language to acknowledge the presence and superiority of the larger animal. However, if the bears are similar in size and strength, body language and bluffing behavior would not always work to scare off the aggressor. Fierce fights then ensue, complete with loud roars and lots of commotion. If you look closely, you will see that many big, old boars carry scars of past battles with their own kind. Access to the viewing area is by permit only, this is obtainable from the U.S. Forest Service in Juneau at 586-8790, or the Alaska Department of Fish and Game in Douglas at 465-4265. Flight services and charter boats in Juneau will arrange for drop-offs and pick-ups at your convenience. Reserve before hand to avoid disappointment.

guarantees a constant food supply. The gathering usually starts in October, with the peak occurring in November, and frequently lasting until February. Up to 4,000 eagles can inhabit the Chilkat valley during this time, and there are

Klondike Historic Center at Skagway.

eagles in the trees, eagles in the sky, eagles on the ground, eagles eating, resting, digesting, eagles everywhere. Of course, there is more to **Haines** than eagles. The histories of the **Chilkoot** and **Chilkat Tlingit Indians** are commemorated and kept alive in Haines, as well as the days of the **gold rush**. Tourist amenities are plentiful, and the surroundings yet to be challenged. **Dalton City**, Alaska, is a restored set of the movie "White Fang". Located on the fairgrounds a mile from downtown Haines, Dalton City is open seven days a week during the summer. It features the **Alaska Natural Resources Museum**, sled dog and **Tlingit** canoe carving demonstrations, daily performances by local actors in a period melodrama,

Commorants and gulls co-exist at Glacier Bay National Park.

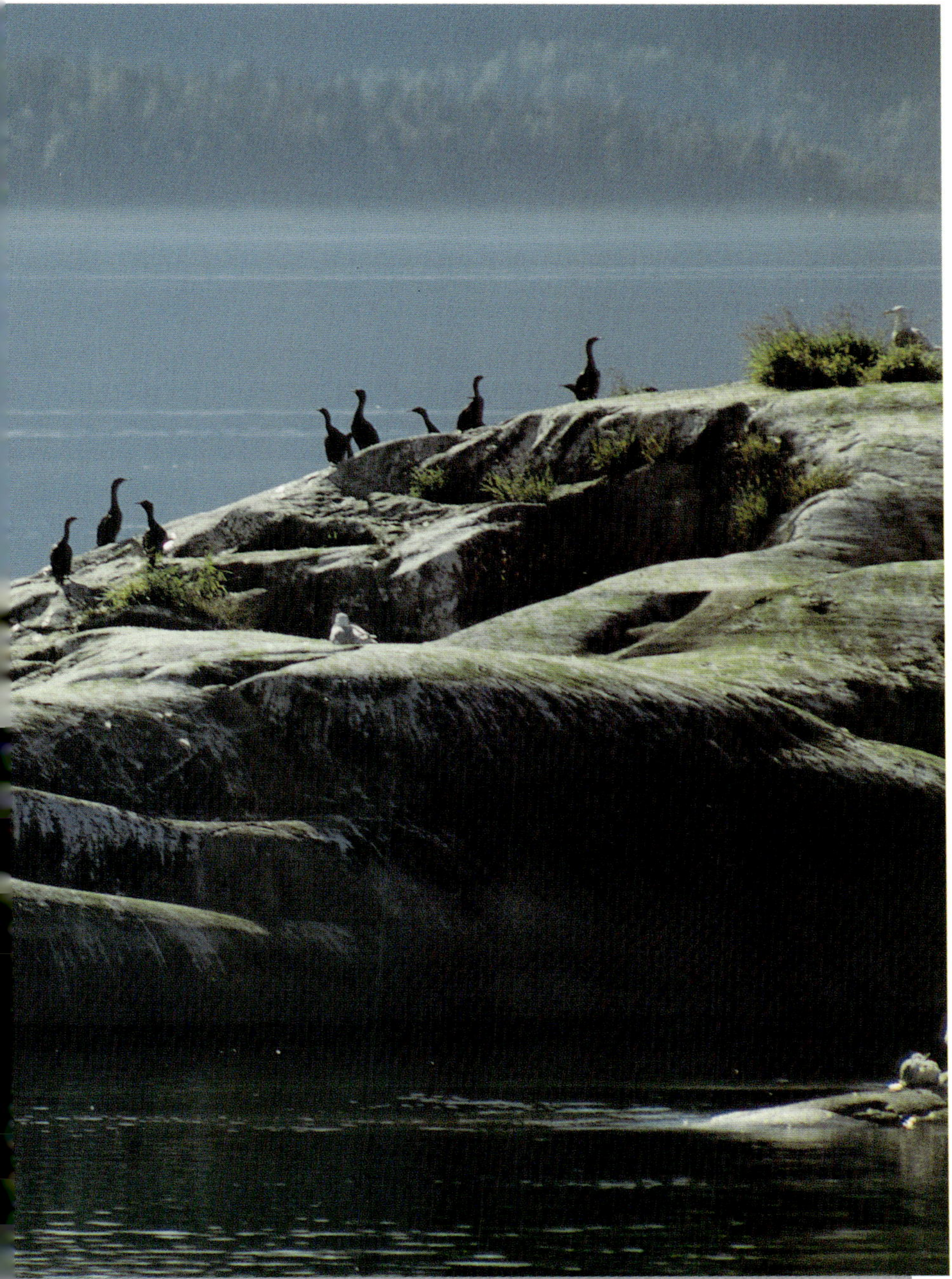

Bartlett Cove amidst the backdrop of Fairweather Mountain Range.

SOUTHEAST ALASKA

167

Canada-U.S. Border Crossings

A breathtaking view of Wrangell mountain range from Highway 4.

Travelers driving to Alaska on the Alaska Highway, or driving from the ferry terminals at Haines and Skagway, have to pass through customs offices. Ordinarily, these transactions are accomplished simply and efficiently, with no problems experienced by either party. However, it is an international border crossing, and as such should not be taken lightly. Although Canada customs are not complicated, there are definite precautions to take before attempting to cross the border.

Failure to have all your papers in order can be cause for the border officials to deny entry, to send you back to where you came from, or even to precipitate an international incident by arresting you. Do not take chances. Do your homework, and have all your ducks in a row before heading for the final border.

Adequate identification should be your first concern. A driver's license is no longer considered sufficient proof of citizenship for United States residents. Remember to carry a copy of your birth certificate or a passport. A passport is not required for United States citizens, but it does provide a handy means of identification, complete with photo. It is also more durable than a flimsy and easily lost piece of paper. Resident aliens of the United States should carry their Resident Alien cards with them. Travelers from other countries must make sure that their passports and visas are in order before reaching the border, especially if they carry a single entry United States visa. Check with the nearest office of the United States Immigration and Naturalization Service or the Canadian Embassy or consulate before you begin your trip. Border officials may also require proof of auto insurance. United States insurance companies can provide policy holders with a motor vehicle liability card as proof of insurance. Border officials may also ask for proof of funds. They do not want indigent types breaking down in Canada with no way to get home. This is rather a judgment call for the border guards. If you are driving a US$100,000 motor home, towing a Range Rover behind, and dressed in a coat and tie, no border guard in the world is going to ask to see the color of your money. On the other hand, if you are traveling with eight of your closest friends in a 1968 VW bus with cardboard boxes strapped to the roof, you can expect a certain amount of scrutiny on the part of the officials of both countries. Of course it is not fair, but that is the way the world works, and expect-

---

food, shops, etc. Nearby **Fort William Seward** served as a home for the army from 1904 to 1946. After its decommissioning by the army, it was purchased by a group of veterans, and now stands restored, serving as a national historical site, and as home to the **Alaska Indian Arts center** and the **Hotel Hälsingland**, among other businesses. A walking tour of the downtown

ing anything different is hopelessly naive.

If you are traveling with pets, carry proof of vaccination against rabies for dogs and cats. Traveling with birds presents potential complications. Some domestic birds are considered endangered species, and international transport and legalisation is problematic. For details, contact the Canadian Wildlife Service in Ottawa at (819)997-1480.

One of the major problems for Americans traveling through Canada is firearms. Rifles and shotguns do not present a problem as long as they are not fully automatic and have legal barrel lengths of (18 1/2 inches) 47 cms then there is no problem. Notify the customs officer that you are transporting long guns, and he might ask to examine them, to see that they are unloaded. The attitudes of the two governments concerning handguns are very different. In Alaska, many outdoors types do not consider themselves fully dressed unless they are carrying the trusty .44 magnum on the hip. However, Canada forbids carrying or transporting handguns unless you acquire a special permit from the government. If you feel you need your sidearm in Alaska, talk to a local gun shop before leaving home. Gun stores are required to possess a Federal Fire arms License (FFL), and only holders of an FFL may ship handguns by mail. Most stores will ship your gun to a license holder at your destination as a courtesy, or for a slight charge. Do not attempt to sneak through customs with a handgun- if you are caught, you have had it. If you have purchased handicrafts in Alaska made of ivory or certain animal parts, a free permit is required to transport them through Canada. Remember to ask for a permit at the time you purchase the craft items, or make sure you obtain one from an office of the United States Department of the Interior or the United States Fish and Wildlife Service.

area will take you by the **Sheldon Museum**, the old city hall and fire station, and other reminders of the city's past. You can take a raft trip through the eagle preserve with **Chilkat Guides**,

Saxman villager exhibiting their handwoven blankets.

(766-2491), arrange a tour of **Haines** or **Glacier Bay** with **Fort Seward Tours** (766-2000 or 1-800-542-6363), travel to Skagway with the **Haines-Skagway Water Taxi** (766-3395), or tour Haines in a horse-drawn carriage with **Haines Carriage Co.** (766-2665).

Skagway calls itself "**The Gateway to the Klondike**", and wholeheartedly embraces its sometimes tawdry but always colorful past. When gold seekers of every stripe first wound up here at the tail end of the 19th century, the town was at times lawless and violent, ruled for a time by the infamous **Soapy Smith**. Somehow the town has managed to survive through boom and bust, and today remains as a popular tourist stop. It is the end of the line for the Alaska

Skagway vintage car.

ferries here. You can connect with the road system, catch a plane out of town, or go back on the ship or ferry you came in on. Alternatively, stick around for a while and take in the ambiance of the Gold Rush days. For a taste of the gold rush, visit the "Days of '98" show, held daily at the **Eagle's Hall** at 6th ST and Broadway. A group of actors and musicians recreates **Soapy Smith**'s days in **Skagway** in what is billed as a one-hour historical comic drama. There are daytime and evening shows, and the evening shows are preceded by a half hour of mock gambling. Railroad buffs, sightseers, and **Chilkoot Trail** hikers will enjoy taking the **White Pass & Yukon Route** trains. The trains offer a variety of excursion possibilities: you can take the train to White Pass Summit and return to Skagway, or take a longer trip to the shores of **Lake Bennett** in neighboring British Columbia. You can also make arrangements to stop at the town of **Fraser B.C.**, and take a motor coach from there to Whitehorse, Yukon Territory. If you are hiking the Chilkoot Trail, you can purchase a return trip ticket in Skagway, and take the train

A lone lighthouse beckons at Lynn Canal.

back from Lake Bennett. The cruise ships visiting Skagway have a number of seats on the train available, so you can buy train tickets on board. Other possibilities in Skagway include sportfishing, flight seeing, and local tours and excursions. Contact **Frontier Excursions** at 983-2512 for tours and shuttles, **Skagway Sportfishing** at 983-2244, **L.A.B. Flying Service** at 983-2471 or **Skagway Air Service** at 983-2218. You will find plenty in Skagway to whet your appetite for outdoor adventure, or fill in any gaps in your traveling experiences.

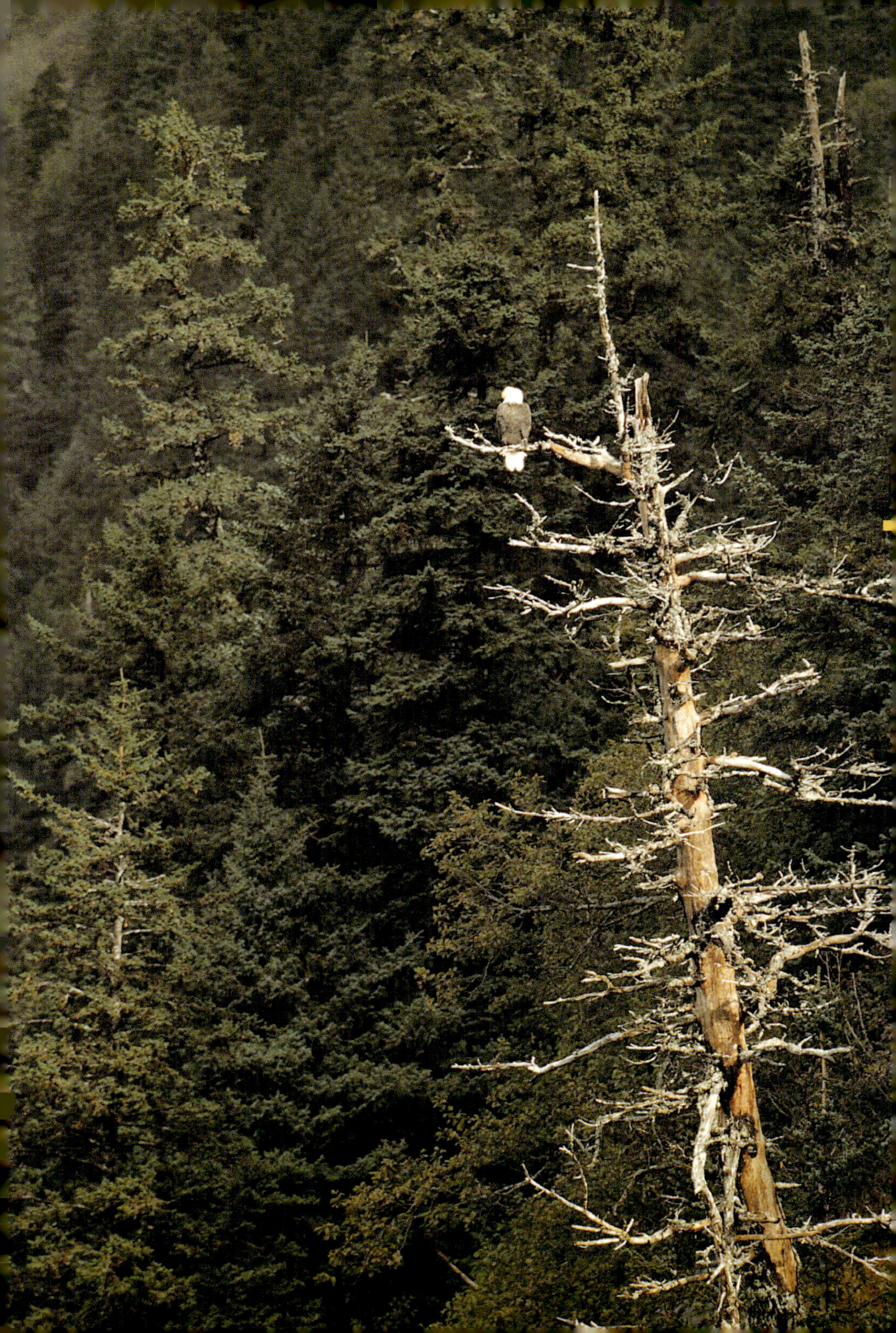

SCENIC SOUNDS

Southcentral Alaska

The most visited part of the state is the **Southcentral** region. Easily accessible by air and by road, this region contains most of the state's people, and a sizable chunk of wilderness and attractions as well. It includes **Prince William Sound (PWS)**, the **Matanuska** and **Susitna Valleys**, the **Anchorage** area, and the **Kenai Peninsula**. Within this section of land, there is lots of room to traverse the wide expanse and still be within reach of the creature comforts and relatively low prices of the Anchorage bowl. Most of this area is road accessible, making for lower transportation costs, but true wilderness is often just a short flight, boat ride, or hike from the road system.

A bald eagle perched up high.

Prince William Sound

Prince William Sound received a lot of unwanted attention and visibility due to the **Exxon Valdez** oil

Prince William Sound

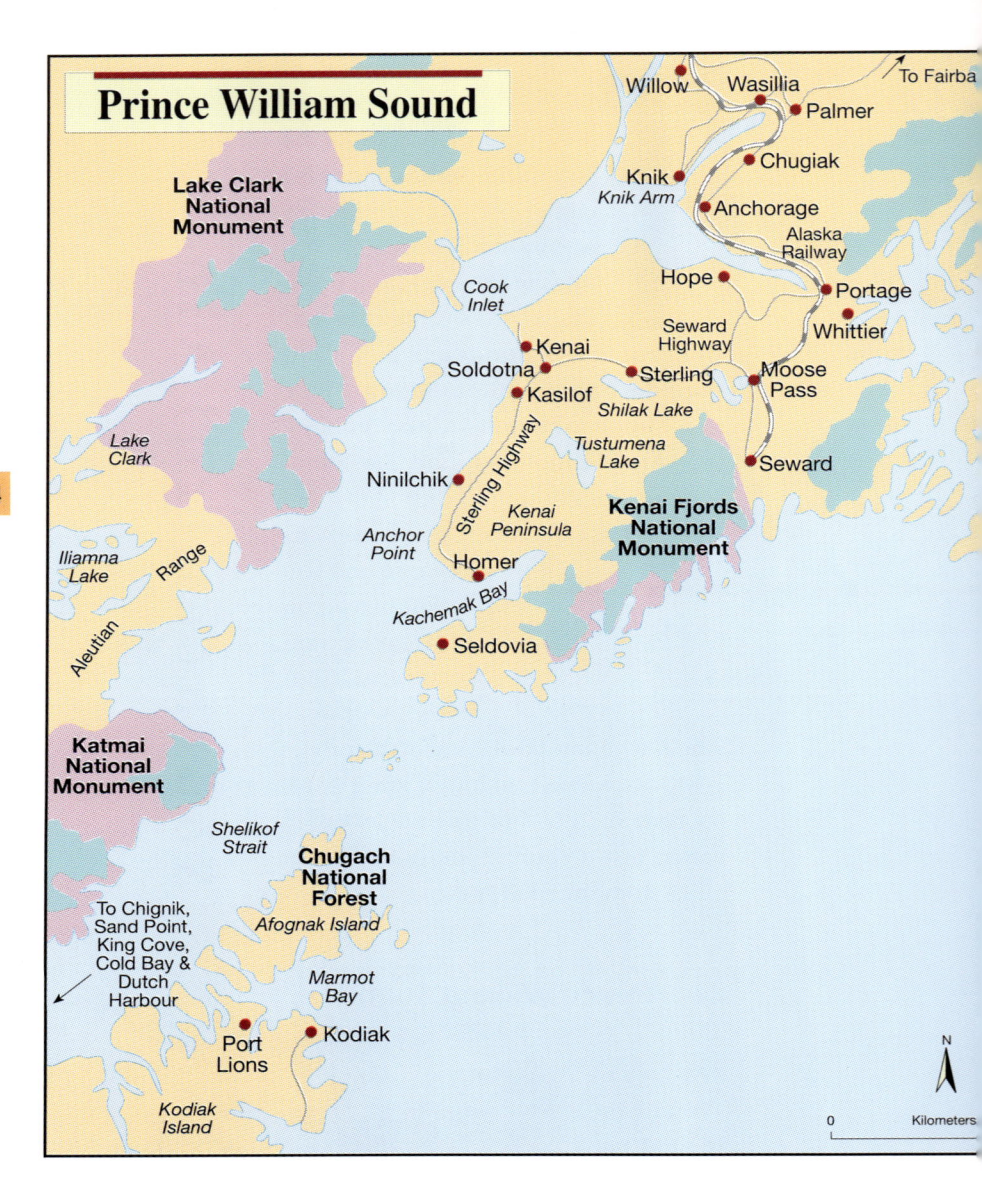

spill. In the years since the spill and its controversial clean-up, the Sound has, to the naked eye anyway, returned to its former nearly unblemished serenity. For the visitor, there is no reason to avoid the Sound, but many reasons to explore it. It is truly one of the most breathtaking regions on the planet, with numerous uninhabited islands, tidewater glaciers, narrow channels and open water. All of these are surrounded by spectacular mountains, capped by snow and ice all year round. Any chance to visit this place should not be passed by. For the

A harbor seal relaxing at Tracy Arm.

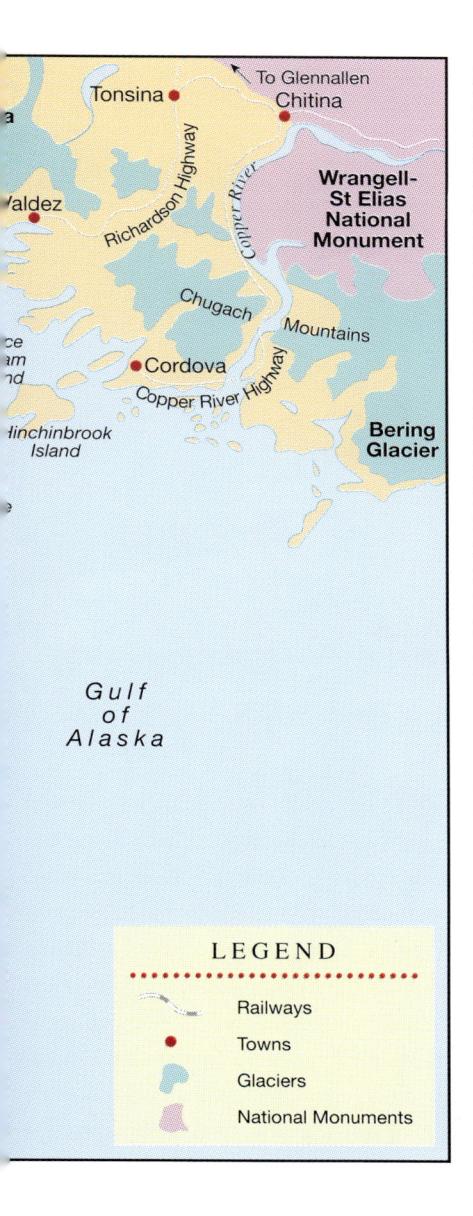

road traveler, access points to **PWS** are at **Valdez** and **Whittier**. Whittier is not road accessible by the strictest definition of the term, since no roads lead there, but the **Alaska Railroad** runs a shuttle train between **Portage** and **Whittier**, a twelve-mile run that passes through two tunnels. Cars and trucks can be transported on the train, and in Whittier you can make connections with the Marine Highway ferries. Whittier is the nearest ice-free deep-water port to **Anchorage**, and during World War II was used extensively by the military. The only glitch in the location was those inconvenient mountains, so the tunnels were blasted through, and an oil pipe line built between Whittier and **Fort Richardson**.

The change in weather between Whittier and the Anchorage bowl is astounding. It can be sunny, warm and clear in Portage, but overcast, raining like crazy, and blowing a gale on the other side of the tunnels. The difference in precipitation levels between the two areas is hard to believe, but Anchorage

Getting ready for a flightseeing spin at Prince William Sound.

receives a mere 15 inches (38 cm) a year, while **Whittier** endures nearly 200 inches (508 cm). This difference is especially noticeable in the winter, when **Portage** can be windswept and barely snow covered, and Whittier buried under 10 feet of the stuff.

The train ride to Whittier is a delight. Between Portage and the first tunnel, look for mountain goats on the cliffs, moose in the lower areas, and ducks in the potholes. As the train emerges from the first tunnel into **Bear Valley**, look for moose near the tracks, and for black bears on the hillsides. Look for sea otters in the bay after you emerge from the second tunnel, and in the small boat harbor. Scan the upper reaches of the mountains, looking for mountain goats on the rocky faces in the area. Occasionally black bears are seen crossing snow fields, or in lower, open areas. Whittier sits on the edge of **Passage Canal**, across from **Billings Glacier**. It is a popular jumping-off point for sea kayakers, fishermen, (both sport and commercial), sightseers, and hunters, and is the closest small boat harbor to **Anchorage**. It is also a popular and convenient place for cruise ships to stop and shuttle their passengers via train and bus to Anchorage. You can book a room or grab a good meal at the **Anchor Inn** (472-2354) or at the **Sportsman's Inn** (472-2352), camp out at the camper park, or catch the ferry. The route to **Valdez** is especially popular, the six hour and 45 minute run passing

Sunset glow at Valdez.

Columbia Glacier provides quite a tour of the Sound. **Valdez** is the southern terminus of the **Trans-Alaska Pipeline**. There are tour boats out of Valdez for guided trips through the sound, fishing, or trips to **Whittier** or Cordova. Campsites and lodging, restaurants, shopping, and tourist services are plentiful in Valdez. You can also tour the **Alyeska Marine Terminal** (835-2686) and see the end products of the oil pumped all the way from the **Arctic Ocean**. Stop by the visitor center at 200 Chenega St., (835-2984) and the **Valdez Museum** (835-2764) at 217 Egan Dr. for local information and background. Visit **Columbia Glacier**- the tour boats provide closer views than the state ferry, along with narration and explanation of the area's wildlife and natural history. Contact **Stan Stephens Charters** at 1-800-992-1297 or 907-835-4731, **Capt. Jim's Great Alaska Charter co.** at 835-2282, or **Gray Line** at 835-2357. The more adventurous might want to try sailing or kayaking in the area, or rafting in one of the local rivers. Call **Keystone Raft & Kayak Adventures** at 1-800-328-8460 or 907-835-2603, **Alaskan Wilderness Sailing Safaris** at 835-5175, or **Anadyr Adventures** at 835-2814.

The Kenai Peninsula

Because of its many varied attractions and road accessibility, the **Kenai** is very popular, for a whole lot of good reasons.

Public Use Cabins

A place of solitude on Growler Island, Prince William Sound.

There is an alternative to travelers looking for low-cost backcountry options, but unwilling or unprepared to spend time in a tent. Alaska State Parks, the United States Bureau of Land Management, and the United States Forest Service maintain cabins available for rent by the public. These cabins are mostly in out-of-the-way locations, usually requiring a considerable hike away from the road system, or access by floatplane or boat. The cabins are very basic, consisting of walls, a floor, and a roof, wooden bunks, tables, and heating stoves. Outhouses are nearby. You must supply your own bedding, cook stove, eating and cooking utensils. There is no running water or electricity, and the cabins with wood stoves usually have saws and splitting mauls for cutting and splitting firewood. Cabins in areas where wood is not readily available have oil or propane stoves, for which you have to supply fuel. The stoves are not practical for cooking purposes, just to get the stove hot enough to boil a pot of water raises the temperature inside the cabin to near-sauna levels!

If you stay in any of the public use cabins, there are a few basic rules of etiquette to keep in mind:

Rules to Remember

1. Leave the cabin in a clean and orderly condition. Even if it was a mess when you got there, sweep the floor, clean out the stove, and remove your trash and any left behind by others.

2. Do not put green wood, plastic, or aluminum foil in the stoves.

3. Do not cut down living trees. Although the areas adjacent to the cabins have been stripped of available dead wood, a short walk will usually turn up an adequate supply.

4. Leave enough cut, dry wood behind for the next person to have at least one good, warming fire. If you have ever arrived at a cabin tired, cold, and wet, you can appreciate the value of being preceded by a thoughtful camper.

5. Do not occupy a cabin if you do not have a permit. To do so makes you subject to a fine if the rangers happen by, and if the person who does have a permit shows up, there is likely to be an unpleasant scene.

6. Do not camp right next to the cabin if you do not have a permit. The people who pay the rent deserve to be left alone to enjoy their privacy.

Row boats and oars are provided for cabins situated on lakes- life preservers are the responsibility of the user. The rowboats can use small outboard motors- obviously only an option if you fly or boat in to the cabin, or you are a very determined backpacker. The Kenai Peninsula, Prince William Sound, Southeast, the Fairbanks area, and Kodiak have cabins for rent. Most are in coastal areas or on lakes, but on the Kenai, the cabins on the Resurrection Pass and River trails are very popular with back packers. Reservations can be made 6 months in advance, by mail or in person, and payment of US$25 per night must accompany the request.

During the height of the tourist and hunting seasons, cabins are booked months in advance, so plan ahead. Balloting are held for some of the most popular cabins during peak times, usually during hunting and fishing seasons. If you are unable to make advance reservations and still want to see the area, check with the office anyway. Cancellations occur, as do holes in the schedule, so it is always good to give it a try. Address inquiries to:

Alaska Public Lands Information Center
605 W. 4th Ave.
Anchorage AK 99501
Attention:Cabin information
Tel: 271-2599

Bureau of Land Management (BLM)
222 W. Seventh Ave #13
Anchorage AK 99513
Tel: 271-5960
Fax: 272-3684

Ketchikan Area- Supervisor
Tongass National Forest
Federal Building
Ketchikan 99901
Tel: 225-3101

Forest Service Information Center
Centennial Hall
101 Egan Dr.
Juneau AK 99801
Tel: 586-8751

Stikine Area Supervisor
Tongass National Forest
Box 309
Petersburg 99833
Tel: 772-3841

Chatham Area Supervisor
Tongass National Forest
204 Siginika Way
Sitka 99835
Tel: 747-6671

USDA Forest Drive Service Information Center
101 Egan Dr.
Juneau 99801
Tel: 586-8751

Refuge Manager Kodiak National Wildlife Refuge
1390 Buskin River Road
Kodiak 99616
Tel: 487-2600

The Alaska Division of Parks and Outdoor Recreation oversees the rental of cabins in the Nancy Lake State Recreation Area, on the Kenai, near Fairbanks, on Shuyak Island near Kodiak, and in Southeast. Contact the Department of Natural Resources office at:

3601 C St. Suite
200 Anchorage 99503
Tel: 762-2261

A scenic bend at Copper River, Kenai Peninsula.

The towns of **Seward**, **Hope**, **Cooper Landing**, **Soldotna**, **Kenai**, and **Homer** offer multiple reasons for a visit, as do several more of the smaller communities along the way. Wildlife includes moose, (the Kenai is said to be the most productive moose habitat in the world), Dall sheep, mountain goats, black and brown bears, wolves, coyotes, fox, etc. Glaciers and ice fields cover the higher reaches of the Kenai mountains, in some cases extending down to tidewater, or to accessible spots on land. The terrain is varied as well. The Kenai mountains

first opportunity to turn off the **Seward Highway**. Taking a right and following the shore of **Turnagain arm**, the village of Hope is 16 miles (26 km) in. Here you can find food, lodging, tourist services, and the northern end of the **Resurrection Pass Trail**. This popular hiking trail runs for 38 miles (61 km) south through the **Kenai** mountains, over **Resurrection Pass**, and down to the south trailhead in **Cooper Landing**. Continuing south towards Seward, the **Summit Lake Lodge** at mile 45.8 is a great place to stop for a meal, or to visit the gift shop and ice cream parlor next door. Eight miles south of Summit Lake is the junction with the Sterling Highway. Continue straight south to Seward, bear right for **Cooper Landing**, **Soldotna**, and **Homer**. Taking the Sterling Highway from the Seward, you hit the long, skinny town of Cooper Landing, strung out along the highway for eight miles. At the end of **Kenai Lake**, the bridge crosses the beginning of the world famous **Kenai River**. The biggest king salmon in the world live in this river, as do the trophy-size rainbow trout, Dolly Varden, red salmon, silver salmon, and pink salmon. You can pursue book guided fishing and float trips in Cooper Landing with **Osprey Alaska** (1-800-533-5364, winter, 1-800-478-0103 in Alaska), or **Alaska Wildland Adventures**, (1-800-478-4100). Stop at mile 52 of the **Sterling Highway** for food, lodging, fishing tackle, fishing information, beer, and a breather. **The Kenai Cache** (595-1401) sells and rents fishing tackle

dominate the peninsula, but in the northwest corner is a huge area of flats and plains. Here the **Swanson River** and **Swan Lake** area provide miles upon miles of canoe trails over a series of interconnecting lakes and streams. You can bring your own canoe, or rent one at **Sterling**, and spend a day or several weeks exploring the canoe system. At mile 56.7 is the **Hope Highway**, your

Clouds gather at Barry Glacier, Prince William Sound.

and gear, and will also freeze and ship your fish. Next door is Gwin's Lodge (595-1266), with a restaurant, bar, liquor store, fishing tackle, and lodging. You can also do book guided river trips or arrange for fly-in trips here, a very popular stop on the highway. If you want to fish in the area, you can get a campsite or park for the day at the Russian River campground a half mile down the road. The campground is always full during salmon runs, but if you have got the time and patience, you can get in line and wait. If you just want to watch at the state's most popular fishing hole, park (for a fee) at the ferry crossing at mile 55. You can watch the shoulder to shoulder fishing action from this side, or get a ticket on the current-powered ferry (US$3.00 per person round trip) and stroll the bank on the other side. The **Kenai-Soldotna** area of the lower Kenai River is the most productive area for king salmon fishing. Numerous guide services are available for half or full day fishing trips to pursue the mighty king. Red and silver salmon are also plentiful during their runs. Kings start the first of their two runs into the river in late May or early June, reds follow with the first of their two runs in mid-June, and silvers make the trip in July and August. On your way out of Soldotna on the **Sterling Highway**, the last stop light is just across the Kenai River bridge. Turn left on the Funny River Road, take the first right and follow the signs to the **Kenai**

A couple wrapped up in fox fur.

National Wildlife Refuge visitor's center. After visiting the center, retrace your route and go straight at the stop light on **Kalifornsky Beach Road**. This takes you south towards **Homer** along scenic bluffs overlooking **Cook Inlet** and providing tremendous views across the inlet to **Redoubt Volcano**, **Mt. Illiamna**, and the peaks of the Alaska range extending south. At the intersection six miles (10 km) from the **Sterling Highway**, take a right towards **Kenai**. There is usually a small herd of caribou in the area, and if you are lucky you will spot one of them in the flats around the **Kenai River** delta. Pull over in one of the turn-outs and look for caribou and waterfowl. Snow geese, Canada geese, ducks, and sandhill cranes frequent the area. Go back the way you came, and turn right at the stop sign. Kalifornsky Beach Road rejoins the Sterling Highway south of Soldotna. The drive to Homer parallels the shoreline, offering occasional glimpses of the Inlet and the mountains on the other side. At **Ninilchik**, there is a restored Russian Orthodox church overlooking the Inlet, worth a stop and look. At **Deep Creek** a semi-permanent campground and settlement thrives on the beach area, with fishermen using the spot for launching boats into the inlet to search for halibut and salmon.

The approach to Homer is amazing. You are driving along, getting used to the scenery, when you turn a corner and there you are, high on a hill over-

The "Eagle Spot" at Homer where eagles are fed in winter.

looking **Kachemak Bay** and **lower Cook Inlet**, with the Kenai Mountains on one side and the Alaska Range on the other. Pull over at one of the scenic overlooks along the road and take in the sights before heading downhill into **Homer**.

Halibut Fishing in Homer

Follow the highway straight through town and out to the **Homer Spit**. When you are at the end of the road, you are really at the end of the road. After Homer would be the deep blue seas. This is as far as you can drive from the Lower 48 without getting wet, or to quote local author **Tom Bodett**, it is as far as you can go without a passport. Along the spit you will find halibut charter outfits too numerous to mention, food, lodging, espresso, obviously, the basic necessities of life is hardly lacking here, at the far end of the United States. Stop by at the **Salty Dawg Saloon** for a nip and some local color. Although Homer is the self-proclaimed "Halibut Fishing Capital of the World", and for good reason too, there is more to do here than just fish for the huge bottom fish. Across **Kachemak Bay** lie the settlements of **Halibut Cove** and **Seldovia**, accessible by ferry from Homer. The ferry, Danny J, a classic wooden boat, leaves Homer every day at noon, and cruises to Halibut Cove, stopping along the way to look at nesting sea birds and whatever other animals of interest present them-

Ships at night in Prince William Sound.

selves. The 2½ hour stay at Halibut Cove is up to you to fill – you could have lunch at the Saltry, dining on fresh local seafood, hike the trails on **Ismailof Island**, and board the Danny J at 4:00PM for the return to Homer.

The boat makes a second run to the cove, leaving Homer at 5:00 PM for overnight guests on the island and for dinner at the Saltry. Call **Central Charters** at 907-235-7847 or the **Kachemak Bay Ferry** office at 907-296-2223 for ferry information, and the **Saltry** at 296-7847 for early reservations at the restaurant to avoid disappointment.

Also on the other side of the bay from **Homer** is the town of **Seldovia**. This picturesque little fishing community is served by the Alaska state ferry, and by tour boats in Homer. Seldovia has stores, visitor services, a small boat harbor, camp sites and lodges to soothe the weary traveler. You can take a vehicle over on the state ferry, fly over with a Homer air taxi or by scheduled aircraft from Homer and Anchorage. **Alaska Maritime Tours** (235-2490) and **Kachemak Bay Adventures** (235-6669 or 235-8206) conduct nature tours of the area, with stops to visit Seldovia.

Seward

Continuing south past the **Sterling Highway** junction takes you to **Seward**. Just past the Sterling highway turn-off, watch the mountainsides along both

Columbia Glacier

A panoramic view of Columbia Glacier.

The dynamics of glaciers continue to intrigue and at times to mystify scientists. These enormous rivers of ice hardly seem, at first glance, to merit much study. A bunch of snow falls, it accumulates and forms ice sheets, then obeys the laws of gravity by flowing downhill and then melting. What is the big mystery? As with so many other things in life, what seems simple on the surface is actually complex and multi-layered once you start to study the subject in depth and get behind the easy and obvious. Glaciers that reach an arm of the sea are referred to as tidewater glaciers. They meander down out of the mountains, reaching their terminal points at salt water. There the action of the (relatively) warm water erodes the base of the ice face, causing an action known as calving. Large spires of ice break away from the main body of the glacier and tumble into the water, with a sound and a splash that is absolutely awe-inspiring. (Tour boats that visit glaciers will often sound their horns to try and initiate this action). As these ice chunks get pulled away from the glacier's face by the tide, they float out into the water as icebergs. They drift around the ocean, disintegrating slowly as they melt into the sea. It is dangerous to approach icebergs- they tend to melt from underneath as the warmer salt water works on the ice, and they will destabilize and roll over, giving no notice beforehand.

sides of the road – sheep and goats are almost always present along here. In Moose Pass, food, lodging, and visitor's services are available at the **Crown Point Lodge** (288-3136) and the **Trail Lake Lodge** (288-3101). At the end of the

Columbia Glacier is the largest glacier in Prince William Sound. Over 400 sq miles (1,032 sq km) in size and nearly 40 miles (64 km) long, this is one big chunk of hard water. Columbia Glacier was first photographed in 1899. Scientists have been able to chart its progress by comparing photos taken periodically since then. Glaciers go through cycles of advancing, resting, and retreating that depend on a variety of complex and interconnected factors. Columbia advanced down Columbia Bay slowly during this century, occasionally making small retreats as well. Its structure and behavior caused glaciologists in the 1970s to suspect that it was getting ready to enter a phase of retreat. In December of 1984, Columbia Glacier began a phase of irreversible retreat. When you consider that these behemoths advance at a rate of something like one mile every hundred years, the rate of retreat is impressive indeed. Three years after it began its retreat, Columbia had backed up two miles, at one point traveling 3,000 ft (315 meter) in two months. Eventually it is expected to retreat to a point above tidewater, exposing a new 25 mile-long fjord.

The best way to view the Columbia Glacier is via tour boat from Valdez. The boat operators can take you to within a mile of the glacier's face, where you will be able to see and hear the icebergs calving off its face. The bay lies about 40 miles (64 km) from Valdez and 60 miles (97 km) from Whittier- you can charter boats out of either port, although Valdez offers more outfits to choose from. You can also arrange flightseeing trips from Valdez in helicopters or fixed-wing aircraft. The Columbia glacier is also visible from the deck of the Alaska state ferry as it travels between Valdez and Whittier. Some commercial operators offering views and tours of Columbia: Honey Charters Box 708 Whittier 99693 344-3340 Stan Stephens Cruises Box 1297 Valdez 99686 1-800-992-1297 907-835-4731 Era Helicopters 1-800-843-1947 Ketchum Air Service 1-800-433-9114

A totem by the corner of a lodge at Fort Seward, Haines.

road, by rail, by ferry, and of course by air, making it one of the most accessible cities in the state.

Fishing charters are available here, halibut, salmon, and ling cod among the more popular fish. Check in at The Fish House at the small boat harbor (1-800-478-8007 or 907-224-3674) for charter and fishing derby information.

If you are in the neighborhood on the 4th of July, be sure to catch the annual run to the top of nearby **Mt. Marathon**. This event attracts contestants from all over the state, and from outside as well, as they try for the fastest time to scale to the top of the 3,022 ft (922 meter) mountain, and back. **Seward** is also well known as the access point to **Kenai Fjords National Park**.

road lies the seaside town of Seward, sitting on the shores of beautiful **Resurrection Bay**. Seward is accessible by

Rugged cliffs loom large around Resurrection Bay.

Several tour boat companies offer half-day and full day cruises affording the visitor a chance to view sea otters, seals, sea lions, whales, glaciers, sea bird rookeries, and some of the most fantastic scenery in the state. Do not pass up a chance to see this collection of natural wonders. Call **Major Marine Tours** at 1-800-764-7300, **Mariah Charters** at 224-8623 (summer) or 243-1238 (year round), **Kenai Fjords Tours** at 1-800-478-8068 or 224-8068, or **Kenai Coastal Tours** at 907-277-2131 or 1-800-770-9119.

(Southcentral) North of Anchorage

Heading north from **Anchorage**, the remainder of the southcentral region is accessible via the **George Parks Highway** and the **Glenn Highway**. The Parks Highway runs from **Wasilla** to **Fairbanks**, and the Glenn runs from Anchorage to **Tok**. The **Hatcher Pass** area offers an opportunity to take a slow round loop through picturesque

Harbor and boatyard on Resurrection Bay.

mountain habitat, following the twisting mountain road up across the 3,886 ft (1,185 meter) pass. From the Parks Highway mile 71.2, turn right and follow the road. The pavement ends after a while, and the road climbs, paralleling **Willow Creek** through the valley, switching back as it heads for the summit. After breaking out above treeline, the terrain is open tundra, providing sweeping views of the area.

There are several working gold mines in the area, as well as some abandoned sites. You can alight, take a stroll or hike anywhere your spirit moves you, climbing the hills for even better views of the Southcentral, stopping for a picnic lunch along the road, or taking one of the side roads for an even more secluded visit.

On the other side of the pass, there is the **Independence Mine State Historical Park**, an abandoned gold mine offering walking tours and a glimpse into the past. The **Hatcher Pass Lodge** (745-5897) is nearby, offering lodging, food, and a bar.

As the road continues down the hill, the **Motherlode Lodge** (745-6182 or 1-800-725-2752) is near the bottom, also providing lodging and food as well as horseback riding, gold panning, and nature trails. The road then continues out and connects with the **Glenn Highway** at mile 49.5 from **Anchorage**. A left on the Glenn takes you towards **Glennallen**, **Tok**, and **Valdez**, a right goes back to **Anchorage**.

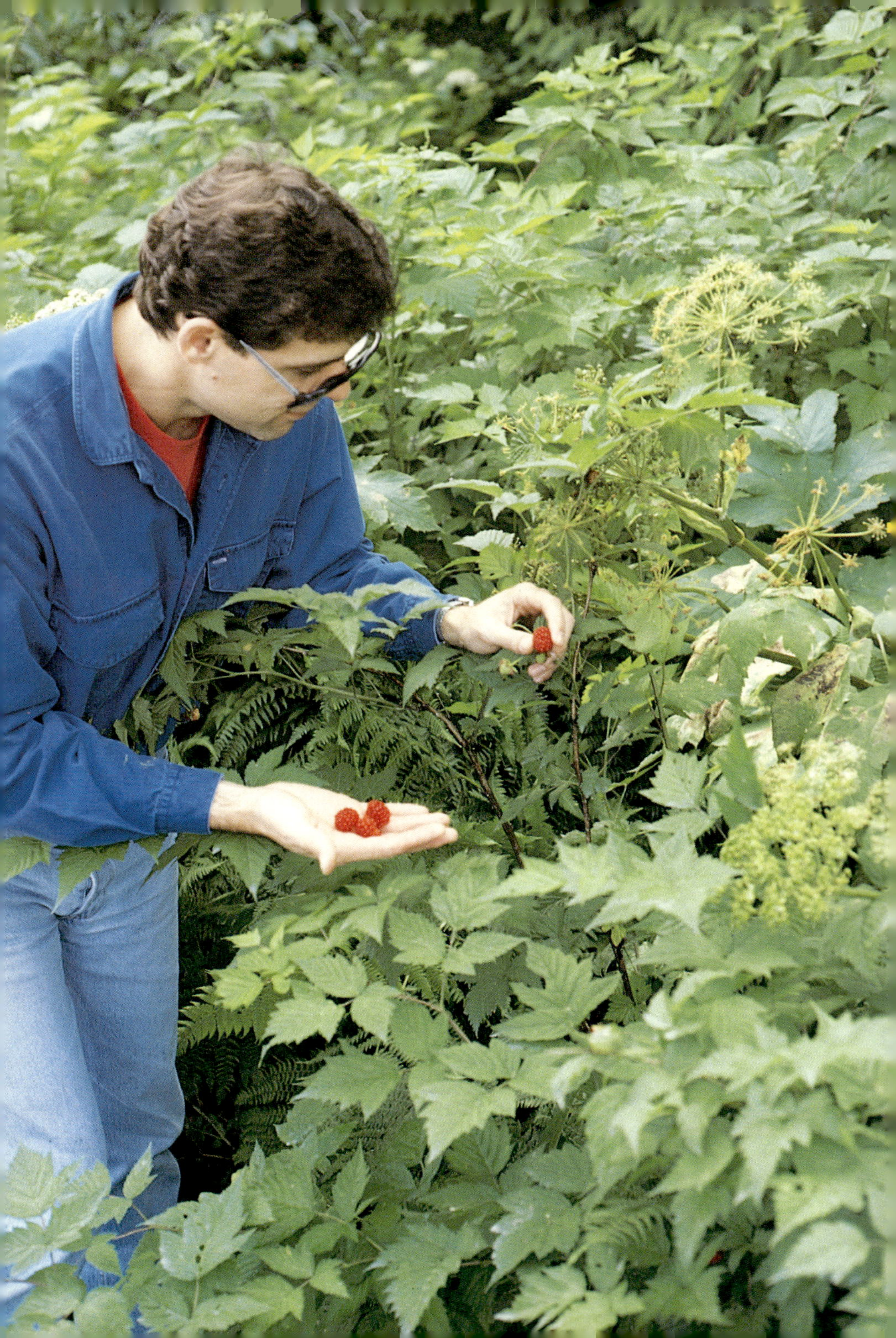

SPORT FISHING IN BEAR COUNTRY

Kodiak Island

The **Kodiak Island** group, consisting of **Kodiak**, **Afognak**, **Raspberry**, **Shuyak**, and numerous smaller islands, is an extension, geologically speaking, of the **Kenai Peninsula**. Sitting in the **Gulf of Alaska**, Kodiak is strategically placed in some of the world's richest fishing grounds. Hundreds of fish boats call Kodiak home, and numerous fishing and processing boats from the Lower 48, as well as from Asian countries, spend a considerable amount of time and money in the port of Kodiak. Locally based boats ply the surrounding seas in search of salmon, halibut, king, tanner, and Dungeness crab or shrimp. There are canneries in town to handle this influx of protein from the sea, providing jobs for numerous seasonal and year round employees. This dependence on fishing has buffered the people of Kodiak from some of the extreme fluctuations of Alaska's boom and bust cycles. While the oil and gold rushes on the mainland did not enrich the locals to the extent that it did many people

Salmon berry picking season.

Small craft parked in placid waters.

farther north, the subsequent downturns were not as sorely felt here either. The **Kodiak** economy is much more stable than that of the rest of the state. Oil and gold booms will come and go, but people will always have a taste for seafood. While tourism is also a factor in the local economy, it is not as significant as it is elsewhere in the state.

The **Kodiak Visitor Information Center** (486-4070) is on the waterfront next to the ferry dock. They can arrange walking and driving tours, as well as give you more detailed information on local attractions and what is the best route to get there.

Getting there

Due to Kodiak's far-out location, you pretty much have to go there on purpose – it is not on the way to anywhere else, moreover, the cost of transportation to the island is a deterrent to many casual visitors.

Air connections from Anchorage and Homer are available. Ferry service on the **Alaska Marine Highway** is an-

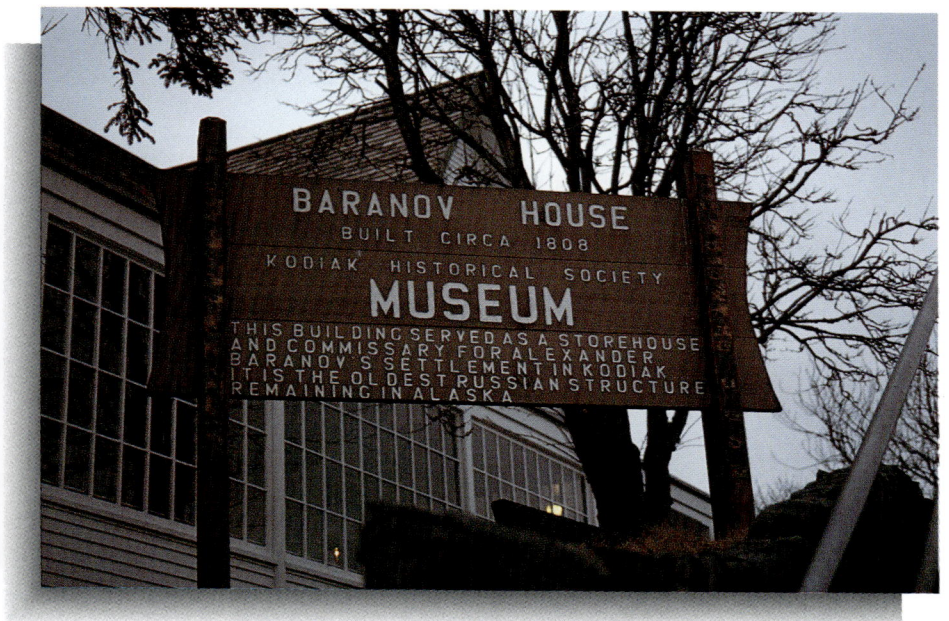

Russian Rememberance – the Baranov House Museum at Kodiak.

other option, with ferry runs carrying vehicles and passengers connecting Kodiak with **Seward** and **Homer** on the mainland, and to ports in the **Aleutians** as well. Climate on the island is mild and maritime, with approximately 74 inches (185 cm) of rainfall every year. Daily temperatures seldom go above 60 degrees, or fall much below 30. Rain, fog, and wind are common, and the well-dressed tourist will supplement his or her wardrobe with rain gear and wool for any Kodiak sojourns.

Disasters, both natural and man-made, have figured prominently in Kodiak's history. In 1912, the **Novarupta volcano** erupted on the Alaska peninsula. This enormous rip in the earth's surface was 10 times as powerful as the **Mount St. Helens** eruption, and was the second greatest volcanic eruption in recorded history. The area near the volcano was buried under 700 ft (214 meter) of ash and pumice, and **Kodiak**, 100 miles (161 km) downwind, received over a foot and a half of volcanic debris covering everything in sight. The ash fall which resulted, blocked out the sun for two days. This natural disaster had severe environmental effects on the island, killing animals and vegetation indiscriminately. Luckily, the mineral content of the ash was good for plant life, and over the next few years the self-healing properties of the earth took over and life on the islands rebounded and thrived again.

The next big catastrophe unleashed

Within the sanctuary of a Russian Church.

by Mother Nature was the **Good Friday earthquake** that devastated **Anchorage** in 1964. The quake itself did little damage on Kodiak due to the distance, but the tsunami generated by the temblor actually reached and devastated villages and the harbor at the town of Kodiak. At least twenty people died, and the fishing fleet in port was all but wiped out with over 200 vessels damaged or destroyed. This was a big blow to the local fishing industry. Again however, the people and the area survived and rebuilt.

The latest disaster to touch Kodiak was not a natural force, but rather resulted from the follies of man. The **Exxon Valdez oil spill** in **Prince William Sound** reached Kodiak in the form of tar balls and oil mousse lining the shoreline in the path of the spill. Fishing was largely unaffected, and today little evidence of the spill remains to be seen.

Kodiak History and Culture

Kodiak's history is interesting and colorful, encompassing as it does the native peoples who inhabited the islands long before white men came along. There are three museums in the town of Kodiak, the **Baranov**, the **Veniaminoff**, and the **Alutiiq Cultural Center**. The Baranov is located at 101 Marine Way in the Erskine House, a National Historic Landmark. The house was built by the Russians in 1808, and underwent

Exhibits at Baranov Museum, Kodiak.

repairs by volunteers before being leased by the **Kodiak Historical Society** in 1966. Today it houses a collection of **Aleut**, **Koniag**, **Russian** and **American** pieces covering the island's past from pre-historic times up to contemporary times. Call the museum at 486-5920 for opening hours and admission prices.

The **Veniaminoff Research Institute Museum** is on the grounds of the **St. Herman Theological Seminary** of the **Russian Orthodox Church**. The museum has a collection of Native artifacts, a book store and a gift shop. The **Alutiiq Culture center** at 214 Rezanoff Dr. was created to study and preserve the culture and language of the local native peoples. They have anthropological exhibits, as well as photo archives and sound recordings of Native languages. Exploring Kodiak by road is an interesting way to see the sights. With fewer than 100 miles of road to explore, you can cover everything driveable in a reasonable amount of time.

Kodiak is also home to the country's largest **U.S. Coast Guard** base. The USCG operations here include four cutters for offshore patrol, search and rescue, and fisheries enforcement work. There are over 1,000 Coast Guard personnel based on Kodiak, along with over 1,500 dependents.

Kodiak Wilds

Besides the town of Kodiak, six other

Kodiak Bears

Brown bear with a salmon catch.

The bears of Kodiak island are often referred to as the largest carnivorous animals on earth. While the polar bear rivals the Kodiak in size, whether one or the other is actually larger on average is a minor sticking point in definition. The fact is, Kodiak brown bears are enormous, and the sight of one in the wild is a truly magnificent occasion. In years past, it was thought that the grizzly bears of the interior, the brown bears of coastal regions, and the Kodiak bear were all separate and distinct species.

Grizzlies ranged in size up to about 500 lbs (225 kg) or so, and the browns and Kodiaks often passed 1,200 lbs (540 kg). This difference in size was attributed to differences in the animals' genetic make-up. However, after much study by taxonomists and biologists, it has been determined that the grizzly and the coastal brown bear of the mainland are really the same animal – it is just that the bears that live near salt water have access to a much more protein-rich diet than do the animals living miles away from salmon streams. But it comes to the Kodiak bear, it turns out there really is a difference. A taxonomist well-versed in bears can tell the difference between the skull of a Kodiak bear and the skull of a mainland brown bear.

Even though the coastal brown bears on the mainland, the islands of Southeast, and the Aleutians are very large, the bears of Kodiak are larger still. The Boone & Crockett club keeps records of North American big game animals taken by hunters, and of the 50 largest brown bears ever killed, 34 of them are from Kodiak. These giant bears roam all over the islands of the Kodiak group. Standing over 9 ft (3 m) tall these bruisers rule the islands. Fearing nothing but man and other, larger bears, they feed on salmon, carrion, berries, roots, and small animals, when they can catch them. Deer hunters on the islands have an especially hard time dealing with these bears. A dead deer and the accompanying gut pile left by the hunters makes a very appealing find for a bear. Deer hunters have to dress out their deer and get them away from the kill site fast. Some hunters even swear that in recent years, the bears have learned to associate a rifle shot with a dead deer, and claim that the bears are attracted by the sound.

To get a chance to see bears on Kodiak, the most reliable method is to book a fly-in or boat charter with one of the local companies specializing in bear viewing. The effect of seeing one of these animals, even at long range and under the constraints of a supervised viewing trip, is difficult to convey. People who have lived their lives in urban areas or spent time in backcountry areas devoid of large predators have no basis of comparison when it comes to seeing large bears. To be walking through the wilderness, standing on the same ground as the largest meat-eater on the planet is indeed a humbling experience. Watching the animals in zoos or on television can hardly prepare you for the visceral, literally breathtaking experience of encountering one of these immense, shambling animals in its own territory. And it is more than just fear that one feels. Seeing big bears in their natural habitat, knowing of their intelligence and power, stirs atavistic feelings long sublimated by civilized man. When we spend our time in cities or areas that have been controlled, developed, and tamed we can pretend that as humans, we are really in command of our world. However, standing within view of a huge bear just some feet away, reminds us that there are things in nature beyond the capabilities of mere puny humans to control.

Sea lions pose proudly.

outposts of civilization exist on the islands: **Karluk, Akhiok, Larsen Bay, Old Harbor, Ouzinkie,** and **Port Lions.** The town of Port Lions is served by the ferry system, while the others can be reached by air and private or tour boats. (Port Lions got its name when the town of Afognak was wiped out by the 1964 quake. When **Lions Club International** assisted the residents of Afognak in moving and rebuilding their town, they renamed it Port Lions in gratitude.)

A large section of the island is given over to the **Kodiak National Wildlife Refuge,** home to the magnificent **Kodiak brown bear.** Besides the giant bears, wildlife on the islands includes, red fox, river otters, and few other native mammals. Exotic species include Sitka blacktail deer, mountain goats, and on Afognak and Raspberry Islands, herds of Roosevelt elk. The deer, mountain goats, and elk were introduced by the **Department of Fish and Game,** and all three species have survived and multiplied in the new environment.

The Surrounding Waters of Kodiak

The surrounding waters support marine mammals, including Steller's sea lions, harbor seals, humpback and killer whales, sea otters, and dolphins. The sea lions have occasionally been the source of problems in the **Kodiak harbor,** since they can be aggressive,

Thick-billed Murres and Tufted Puffins are among the many resident birds.

especially if they have lost the fear of humans. Do not feed, approach, or otherwise molest any wild animals, especially the sea lions. Recent years have seen a significant decline in the numbers of sea lions. The reasons for the decline are not known, but the mammals have been placed on the list as a "threatened" species according to the Endangered Species Act. This listing allows the federal government to limit human activities, including commercial fishing, in the area around sea lion rookeries while further studies are

The petite Arctic Blue Fox on a rocky island.

being conducted to save them.

Sport fishing is excellent, as might be expected of a place that makes so much of its living from the surrounding waters. Salmon migrate into dozens of island streams, the lakes contain trout, Dolly Varden, and grayling, and just offshore lurk large halibut. From May through mid-October, there is always something to fish for in Kodiak. Dolly Varden are available in both fresh and salt water. Halibut fishing is good from May until October, and the salmon runs start with kings and reds around the first of June, and finish off with silvers in October. For the hard-core and serious anglers, the steelhead fishery extends from September into November. Rainbow trout and grayling are stocked in **Abercrombie Lake** by the **Department of Fish and Game**. If you do not have the time, skill, or inclination to catch your own fish, **Seaside Seafood** at 330 Shelikof Ave. (486-8575), can supply you with fish for dinner, to take home with you, or to ship to your friends outside. They will also vacuum pack, freeze, and ship your catch for you. If

St. Paul's harbor at Kodiak.

your friends get the impression that you caught rather than bought the fish, well, no one is exactly under oath when it comes to fish tales.

The **Kodiak Refuge headquarters** and **Visitors Center** is on the Rezanof road, and information about access, activities, wildlife, is available there. **Shuyak Island State Park** is a 50 mile (81 km) flight north from the town of Kodiak. A few trails cross the island, but it is largely covered by thick virgin Sitka spruce forest. The game trails created by deer and brown bears are the main

The beady-eyed Snowy Owl of Alaska.

means of travel through the woods. The shoreline is studded with islands, beaches, inlets, and bays, making it prime country for sea kayaking.

Fishing is good on the island, and the streams hold rainbows and Dollies, and silver and pink salmon during seasonal runs. There are four public use cabins on the island at **Neketa Bay**, **Big Bay**, and **Carry Inlet**, inquire about availability and make reservations with the state parks office at **Ft. Abercrombie Park** (486-6339), or at the **Alaska Public** Lands office in Anchorage (271-2737). Ft. Abercrombie State Park, three and a half miles (5.6 km) out of town on the **Rezanof-Monashka Road**, offers picnic and camping sites, hiking trails, and a great ocean view from **Miller Point**. The State Park Information Center is situated at Ft. Abercrombie.

Four and a half miles (7.3 km) south of town is the **Buskin River State Recreation Site** and the **Kodiak National Wildlife Refuge Visitor Center**. The Buskin River is a favorite for fishing the salmon runs, and for trout and Dollies. Forty miles (64 km) south of town is the **Pasagshak River State Recreation Site**,

A Day in the Life of a Kodiak Fisherman

What a catch!

Before the fishing season begins, the boat is "dry docked" for repair and maintenance work. After the boat is ready, the captain must buy licenses and permits for the areas and species he intends to fish. Next, captain and crew must ensure that the boat is equipped with all of the Coast Guard-required safety gear. The boat must carry a survival suit for each crew member. Survival suits are designed to keep people dry and warm in case they have to abandon the boat. To enable rescue vessels or aircraft to quickly home in on a boat in distress, fishing boats are also required to carry an EPIRB (Emergency Position-Indicating Radio Beacon). Once the boat and crew members are prepared, they head out to their favorite fishing spots. In salmon fishing, it is not unusual for many boats to compete against each other in the good places, and sometimes boats can wait for more than six hours for a turn to fish. The boat uses a skiff to encircle the fish with a net. The net is closed and the salmon captured inside it. The boat then hauls the net and fish aboard, and the fish are placed on ice in the boat's hold. At the end of the day, the boat takes the day's catch to a "tender", a boat owned by a cannery or sea food company. The fish are taken on board the tender, weighed, and the tender personnel keep track of how much each boat brings in. At the end of the season, the vessel is paid according to how many pounds of fish she caught.

In fishing for halibut, the day begins by sharpening hooks and preparing the bait, which can include herring, salmon parts, cod, or octopus. Halibut gear is essentially a long rope, or skate, up to 1,800 ft (549 km) long, with hundreds of baited hooks attached. The hooks are snapped onto the skate as the line is paid out from a large spool run by a powerful hydraulic

offering beach access, camp sites, and river fishing for kings and silvers.

Hiking the developed trails on Kodiak, or through untracked country above treeline or along the beaches presents the opportunities for other pursuits besides merely putting one foot in front of the other.

Bird watching, berry picking, photographing wild flowers, and beach combing offer chances to involve yourself in the subtleties of your surroundings. Visitors to Kodiak have the chance to see a variety of bird life unlike that found anywhere else in Alaska. The island's location at sea, its proximity to the seldom seen species that inhabit the **Aleutians**, and its population of upland nesting species combine to make a home or a resting spot during migration

winch. The skate sits on the bottom, and the ends are marked with buoys so the skipper can find it again. After all the skates are set, usually three to five of them, the boat returns to the first one set, which has been soaking for several hours, and the line is picked up, attached to the spool, and winched aboard. Male halibut can weigh up to 150 lbs (68 kg), and females can top 500 lbs (225 kg), and even with the aid of hydraulic equipment, handling the fish, especially in rough seas, is difficult and dangerous work. As the fish are brought aboard, they are gutted, and the body cavities filled with ice. The fish are then placed on ice in the hold. At the end of the fishing opening, usually 24 hours, the fish are brought back to the processors, weighed, and the boat paid according to weight of the fish. Currently, fishing boats have a maximum quota of halibut that can be taken from each sector, or fishing area. Usually, two 24-hour openings per year are all it takes to fill these quotas. Due to the increase in fishing pressure and diminishing numbers of fish, fishermen are not making as good a living as they used to. Alaskan fishermen have to deal with foreign markets, farm-raised fish, and quotas and regulations set by the Department of Natural Resources. Each year, more and more fishermen are going out of business, and looking for other ways to make a living.

(This account of the details of commercial fishing was written by Laurence Anderson, a long-time Kodiak boat owner and a resident commercial fisherman.)

for more than 200 kinds of winged creatures en route to the mainland.

Seabirds nest on the islands, the rich seas nearby providing plenty of potential food for rapidly growing nestlings. Resident seabirds and sea ducks include puffins, murres, cormorants, gulls, guillemots, scoters, many of them inhabiting large colonies on the smaller outlying islands. Migrating waterfowl

An Alaskan Ptarmigan.

pass through in the fall and spring, including ducks such as mallards, pintails, and teal, Canada, white fronted and brant geese, and tundra swans. Other, miscellaneous birds include the small passerines such as chickadees, warblers, and thrushes, golden and bald eagles, shorebirds and magpies.

Observing and photographing wildflowers could turn into a full-time job, if you were so inclined. The variety of habitats supports a variety of plant life, and the abundance of wild flowers gives the hiker a convenient excuse to stop, catch a breath, and "smell the roses" on the way uphill.

Beginning in late May and continuing through the summer, Kodiak's moderate temperatures and steady rain-

A sultry winter at Kachemak Bay and Homer Sand Spit.

fall provide an excellent environment for an array of blooming plants. Open meadows, deep forests, stream sides, oceanfront, and alpine areas all play host to differing types of flowers, and the observant visitor will take the opportunity to enjoy, photograph, and remember this unusual juxtaposition of plant types and color.

If you are more inclined to eat the plants you encounter rather than just enjoy their aesthetic qualities, there is ample opportunity for that as well. Salmon berries, blueberries, and cranberries grow well here, and give weary hikers a chance to sustain themselves by living off the land, although on a small scale. Be

A Red-throated Loon resting.

Native children frolicking in the summer.

advised, however, that bears find the summer berry crops just as attractive as you do so keep your eyes and ears open at all times, and do not become so immersed in your grazing that you fail to pay attention to your surroundings.

Beachcombing

Beachcombing can also provide the opportunity to stretch your legs and pick up a few souvenirs along the way, souvenirs that you do not have to pay for. At **Monashka Bay**, **Jewel Beach**, **Buskin Beach**, and **Pasagshak**, among others, you can wander along the tideline, picking up fossils, driftwood, sponges, shells and the like. Be sure to check the tide tables before you go, and pay attention to your surroundings and the state of the tide as you walk. If you want to explore the archipelago beyond the road system, there are numerous air and marine charter outfits to cater to your wishes. Hiking in the area away from the road system and off the established trails is a problem, since the brush is thick and unyielding in many places. However, for exploring beaches, inlets, and fjord-like territory, Kodiak is unsurpassed. For getting out of town and sightseeing, or for extensive wilderness excursions, you will need either a boat or an airplane. There are quite a few such services in Kodiak. Check and compare rates and services provided before laying out your money.

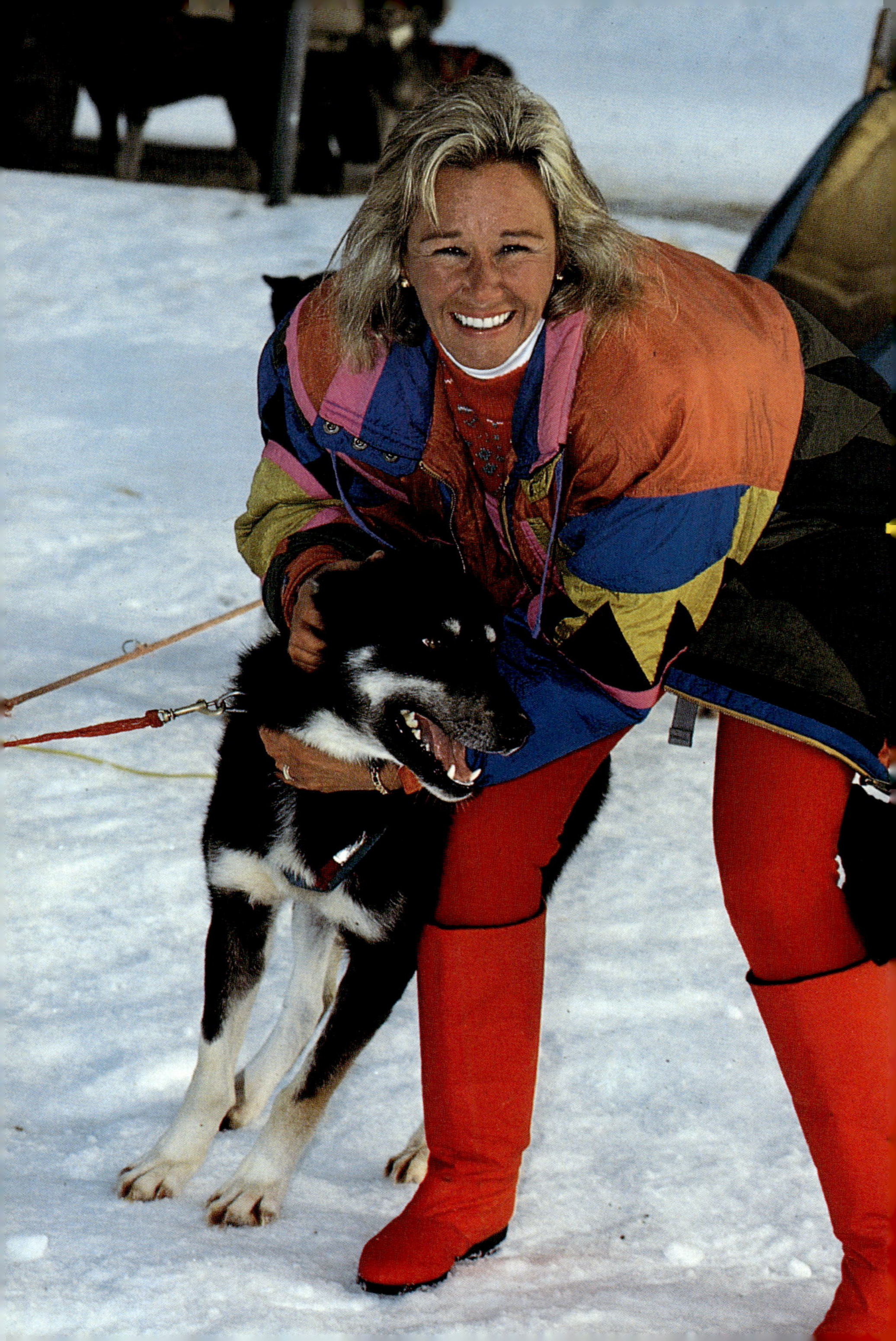

Anchorage

With a population of about 260,000, approximately 40 percent of the people in the state, **Anchorage** is by far the largest city in the state. As Alaska's financial, transportation, and commercial hub, most of the state's economic activity is centered here. The majority of visitors to the state, except for those whose visit are limited to a cruise in **Southeast**, come to Anchorage, in the main to arrange transportation to other areas. Many tourists use Anchorage as a kind of base camp, for stocking up on supplies and other necessary items before branching out to less civilized areas of the state. Anchorage's size guarantees competition among merchants for the tourist dollar, a feature often not found in smaller communities.

The surrounding area is spectacular, as the city is hemmed in by the **Knik** and **Turnagain Arms** of **Cook Inlet** and by the **Chugach Mountains**. These geographical

Lady Musher with her canine friend at the Chugiak Sled Dog Park.

Winter wonderland at Earthquake Park, Anchorage.

boundaries define the municipality, encompassing nearly 2,000 sq miles (5,200 sq kms) of land. From **Portage** on the south to the head of **Knik Arm**, it is a 50 mile (130 kms) drive from one end of the city to the other.

Besides its obvious advantages of convenient shopping and information gathering, there is a wild part to Anchorage as well. **Chugach State Park**, Anchorage's back yard, is 495,000 acres of wild tract right at the edge of town. Besides the ubiquitous moose, the park contains brown and black bears, coyotes, Dall sheep, mountain goats, wolves, wolverines, eagles – the symbols of Alaskan wilderness.

Anchorage has a wonderful system of parks and greenbelts. If you are spending time in the city, make an effort to explore these little pockets of green. The parks provide picnic sites, bike trails, ball fields, plenty of opportunities to relax and unwind.

The Coastal Trail meanders along the fringe of the city, allowing walkers, bike riders, and joggers a chance to get away from the urban environment without traveling too far. Numerous access points allow you to hop onto the trail and walk or jog along while catching some great views of downtown Anchorage set against the magnificent **Chugach Mountains**. A couple of convenient and inviting spots to reach the trail are at **Earthquake Park** on **Northern Lights Blvd.**, **Westchester Lagoon** at **Spenard Rd.** and **Chester Creek**.

A golden hue settles over the autumnal Anchorage skyline as evening arrives.

Downtown

Anchorage's downtown area is laid out in a relatively comprehensible grid, making directions easy to give and follow. Starting with 1st Ave. at the north end of town, the avenues run east-west, the numbers going up as you progress southward. Then starting at A St. (Street), the letter-named streets progress alphabetically to the west. Going east from A St., the north-south streets are alphabetically named after Alaska towns,

The spacious interior of Anchorage Museum of History and Art.

(Barrow, Cordova, Denali, Eagle, etc.).

Start at the town square with the **Visitor Information Center** located in the log cabin at 4th Ave. and F St. Everything you need to know about Anchorage is available either in the racks of information pamphlets, or from the always helpful volunteers behind the counter.

Cater-corner from the log cabin is the **Alaska Public Lands Information Center** at 605 W. 4th Ave. (271-2737, or 258-7275 for a recorded message). Here you will find exhibits pertaining to all the public lands in Alaska, the **Alaska Natural History Association** bookstore, and helpful personnel to dispense information on the National Parks and National Forests. You can reserve United

Jamboree time at the Fur Rondy Carnival, Anchorage.

Beautiful sidewalks grace the Anchorage Performing Arts Center.

States Forest Service public use cabins here, and research on trips into the exigencies of backcountry travelling.

While you are downtown, stroll around the area, perhaps, fortified with a lunch of hot dogs and espresso from one of the many street vendors. Visit the 4th Ave. Theater just across from the Public Lands Center. Then go to the end of E St. at 2nd Ave. to the dockyard overlook. You can see the **Port of Anchorage docks**, the **Alaska Railroad station**, and **Ship Creek** from here, as well as a view across the inlet to **Mt. Susitna**, also known as the Sleeping Lady, and watch the aircrafts on their final approach to **Elmendorf Air Force Base**.

Other spots to visit on your downtown sojourn are the **Captain Cook Monument** at 3rd and L St., the **Oscar Anderson House** at 420 M St., the **Imaginarium** at 725 W. 5th., the **Alaska Center for the Performing Arts** at 621 W. 6th Ave., and finally the **Anchorage Museum of History and Art** at 121 W. 7th Ave. Plan on spending some time here. The museum has a collection of contemporary artworks with Alaskan and northern themes, and exhibits on Alaska history, Native contributions to history and art, as well as a schedule of 30 new shows and exhibits annually. There is also a gift shop and a cafe. Do call the museum at 343-4326 for information on exhibits.

If you have got wheels, you can head out from downtown and visit the rest of the city. If you do not have transportation, quickly check out the tour companies around the square for tours of the city and the surrounding countryside.

If there is one thing Alaska's got plenty of, it must be airplanes. To see the largest floatplane base in the world, head out to **Lake Hood** and **Lake Spenard** near the International Airport. Most of the flight services that ferry hunters, fishermen, and flight seers out to the surrounding countryside have their bases of operation there, as do a multitude of private pilots. You can circle the lakes, looking at all kinds of planes on floats, and watch the constant stream of incoming and outgoing traffic.

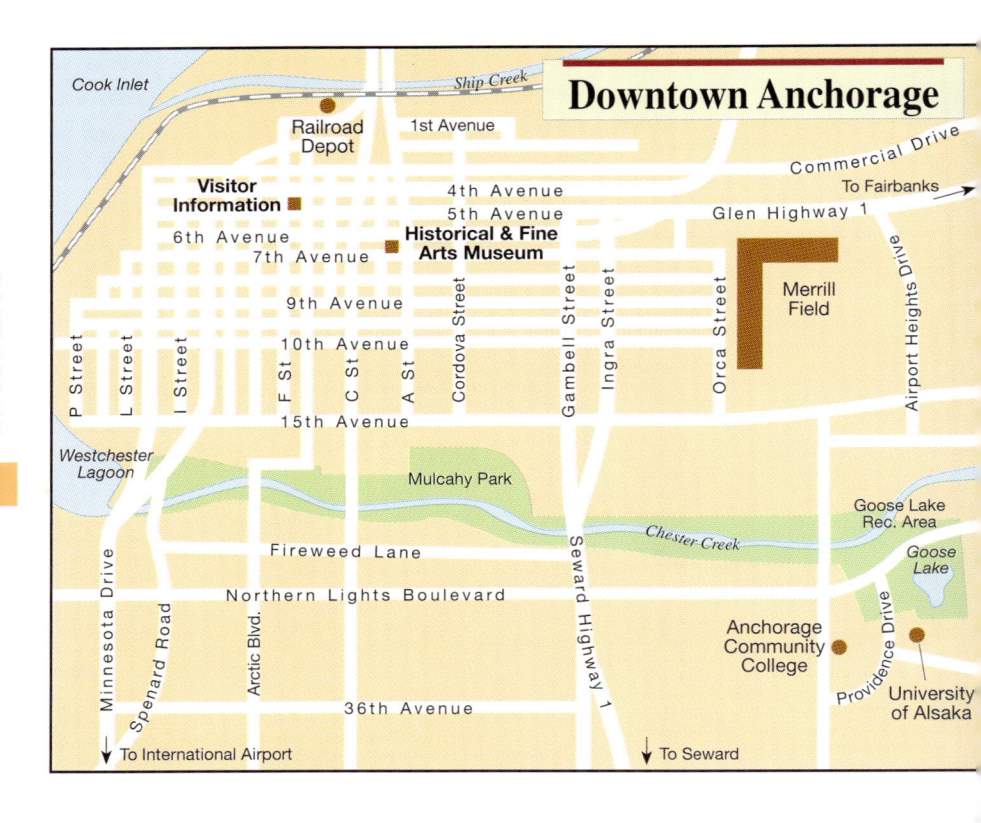

Chugach State Park

Chugach State Park is a terrific place for a day hike, for a backpacking trip into the backcountry, or to just sit on the edge between city and wilderness. The best view of the area can be had from the **Glen Alps** overlook, at the base of **Flattop Mountain**. Take the **Seward Highway** to O'Malley Road, and turn right on Hill side Dr. then take a left on Upper Huffman Rd., and follow the signs to the park entrance at Glen Alps. The drive itself is spectacular, and once you get to the parking lot, follow the path out to the overlook. On a clear day you can see from **Mt. McKinley** in the north to **Illiamna Volcano** in the south, the two peaks lying 220 miles (354 km) apart. In between you can see **Mt. Foraker**, **Mt. Susitna**, **Mt. Spur**, and **Redoubt Volcano** as your eyes trace the Alaska range from north to south.

Mt. Spur sunset, still releasing steam after its 1992 eruption.

If you are in reasonably good shape and wear decent shoes or boots, you can head up the trail to the top of **Flattop Mountain**, the most-climbed mountain in Alaska. The trail to the top is a trek up, with some scrambling required near the top. Tourists and residents of all ages make the trip regularly, so do not let the trail intimidate you.

The trek will take two to four hours and it is best to carry a quart of water each person and take along a rain gear and warm clothings to put on once you reach the top. The view on a clear day is amazing, but if you do not bring warm and windproof clothing, there is a good chance you will have to leave before you can fully enjoy the scenery.

Other good access points to the park

A birding outpost at Potter Marsh.

The popular Alyeska Ski Resort during the holiday season.

are at the **Eagle River Visitor's Center** in **Eagle River** and **Lake Eklutna**, north of **Anchorage**, and at the **Crow Pass** trailhead in **Girdwood**.

Anchorage Outskirts

A good day trip out of Anchorage starts at **Potter Marsh**. Take the Seward Highway south. The turn-off to the marsh is just south of the **Old Seward highway** interchange. There is a long boardwalk extending into the marsh, complete with interpretive signs identifying some of the local birds. Numerous waterfowl, shorebirds, and gulls use the marsh as feeding and nesting habitat, and during the summer ducklings and goslings are numerous. There is also a run of salmon into the marsh every year, visible from the boardwalk.

Continuing south on the Seward Highway, the **Potter Point Section House** is just past the end of the marsh, on the right. Park information is available here, along with a restored train engine which was formerly used to clear snow from railroad tracks, and that rare commodity along Alaska highways – the rest rooms.

As you continue south, **Turnagain Arm** is to your right. With a tide range in excess of 35 ft (11 meter), it has the second highest tide range in North America, exceeded only by the **Bay of Fundy's** 50-foot (15 meter) range. This extreme range is the main reason why you do not see pleasure boats in the upper reaches of **Cook Inlet**. At low tide, large areas are left high and dry, and when the tide comes back in, it comes in with a vengeance. These flats are extremely dangerous, and the seemingly solid mud can turn to a quicksand without warning, trapping the unfortunate in a vice-like grip as the tide rolls in. This has happened with tragic results, so no matter how firm the footing seems, or how many other people you might see wandering out there, do not join them. In most cases, help cannot be summoned quickly enough to thwart the forces of nature.

One form of waterborne recreation that is possible on **Turnagain Arm** is windsurfing, and the conditions here are said to be among the best in the country. Especially on weekends, when conditions are right, you will see the multi-colored sails of the boards zipping across the inlet at phenomenal speeds. Turnagain Arm is one of the few places in North America to see tidal bores. Two hours after low tide the incoming water forms a wave that can reach six feet in height. To see the bore at its best, pick up a set of tide tables from a sporting goods store to pinpoint the time of low tide. Park along the highway at any good viewpoint between **McHugh Creek** at milepost 112 and **Bird Creek** camping ground at milepost 101.

Watch for beluga whales in the Arm if the tide's in. These snow-white whales follow schools of salmon and hooligan (a type of smelt) into the arm,

Frosty trees at Turnagain Arm.

and pods of belugas are a common sight. Less common but still regular visitors are killer whales. Several times each summer a pod of orcas visits the area, much to the delight of lucky travelers. If you see cars pulled off the road and looking out across the inlet, carefully pull over, watch the traffic as you get out, and check out the attraction.

At milepost 107 you will find the best chance in Alaska for a close-up view of Dall sheep. There is a wide turnout area on both sides of the road, and the sheep often come down next to the highway to feed. When they are near the road there is usually a traffic jam, with cars and tour buses pulled over, people trying to ogle the sheep while driving, tourists crossing the highway

Anchorage Fishing Opportunities

An idyllic fishing spot where even fishes oblige.

While the wilderness fishing in Alaska is justifiably world famous, you do not necessarily have to travel hundreds of miles from the road system by way of expensive bush plane flights just to catch a fish or two. Within the confines of the Municipality of Anchorage, you can catch wild salmon, trout, and Dolly Varden, as well as stocked fish, including arctic grayling. Your best chance to catch a big fish in town is during the king salmon run in Ship Creek. These fishes are returning to the hatchery at Elmendorf Air Force base, and the numbers of returning fish are much greater than the hatchery needs to perpetuate the run. These "excess" fish are available for taking, under certain limitations, of course. The run is usually fishable in June and July, from the mouth of the creek upstream to a set of markers near the dam. The area open to fishing is visible from downtown, and lies parallel to the railroad tracks down in the flats near the port facilities. When the kings are running, just look for the crowd of fishermen lining the banks of the creek down near the railroad station. There are few tackle restrictions in this fishery, and most of the successful anglers use clusters of salmon eggs, Spin-N- Glos, and Pixees. Because of the somewhat crowded conditions, use a stout rod and 20-30 lb line. Chasing a big king up and down the bank, playing him out on light tackle will not make you popular with your fellow fisherfolk. Fish the incoming tide, and although it is far from being a wilderness experience, 40 lb fish are not unusual, and the atmosphere is friendly and sometimes even party-like. Later in the summer, there is a run of silvers in Ship Creek, and another one in Campbell Creek. Campbell Creek winds through town and is fishable from the Dimond Boulevard bridge near the Fred Meyer store up as far as the weir off Tudor Rd. The smal

with cameras and video equipment - it is a great opportunity to see sheep, but be very careful of traffic and distracted pedestrians along the way.

Alyeska Ski Resort

At milepost 90 is the **Girdwood-Alyeska** road. The little strip mall on the corner has gas, a convenience store, and a cafe. The road takes you to the popular Alyeska ski resort and to the **Crow Pass** road, where you will find the **Double Musky** restaurant, **Raven Glacier Lodge**, and the **Crow Creek Mine**.

At Alyeska, you can wander through the resort area, catch a bite to eat at **The Bake Shop** or the Chair 5 restaurant, or take the tram up the mountain to a

run of kings in Campbell Creek is off limits, but there are legal rainbows and Dollies in residence. The Department of Fish and Game stocks rainbows, arctic grayling, arctic char, and king salmon in most of the lakes in town, with the clear intention that these fish be caught and eaten. Do not worry about diminishing the resource here – just stick to the catch limits and have a ball. A complete list of the lakes and other fishing information and suggestions are available from the Fish and Game office at 333 Raspberry Road. The Department also maintains a fishing hot line, (349-4687) updated every week to tell you when and where to find the best fishing spots in Southcentral. If you want to get away from the city proper but still do not have the time or inclination to get all the way out of town, Bird Creek, south of town at mile 101 of the Seward Highway, offers more fishing opportunities. Known mostly for its runs of pink salmon, especially in even-numbered years, there are silvers, chums, and Dollies present as well. Fish the incoming and high tides for best results. North of town you can fish rainbows in Lake Eklutna and the run of kings in Eagle River. Before trying any of these fisheries, check all the regulations carefully for legal fishing locations, size and catch limits, and tackle restrictions. The Alaska fishing regulations are complex, and first-time anglers may find all the details bewildering. However, if you have any questions, the people at the Sport Fishing desk at Fish and Game, (267-2218) are generally very helpful and informative.

Skiers take a breather atop snowcapped peaks.

picnic in a mountain meadow and have a meal at the restaurant at the top of the tram ride, or just enjoy the sweeping view of the **Turnagain Arm** area and the surrounding mountains.

Ten miles (16 km) farther south on the Seward highway is Portage. There is a train station for the Whittier shuttle and the surrounding area shows evidence of the 1964 **Good Friday earthquake**. When the quake hit, the ground dropped about six feet, ruining the structures and allowing salt water to reach the roots of the now-dead trees left standing. At milepost 79 is the turnoff to **Portage Glacier**, Alaska's most-visited tourist spot. The six mile (10 km) drive to the **Begich-Boggs Visitor Center** takes you past hanging glaciers on the mountainsides and over streams full of salmon during the late summer. There are camping grounds and picnic sites along the road, the **Portage Glacier Lodge** and a chance to take a cruise boat out to get a better view of the glacier. The hike to **Byron Glacier** is short and easy, and affords you the opportunity to tell the folks back home that you walked on a glacier.

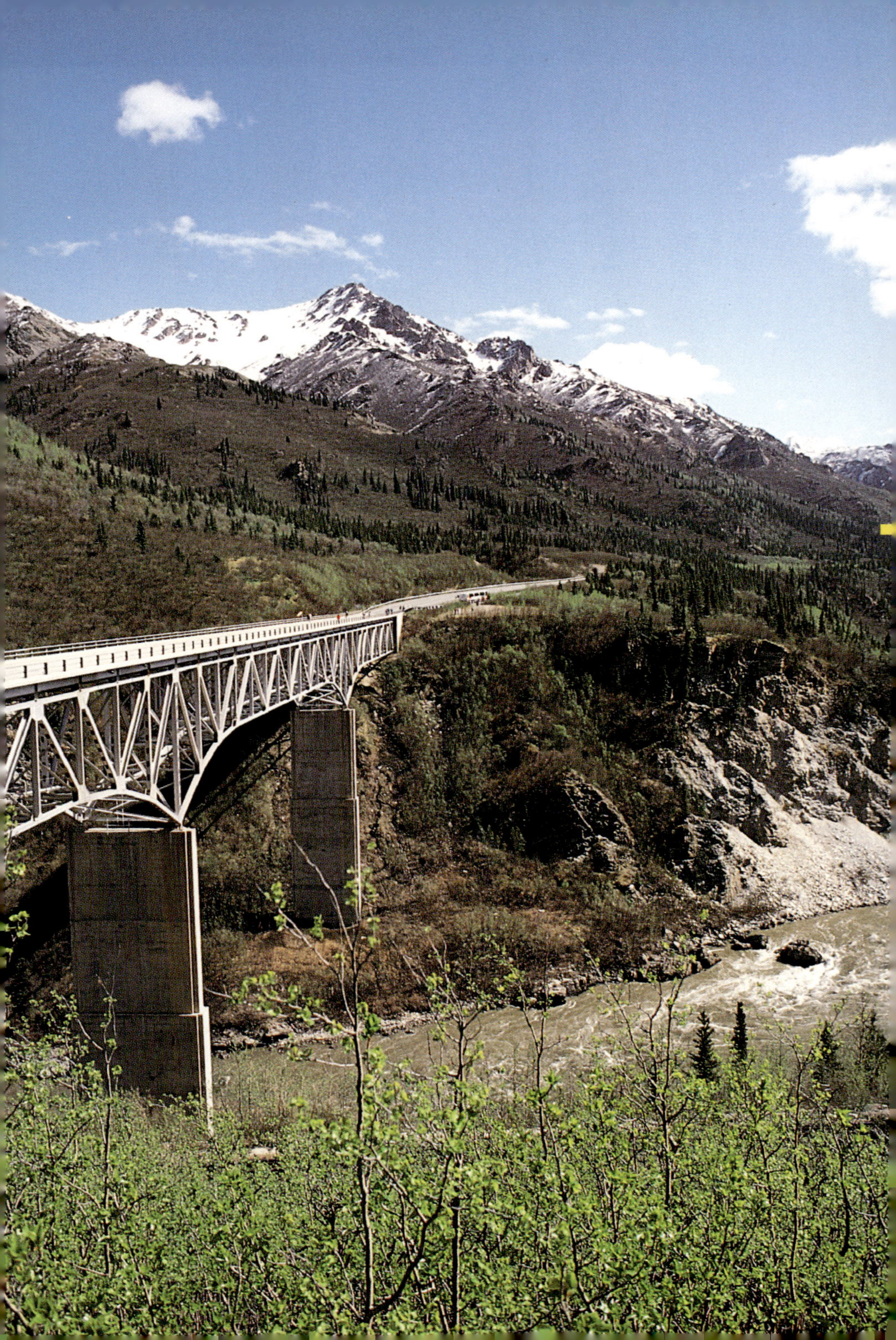

GLORIOUS SUMMERS

Fairbanks & the Interior

Alaska's Interior includes everything that is not **Southeast**, **Southcentral**, **Kodiak** and the **Aleutians** or the coasts. Even though that is a lot of country in itself, there is still an awful lot left over that is considered the Interior. Basically, everything from just north of Anchorage up to the **Brooks Range**, and from the Canadian border west to the coastal regions. This area is estimated at 165,000 sq miles (427,350 sq kms), an appreciable chunk of real estate.

Blue skies and mountain ridges undulating along the road to Denali.

The vast majority of the Interior is roadless and uninhabited. It includes entire mountain ranges, river drainages, national parks and monuments, state parks, **Bureau Land Management** (Native Reserves) or BLM land, thousands of lakes, and vast river deltas. The climate is considered continental, with hot summers and low winter temperatures, and little precipitation.

At the heart of Alaska's great interior lies Fairbanks, the state's second largest city, with a population of 31,000. The Fairbanks North Star Borough has a

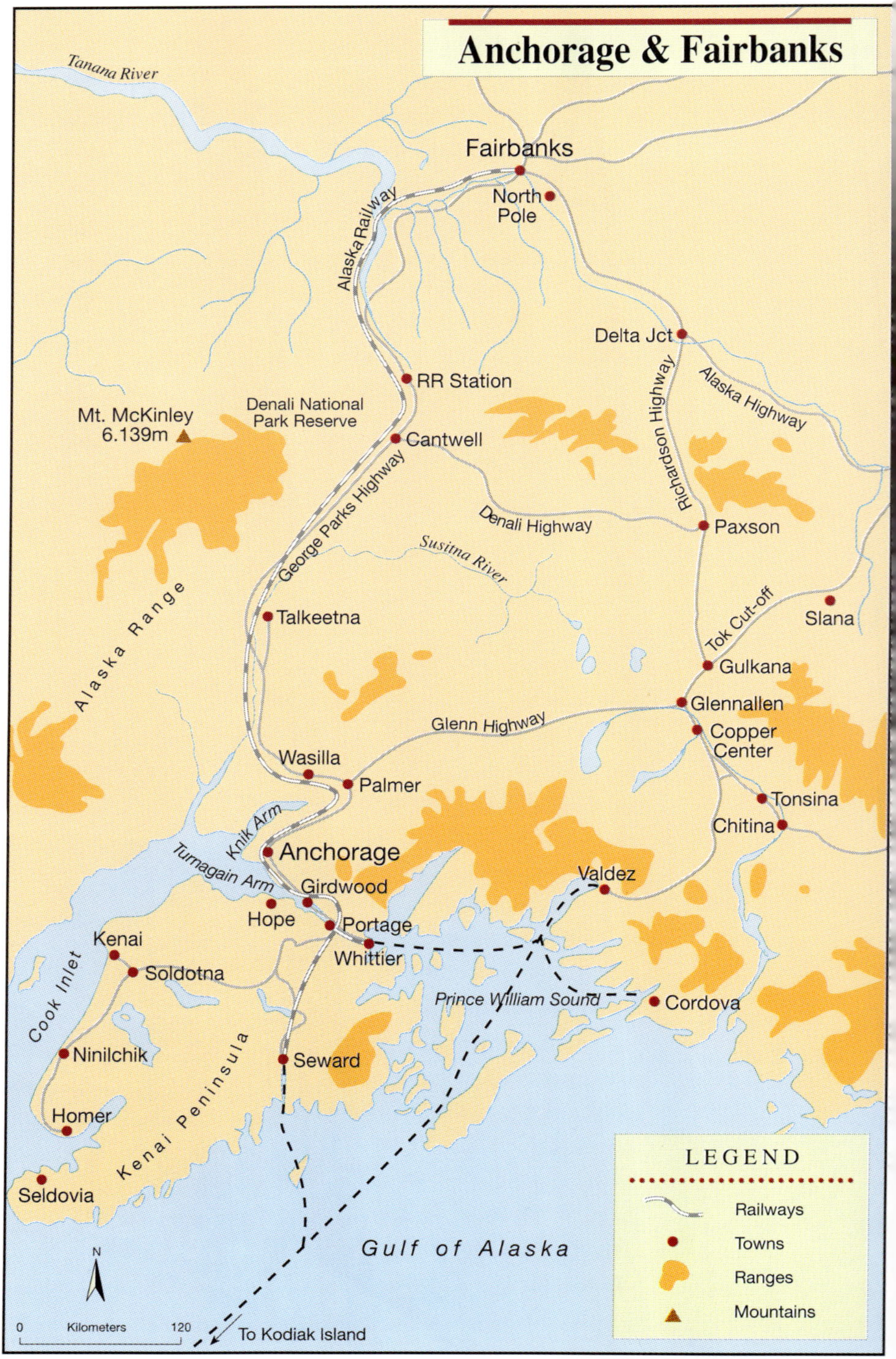
Anchorage & Fairbanks
Tanana River
Fairbanks
North Pole
Alaska Railway
Delta Jct
RR Station
Alaska Highway
Richardson Highway
Mt. McKinley 6.139m
Denali National Park Reserve
Cantwell
George Parks Highway
Denali Highway
Paxson
Susitna River
Alaska Range
Talkeetna
Tok Cut-off
Slana
Gulkana
Glennallen
Glenn Highway
Copper Center
Wasilla
Palmer
Tonsina
Chitina
Knik Arm
Anchorage
Turnagain Arm
Girdwood
Valdez
Hope
Portage
Kenai
Whittier
Soldotna
Cook Inlet
Prince William Sound
Cordova
Ninilchik
Kenai Peninsula
Seward
Homer
Seldovia
Gulf of Alaska
N
0 Kilometers 120
To Kodiak Island
LEGEND
Railways
Towns
Ranges
Mountains

Rafting in the rapids of Nenana River.

population of 78,000, which for Alaska is a lot of people. Considering that the town site was chosen almost by mistake, Fairbanks has done pretty well.

When the **Trans-Alaska pipeline** was proposed and built in the 1970s, Fairbanks was the closest town, and fortunes were made in the ensuing development. Since that time it has managed to stay afloat as the largest town in the Interior where gold mining and oil field services still constitute a large part of the area's economy. Fairbanks is also the end point of the **Alaska Highway**.

Archeological Finds at the Campus Site

Alaska University at Sitka.

Today, it is accepted as a fact that the Native peoples of Alaska and the rest of the North American continent came here from Asia over the Bering land bridge. This was not always the case, however – once upon a time, this hypothesis was mentioned by scientists in the fields of archeology and anthropology as speculation based on very few observations and more than a little guessing. Scientists scrutinized the theory, looked at the materials assembled to support it, and engaged in scholarly debate over the pros and cons that arose. However, other than conjecture based on fossil evidence, there were no artifacts to support the theory.

In 1933, a student digging a post hole on the grounds of the Alaska Agricultural College and School of Mines (now known as the University of Alaska, Fairbanks) uncovered some stone artifacts. He turned them over to the university president, who in turn suggested further excavation of the site. The following year, more study found specimens of arrowheads, hammer stones, and further evidence of stone that had been worked by human hands. Some of the artifacts were then sent to the American Museum of Natural History in New York, suggesting that they were similar in design to other pieces unearthed in the Gobi desert. These stone pieces turn out to be the first hard evidence to support the Asian migration theory.

Over the next few years, more work on the site, now referred to as the Campus site, found more evidence. However, by the end of the decade, interest in the site died down as it appeared that the number and quality of the finds had diminished to the point where further investigation was unwarranted. Although the evidence of prehistoric human habitation at the site was clear, figuring out the approximate dates of the site presented problems. Although the site was referred to by one scientist as "The most important single landmark in the history of interior Alaska archeology", its age has remained an unsolved mystery.

Archeologists use a number of methods to obtain the approximate dates of study sites, measured in years Before Present, (B.P.) They can compare the artifacts to others in the region, use radiocarbon dating of organic materials such as bone or charcoal, or other investigational techniques too complicated to go into here. They also study the "horizontal distribution" and the "vertical distribution" of the artifacts, to try and discover patterns in the layering of the samples and the way they are scattered around the site. They also do a certain amount of educated guessing. After analyzing all of these methods, the approximate ages of the pieces found at the Campus site ranged from 15,000 B.P. to 40 B.P. A recent restudy of the area concluded that most of the artifacts so far uncovered are between 3,500 and 2,725 years old. However, as in any effort to study small fragments of a complicated civilization from prehistoric times, there are inconsistencies and disagreements about the interpretation of the excavated objects. Further study of the objects uncovered so far, and attempts to find more evidence at the site may reveal some answers, or may wind up just provoking more inconclusive questions.

The 20,320 ft Mount McKinley.

Sitting at 65° northern latitude, it is a mere 120 miles (193 kms) south of the **Arctic Circle**. Tourism brings lots of outside dollars to the Fairbanks area. Hunters, fishermen, backpackers, and river runners all use Fairbanks as a jumping off point to the **Brooks Range**, to interior river systems, and to the far out areas of the **Gates of the Arctic National Park**, the **Yukon Flats National Wildlife Refuge**, the **Yukon-Charley Rivers National Preserve**, and the **Arctic National Wildlife Refuge**, among others. If you are venturing into the interior, stock up on supplies before leaving Fairbanks. Goods arrive here by jet and by rail, and prices are certainly lower than anywhere in the Bush.

Visiting Fairbanks during the sum-

Dandelions and buttercups pepper the countryside in summer.

Downtown Fairbanks

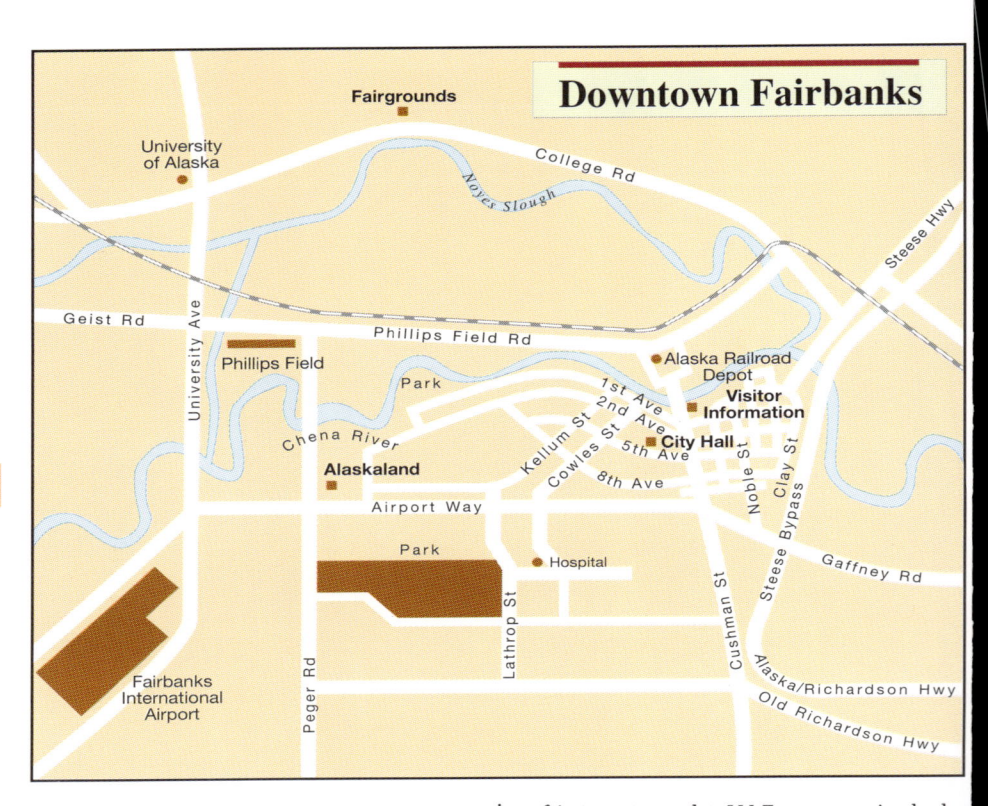

mer can put to rest many misconceptions about Alaska. Sunny skies, temperatures in the 80s, and greenery everywhere you look does not exactly fit the popular stereotypical Alaskan scene. Within the Fairbanks boundaries, you will find Alaska's only theme park, its largest university, a resting spot for thousands of migratory waterfowl, and numerous tastes of city life, tourist attractions, and bits of raw nature as well.

Make sure to visit the campus of the **University of Alaska**, and check out the **University Museum** at 907 Yukon Dr. (474-7505). A visit here will give you a taste of Alaska's history and its people. No visit to Fairbanks is complete without a visit to this museum. Other points of interest on the UAF campus include the **Large Animal Research Station**, the **Geophysical Institute**, and the **botanical garden**. Tours and maps can be obtained at the **Wood Campus Center**. For planning ventures into the surrounding countryside, stop by the Public Lands Information Center at 250 Cushman St. down town, (451-7352). A museum, interpretive center, and information desk are open seven days a week during the summer. At 1st and Cushman you will find the **Fairbanks Visitor's Information Center**, (907-456-5774 or 1-800-327-5774). They can supply you with more information on the town and its surrounding places of interest.

Next to the Visitor's center is **Golden**

Visitors enjoy the snow-swept scenery from a luxury car on the Alaskan Railway.

Heart Park, opened in 1987. A series of bronze plaques surround a sculpture of the Unknown First Family. For more education on Alaska history, visit **Alaskaland**, the state's only theme park. Here you can find a lot of feast your eyes upon – re-creations of a Native village, a gold rush town, and a gold mine, along with a restored riverboat and a pioneers museum. Food for the body is available as well at the salmon bake.

Highway 'Hike'

Methods of transportation out of town to explore the interior are varied. By car or tour bus, the Fairbanks area has more highways to adventure than any other town in Alaska.

To the north, you can drive the **Dalton Highway** alongside the pipeline all the way to the Arctic Ocean, if conditions and the current state of law enforcement will allow. Access to the entire Dalton Highway, also known as the **Haul Road**, varies according to the whims of state politicians. Originally, passenger vehicles were only allowed as far north as the **Yukon River bridge**, but in recent years, access to points farther north has been possible.

Check with the Visitors Center or the **Public Lands Information Center** in Fairbanks for current regulations. At any rate, the drive is not one to be undertaken lightly, as the gravel road was constructed for and is traveled

Sternwheel riverboats ply the Chena and Tanana rivers.

mainly by tractor-trailer rigs moving supplies between Fairbanks and the **North Slope** oil fields. The road is rough and services are few and far between. Carry spares of everything, and be as self-contained as possible. To the west of Fairbanks, the **Elliott Highway** runs for 150 miles (242 kms) to dead-end at the town of **Manley Hot Springs**. To the east, the **Steese Highway** ends in the town of Circle on the **Yukon River**, 160 miles from Fairbanks.

Leaving town to the south, you have actually got a choice between two roads, the **Alaska Highway** or the **Parks Highway**. The Alaska Highway runs down to Delta Junction, and from there you can head east to Canada, or south on the **Richardson Highway** towards

"Cabin Nite" huts are a great way to be with nature.

A friendly wave from the Riverboat Discovery III.

Glennallen and Valdez.

At Paxson, you can pick up the **Denali Highway** and cut back west towards the Parks Highway. From there go north to **Denali National Park**, or head south to **Anchorage**. At **Glennallen**, you can either keep going south towards **Valdez** and **Prince William Sound**, or take the **Glenn Highway** west and south to Anchorage.

The Parks Highway runs south past Denali National Park and then into Anchorage. A quick glance at a map discloses several options for making loop trips or just wandering over different roads, exploring varied parts of the state and just taking in the everchanging landscape of the vast Interior. Another way to travel from Fairbanks is via the

Alaska Railroad. From Fairbanks, the railroad runs south, paralleling the Parks Highway past Denali and on to Anchorage. You can take the train one-way or round-trip between Fairbanks and Anchorage or Denali, and use the cars operated by the railroad, or book space on the luxury rail cars operated by **Gray Line** (800-544-2206) and by **Princess Tours** (800-835-8907). Check with the tour companies, or with the railroad offices in **Anchorage** (907-265-2494) or **Fairbanks**, (907-456-4155).

Water and Air Travel

Water travel from the **Golden Heart** city is available on sternwheel river

Denali National Park

Alaskan paradise at Horseshoe Lake, Denali National Park.

There are two ways to see the sights in Denali National Park. You can book a tour with one of the park concessionaires and have all the trip details taken care of for you. Or you can travel independently, using the park's visitor access facilities and planning your own trip.

Tour companies minimize inconveniences such as finding a room or campsite and planning meals. However, the cost can be considerable, and you will not be able to take off across the tundra when the mood strikes you.

For more information on package tours of Denali call Alaska Sightseeing/Cruise West in Anchorage at 276-1305; ARA, the park concessionaire at 276-7234 in the winter, or 683-2215 in the summer; or Destinations in Travel at 1-800-354-6020.

Independent travel is cheaper, and allows you to set your own itinerary. You can plan day hikes or backpacking trips into the backcountry, camp in one of the campgrounds, and adjust your plans to suit your mood, the weather, and other variable conditions. Disadvantages include difficulty in obtaining campsites and bus passes.

This six million acre park is served by one thin ribbon of road extending 85 miles (137 kms) into the park. The first 14 miles (23 km) of the road is paved and open to passenger vehicles. Beyond the 14 mile (23 kms) point, only park vehicles and tour buses are allowed. Hikers, campers, backpackers, and sightseers use the shuttle buses to explore the park. Free tokens for shuttle bus rides are available at the Visitor Access Center (VAC) near the park entrance. Most of the drivers are very familiar with the park and its animals, and often narrate as they drive. They will stop to look at animals along the way, but stopping and looking time is somewhat limited, since they have schedules to keep. If you want to explore the countryside on foot, just let your driver know where you want to get off. When you are ready to return, after an hour or a week, wait next to the road and flag down a bus going your way.

The commercial tour buses offer more extensive nature talks, and their schedules are

boats. The longstanding **Discovery** riverboats (479-6673) offer tours of the **Chena** and **Tanana** rivers, along with a glimpse into the backcountry lives of Native fishermen along the shores.

The most efficient way to travel from Fairbanks, albeit the most expensive, is again by air. Numerous air taxi and scheduled air lines operate out of the Fairbanks airport with both wheeled and float-equipped aircraft. Flightseeing tours offer trips over the area to Bush villages, above the **Arctic Circle**, into the **Brooks Range**, and to remote fishing and backpacking locations. Call **Wright Air** (474-0502), **Warbelow's Air**

more flexible, so they can linger longer over especially noteworthy animal sightings.

Camp sites in the park's seven campgrounds are reserved at the VAC. A few have RV access, others are limited to tent camping. Advance reservations for a limited number of sites and shuttle bus rides can be made in advance by calling 907-278-2327 or 1-800-622-7275 from Outside. Most of the accommodations are made on a first-come, first served basis at the VAC near the park entrance. If you do not have campsite reservations, plan on spending at least one night in a commercial campground near the park entrance while you wait for a spot in the park to open. All overnight backcountry trips into the park's interior require a permit, and must be arranged at the backcountry desk at the VAC. The park is divided into sections, and the number of backpackers allowed into each section is limited. Rules concerning camping practices will be explained by the desk personnel. In most areas, backpackers are required to carry their food in bear-resistant food containers, provided by the park at no charge. Day hiking does not require a permit. Visitors can almost always count on seeing moose, grizzly bears, caribou, and Dall sheep, and luckier or more observant people will see the occasional wolf, fox, or wolverine.

The VAC has an extensive bookstore for those seeking to educate themselves about the park, its inhabitants and history. Evening informational talks are a regular feature at the park hotel and in some of the campgrounds and at the hotel. In addition, rangers conduct nature walks several times a day – check the bulletin boards for topics and locations.

Ventures (474-0518 or 1-800-478-0812), or **Frontier Flying Service** (474-0014) for prices and details.

Hot Springs Resorts

Another interesting and relaxing recreation possibility is a visit to one of the area's hot springs resorts. Three such resorts are road-accessible from Fairbanks, and you can visit by means of private auto, tour company bus or van, or fly in with one of the Fairbanks air taxi services.

Chena Hot Springs Resort (452-7867) is 62 miles (100 km) from Fairbanks, the closest of the three resorts. Take the **Steese Highway** to the Chena Hot Springs Road underpass at mile 4.9, head east on the paved highway through the **Chena River Recreation Area** to the resort at the end of the road at mile 56.5. Open year round, the resort offers hot springs pools and spas, rooms, cabins, campground, restaurant, and bar. Outdoor activities include fishing, canoeing, horseback riding and hay rides in the summer, and sleigh rides, dogsled rides and cross-country skiing in the winter.

To reach **Circle Hot Springs**, take the Steese Highway out of Fairbanks to mile 127.8 and the intersection with Circle Hot Springs Road. The Steese parallels the **Chatanika River**, and is unpaved for most of its length. The **Chatanika Lodge** (389-2164) at mile 29 offers lodging, and a restaurant and bar. Campsites along the road include the commercial operation at Farthest North Chatanika RV Park at mile 31 and the **Cripple Creek Bureau Land Management** campground at mile 60.

At mile 128 lies the town of Central, and the turn-off to **Circle Hot Springs**. The **Central Motor Inn** (520-5228) of-

E. T. Barnette and the founding of Fairbanks

A sturdy trading post at Fairbanks.

In 1897, Elbridge Truman Barnette, age 34, was living in Helena, Montana when a shipment of Klondike gold worth $200,000 arrived and went on display in 1897. Twelve days later, he was on a train to Seattle.

Barnette captained a small steamer up the Yukon and spent the next couple of years managing mines in Dawson. In 1901 he bought $20,000 worth of supplies, and chartered the steamship *Lavelle Young* to get his goods into the interior. He had to take on a James Causten as a partner to sign notes guaranteeing payment of the shipping bill.

The *Lavelle Young* traveled up the Yukon and up the Tanana to the mouth of the Chena. Barnette talked the captain into proceeding up the Chena River. They finally unloaded Barnette's goods at a point about six miles up the Chena, much to his chagrin. As unpromising as the location seemed, there were a few prospectors in the area, and Barnette was, for the time being anyway, stuck. Then, the following summer, a prospector named Felix Pedro struck gold there. Word got out, as it always seemed to do when gold was involved, and more miners flocked in. By November of 1903 there were enough residents that a vote was held to incorporate the city of Fairbanks. Barnette managed, by means of some back-room shenanigans, to get himself elected mayor.

Barnette opened a bank in 1904, and a steady stream of hopeful miners into Fairbanks fueled its growth. By 1906 annually gold production stood at $6,000,000, and the town managed an electric power plant, telephones, a hospital and other basic facilities.

In 1906, things began to go bad for Barnette. He was sued by Causten, who claimed that his underwriting of the *Lavelle Young's* trip made him Barnette's partner, and entitled him to half of Barnette's earnings and property. During the course of the suit, it came out in court that

---

fers campgrounds, a restaurant and rooms for rent.

The **Circle Hot Springs Resort**, (520-5113), eight miles (13 kms) from Central, is open year round. In addition to the hot spring spa, the resort has a full-sized swimming pool, restaurant, rooms, cabins, and bar. At the end of the **Steese Highway**, 34 winding miles from Central on the banks of the **Yukon River** is the town of Circle. The town got its name from the mistaken belief by the town's founders that it sat on the **Arctic Circle**, 50 miles (81 kms) to the north. Camping and visitor's services are available in Circle.

The third hot spring resort is at the town of **Manley**, made famous by resi-

Barnette had done time in Oregon for larceny. This revelation was publicized in Fairbanks by a newspaper that held no love for the mayor, whose manner and tactics were considered overbearing and somewhat shady by some of the local folks. Barnette lost the suit and he was forced to pay off with an undisclosed, but apparently hefty, sum.

By 1910, banking was no longer profitable, as the gold boom had passed its peak. Barnette quietly resigned his position at the bank, and left for Los Angeles. Shortly thereafter, the bank failed, and everyone in Fairbanks blamed Barnette for it. There had been more than a few shady dealings in the bank's past, and as they came to light after the failure, people blamed everything on Barnette. He returned to Fairbanks and stated his intention of straightening out the bank's problems. A grand jury was convened, but could not find sufficient evidence to indict Barnette. Barnette and his wife then stole out of town under the cover of darkness rather than face a mob of angry townspeople who had lost money when the bank went under.

Barnette was arrested in Los Angeles, and in December of 1912, went on trial in Valdez. In spite of being charged with numerous serious violations, he was convicted of a misdemeanor charge of making a false report, and he was fined $1,000.

Most of the folks in town were convinced that Barnette was a con artist, and as late as 1960, when a grade school in Fairbanks was named for him, old timers still harbored ill feelings, and objected to naming a school after a convicted swindler.

dent dog mushers **Susan Butcher** and **Dave Monson**. Manley is at the end of the Elliott Highway, 152 miles (245 km) from Fairbanks, 125 of those miles are still unpaved.

In Manley you will find the **Manley Hot Springs Resort** (672-3611), the **Manley Trading Post**, and the **Manley Roadhouse** (672- 3161). This little town of under 100 residents offers camping, gas, supplies, and other visitor services. In addition, the Resort has both hot springs and a swimming pool, restaurant, bar, laundromat, showers and other facilities. Salmon and northern pike swim the local waters tempting the eager fisherman.

The Denali Highway

Visitors with their own transportation and a desire to see a "non-tourist" section of the interior should plan a drive across the Denali Highway. This 136 mile (219 km) long road, running east-west, unpaved except for short sections at either end, takes you through the heart of the interior. The terrain is very similar to **Denali National Park**, without the tour buses and traffic restrictions found there. Views across the tundra and to the peaks of the **Alaska Range** to the north are spectacular. There are a few campgrounds and lodges along the road, and many other undeveloped campsites. You can stop and make camp anywhere there is a flat spot, but of course there are not picnic tables, developed water sources, or trash pick-ups (so bring your own trash bags).

Wildlife includes moose, caribou, grizzly bears, fox, beavers, wolves, although not in the numbers found inside the park. This area is open to both sport and subsistence hunting, so the animals tend to be much more people-anguish than the protected populations

A musher and her sled dog.

at Denali. However, a sharp eye and constant vigilance should turn up some interesting critters.

Good fishing is available along the way. Most of the streams contain Arctic Grayling and Dolly Varden, and the larger lakes hold populations of good-sized lake trout. Accommodations and visitor services are available at the following locations, miles measured from Paxson at the east end of the highway: **Paxson Lodge**, (822-3330) at the intersection with the Richardson Highway has lodging, gas, food, and a bar; **Tangle River Inn** (895-4439 summer, 895-4022 winter) at mile 20 has gas, lodging, fishing, and bar; **Tangle Lakes Lodge** (688-9173) at mile 22 has lodging, food, fishing, canoe rentals, and bar; the Maclaren River Lodge at mile 42 has food, bar, lodging, and offers guided fishing and glacier trips; **Gracious House Lodge** (333-3148) at mile 82 has gas, rooms, camping, bar, food, repair and towing services, and an air taxi service. At the Cantwell end of the road, services and lodging are available at Adventures Unlimited Lodge at mile 99.4 and the **Cantwell Lodge** (768-2300). Before setting out across the Denali Highway, check your general state of readiness, including fuel supply, food and drinking water, spare tire condition. The services available are far apart and traffic is usually light, so be prepared to fend for yourself if necessary.

Wrangell-St. Elias National Park

While Denali may be the most popular national park in Alaska, **Wrangell-St. Elias** is the largest national park in the country. Three mountain ranges, extensive glaciers, some of the highest peaks on the continent, and rivers and lakes galore, make this 13 million acre park an adventurer's dream.

Quiet vistas at Harper Lodge – Nenana River.

However, while the absence of crowds and tourist development certainly adds to the quality of one's solitude, there is the slight downside of inaccessibility. Road access via the Nabesna Road out of the town of Slana and the McCarthy Road near **Chitina** provide the tiniest of nibbles around the very edges of the park's vastness. To visit the park's interior, an airplane is the only way to go. Air taxis are available in **Glennallen, McCarthy,** and **Slana**. Call the **Wrangell-St. Elias** office in Glennallen at 822-5234 for more park information. Speaking of McCarthy, a trip to this little town surrounded by Wrangell-St. Elias is worth the effort, especially if your vehicle is a rental. The rough and twisty 60 miles (97 kms) gravel road from Chitina is not recommended for large RVs, or for vehicles pulling trailers. At the end of the road, the town of McCarthy and the old **Kennecott copper works** lie across the **Kennicott River**. (The different spellings for the town and the river are attributed to the rather casual attitude towards spelling accuracy by the founding fathers of the area). To cross the river, you will have to get aboard one of the hand-pulled trams and use muscle power to get to the other side. Thrilling and unique, to say the least. Visitor services, including food, lodging, guided tours, are available from the **McCarthy Lodge** (333-5402) and the **Kennicott Glacier Lodge** at 800-478-2350 inside Alaska, or 800-582-5128 from outside.

Caribous grazing at Denali National Park.

At the town of Chitina, 33 miles (53 kms) from the **Richardson Highway**, you can watch fishing techniques not often seen elsewhere. The **Copper River** sustains large shoals of red and king salmon, and during the summer, subsistence fishermen employ both nets and fish wheels to gather their fish.

Under sport fishing rules, taking salmon from Alaska's streams is strictly regulated both in numbers of fish taken and the means by which they can be caught. However, in some locations Alaska residents may use traditional

An old Episcopal Church amidst the highlands of Nenana.

means to engage in subsistence fishing. At Chitina, most people use long-handled dip nets, wading out into the river as far as they dare and plunging the nets into the current, pulling out fish in much the same way the local Athabascan Indians did centuries ago.

The other method employed is the fish wheel. These floating contraptions are secured to the shore close to the bank. The current turns the arms of the wheel, scooping up salmon and dumping them into a holding pen, as effortless a way to catch fish as you are ever likely to find. Alaska's Interior is huge, and although you can only see a small part of it from the road, you can definitely see enough to give you a taste of its true nature.

An Athabaskan lady cuddles her pet dog.

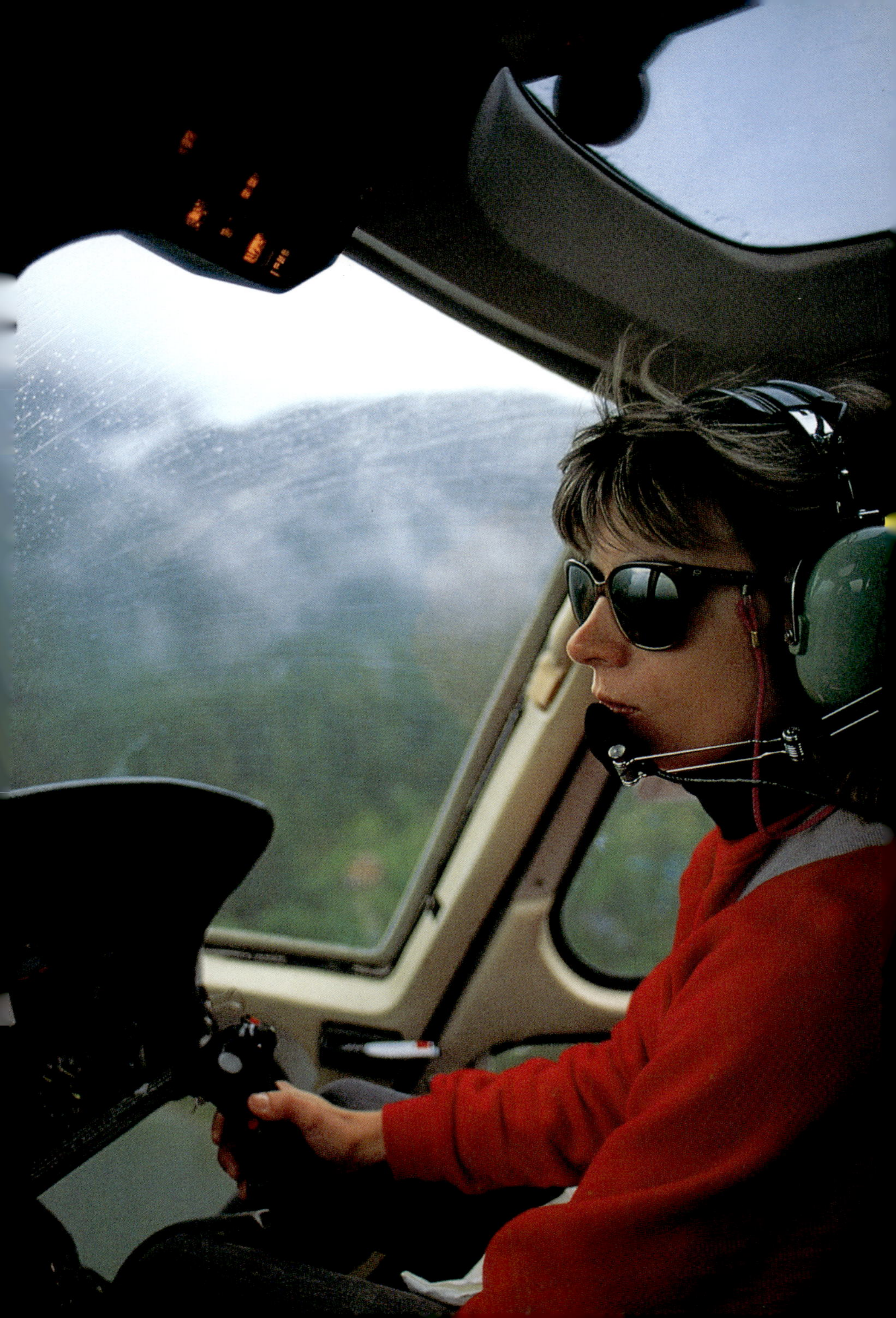

The Bush

Although there is no exact definition of the Bush, generally the term refers to towns, villages and areas not accessible by road. Some folks include the small villages in Southeast and the smaller communities on the road system, but generally speaking, you cannot go wrong using the road system as a guide.

A look at any map tells you that the vast majority of Alaska is not road accessible. The highways run from the Canadian border to **Fairbanks** and **Anchorage**, to the edge of **Prince William Sound**, and down the **Kenai Peninsula**. That is it. Everything else is Bush or Southeast, the true wilderness.

Originally these villages were Native communities, and were established on the coast or on rivers, to make travel possible. In the summer, river travel is possible and mostly by boat whilst in winter the rivers are used as highways for snowmachines. Since the coming of the snowmachine

The true wilderness of the Bush can only be reached by flying.

Arctic Circle Area

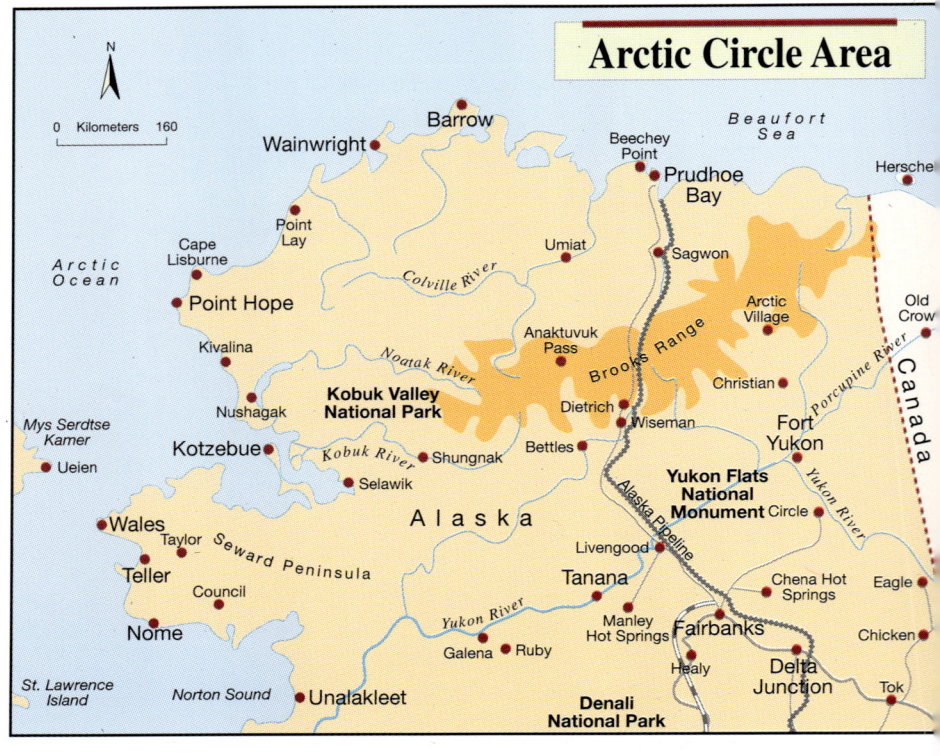

(Map showing locations including Barrow, Wainwright, Point Lay, Cape Lisburne, Point Hope, Kivalina, Nushagak, Kotzebue, Ueien, Mys Serdtse Kamer, Wales, Taylor, Teller, Council, Nome, St. Lawrence Island, Unalakleet, Galena, Ruby, Tanana, Manley Hot Springs, Livengood, Fairbanks, Healy, Delta Junction, Tok, Chicken, Eagle, Chena Hot Springs, Circle, Fort Yukon, Christian, Arctic Village, Old Crow, Wiseman, Bettles, Dietrich, Shungnak, Selawik, Anaktuvuk Pass, Umiat, Sagwon, Beechey Point, Prudhoe Bay, Herschel; features including Arctic Ocean, Beaufort Sea, Colville River, Noatak River, Kobuk River, Yukon River, Porcupine River, Brooks Range, Seward Peninsula, Norton Sound, Alaska Pipeline, Kobuk Valley National Park, Yukon Flats National Monument, Denali National Park, Alaska, Canada)

0 Kilometers 160

to the Bush, the number of people using dog teams for day-to-day travel has declined significantly.

Most of the residents of the Bush are **Alaska Natives**, but then again, not all. Whites have relocated into the villages for a variety of reasons, including employment opportunities, marriage to Natives, or a desire to live the village life, far from the technological clutter of the modern era.

The allure of life in the Bush is often romanticized, but the harsh realities are not always obvious. While a desire to "get away from it all" can hold quite an appeal for beleaguered citizens, the full implications can hit hard on a person not prepared for it.

We take so many things for granted in our modern day lives, so many of the basic necessities of life as well as the things that we have come to think of as necessities, that to suddenly survive without those things can result in a state of shock for the unprepared and uninitiated city-dweller.

Things like electricity,

The vast tracts of land and rivers offer many a sporting fun to young children.

heat, running water, sanitation systems, medical care, stores, TV and radio, banks, that many of us assume are universal by today's standards are often either not available in the Bush, or at the very least available in rudimentary forms.

Travel by Flying

Travel to Bush towns and villages and to remote wilderness recreation sites is almost exclusively done by aircraft. The larger towns such as **Nome**, **Kotzebue**, **Barrow**, **King Salmon**, have regularly scheduled jet flights from cities on the road system such as **Anchorage** and **Fairbanks**. From medium-sized towns, scheduled travel by propeller-driven airplanes is available. Access to the smallest villages and to backcountry recreation spots is done by charter operators or air taxis, the legendary Bush pilots of Alaska. As you travel from your home to a remote backpacking destination, you will find yourself getting into a series of smaller and smaller airplanes. Finally, it could be just you and the pilot in a very small plane indeed.

Traveling to and between Bush locations involves planning, flexibility, and cost. Scheduled flights are often full during the tourist season, as are hotels and lodges. If you want to spend a week backpacking in a remote corner of a national park, you cannot just show up at an airport with a pile of gear and start looking for a ride. You *might* find one,

Saharian look-alike muskegs are found across the land.

The Aurora Borealis

The aura of the midnight sun is one of the enchantments sought by visitors to Alaska.

Although not unique to Alaska, the aurora borealis, or northern lights, is certainly part of the romantic tradition of the state. The aurora has a place in the legends and myths of native peoples of the circumpolar areas, and once you have seen one of these spectacular displays, you can certainly understand the age-old fascination with this amazing and mysterious natural phenomenon of the skies.

Some native peoples equated the appearance of a light display with the coming of a battle, while others saw them as the manifestation of spirits of the dead. Still others considered the aurora to be a predictor of weather, especially of changes in the wind.

The scientific explanation for the aurora borealis, (and the aurora australis, the southern lights) is that the interaction between the "solar wind", electrically charged particles emitted by the sun, and the earth's magnetic field produce a gigantic electrical display in the sky. Usually taking a form similar to gigantic curtains of light, these astonishing phenomena shift, dance, and pulsate in the night sky, continually changing form and intensity.

A number of conditions have to converge for the northern lights to be visible to observers on the ground. First, of course, there has to be a display in the air. Auroral activity changes with sunspot activity and other atmospheric factors, and on some nights the aurora is very active, some nights not so active, and on still other nights, not active or visible at all. While the 11 year sunspot cycle has a definite effect on the intensity of the lights and on how often they occur, there is a large measure of unpredictability – this light show does not have regularly scheduled appearances.

The sky has to be clear, since the aurora takes place hundreds of miles in the air. And, it does have to be completely dark as nearby city lights or even the light of a full moon can obscure a relatively weak display. Since most tourists visit Alaska in the summer when the nights are short, most do not get a chance to see a demonstration. However, if you visit in the fall, winter, or early spring, a clear night should prompt you to make an effort to check out the sky from time to time. The displays are not constant even on a given night. Often they will grow, wave, pulsate and exhibit amazing vigor, then die down and sometimes disappear completely before suddenly reappearing and starting all over. So if you have got a clear night sky, check it often, especially if there has been recent activity.

Sometimes the beginnings of a display look like wisps of cloud in the sky, possibly illuminated by nearby city lights. However, once they begin to move, there is no mistaking the northern lights for anything else. They will grow in size as you watch, and can change form with amazing speed. When the display is especially strong, you will be able to make out colors, either a pale greenish white, or a fringe of red.

So if you happen to find yourself in the northern latitudes on a clear, dark night, make an effort to go outside and scan the sky but be patient – and you will find that the stars are not the only attractions in nature's midnight show.

Ice fishing at Nome's Bering Sea, help solve some of the problems of subsistence.

and then again you might not. Most pilots and air taxi services have their clients booked months in advance, and drop-in customers are not easy to accommodate. Also, you do not want to hire someone whose reputation and background are unknown to you. There might be a good reason why a pilot fails to have any customers as flying into the Alaskan Bush is a highly specialized art form, demanding skill, intelligence, and experience coupled with the proper equipment so check out your pilot first.

Flexibility in scheduling your travels is another requirement. Alaska's quirky weather can ground airplanes for days at a time, leaving people stranded all over the state. You can experience delays on either end of your planned trips, leaving you stuck hanging around an airport, or feeling abandoned in the backcountry, anxiously scanning the skies for your ride. Then when the weather clears, the backlog of passengers has to be cleared up before things can get back to normal. Do not plan on flying out of the Bush on the day before you are scheduled to fly home from Anchorage – leave some slack in your schedule here and there to factor in the inevitable glitches.

Cost is another factor to deal with. Flights within the state to the larger communities are expensive and on the smaller commercial airplanes are more expensive still. There is not much competition on flights to small communities, so the air carriers can pretty much name their price.

Charter flights can be pricier still, depending on a number of factors. While some operators will have to set fees for flights to the more popular locales, the majority of them charge according to flying time. You pay so much per hour, with the cost per hour dependent largely on the size of the aircraft. And, you pay for all the time the engine is running, whether you are in the plane or not. If you want to fly to a spot an hour's flying time from the airfield, get dropped off, and then picked up again at a later date, you will pay for four hours of engine time. The pilot flies an hour out to drop you off, an hour back, another hour out to pick you up, then a final hour back again.

When making inquiries about flights and comparing prices, make sure you are comparing apples and apples, so to speak. Some airplanes are cheaper to operate because they are smaller, and if all of your gear and personnel cannot fit into the plane, multiple trips will have to be made with the clock ticking and charges accumulating the whole time. On the other hand, there is not much sense paying for a larger plane than needed.

For example, a **Super Cub** is a very small plane, carrying pilot, one passenger, and some gear. Charges for Cub flights are often in the US$50-$60 per hour range. Near the other end of the spectrum, the **De Havilland Beaver** can carry payloads of a half ton at a time, but costs in the neighborhood of US$300

An exciting float trip down the river.

an hour. There are numerous plane sizes and configurations (and prices) in between. When making plans, you need to know how many people will be in the party, how much they weigh, how much gear (in pounds) you plan on carrying, and exactly where it is you want to go. Be as precise as possible with your information, and avoid surprises such as showing up with an unexpected guest who decided to tag along at the last minute. Your pilot will *not* be amused, and may not be able to accommodate your change in plans.

Learn as much as possible about your destination before departing. You will need to know whether you need an airplane equipped with floats, wheels or skis. Some operators have a variety of

An "Argo" – tundra vehicle, a main form of transport for natives at Anaktuvuk Pass.

aircraft to choose from, while others are just one- or two-plane outfits.

Get as close as possible to your final destination by road or scheduled airline. You *can* fly to the **Brooks Range** from **Juneau** in a small plane, but it is less expensive and much less hassle to fly there from **Fairbanks**.

Packing for a flight into the Bush requires some forethought and planning. Scheduled airlines can accommodate standard luggage, usually. If you are traveling to smaller towns or villages, leave your set of matched and

Cargo areas of Bush planes usually have several nooks and crannies, so it is better to have a lot of small pieces of gear rather than one or two great big ones. Weight balance is critical on these aircraft, and breaking your gear down into small bundles allows the pilot to position things exactly where he or she wants them to balance the aircraft.

Accommodations

Accommodations in communities removed from the road system range from luxurious to primitive to non-existent. Do not just drop into an interesting looking dot on the map and expect to find a Holiday Inn, McDonalds, and a Safeway store. Be prepared for anything, and try to keep your sense of humor at all times. Before booking a room in a lodge, hotel or rooming house, especially if it is not on the road system, ask about the nature of the place. Does each room have a private bath? Is food service provided, is there a restaurant on the premises or nearby. In many of the smallest villages, accommodations are indeed rustic but this should not be a turn-off for those eager to experience the true nature of the Bush. If you know that before going in, you will be better prepared to enjoy your experience instead of ending up disappointed. On the other hand, some of the backcountry lodges are very plush. Prices will give some indication of what to expect, but be prepared to pay quite a lot even for

personalized Louis Vuitton hard-sided suitcases at home. Instead, opt for soft luggage or duffel bags, especially if you are chartering a small plane. Flights to the Bush, even aboard scheduled flights, often carry machine parts, dogs, big game trophies, fish, used nets none of which you will want to come in contact with your expensive stuff.

Pilots of the Bush

A Bush pilot and his prized aircraft, all geared up for a fly-in fishing trip.

Alaska has more airplanes and more pilots per capita than any other state, and for good reason. Where there are no roads, and where overland travel is at best difficult and at worst impossible, the airplane is sometimes quite literally the only way to go.

Flying into the Bush can take any one of many different forms. A pilot could find himself flying passengers and freight on regularly scheduled flights into Bush communities, or dropping hunting, fishing, or camping parties onto far out lakes. Climbing groups often require pilots to drop them and their gear onto glaciers high up on the sides of mountains. Remote communities sometimes need to have people with medical emergencies ferried out to hospitals in the bigger cities.

This kind of flying presents an infinite number of variables and challenges. Different types of airplanes have varying capacities and idiosyncrasies, and the pilot must always be familiar with his craft.

A Bush plane might be equipped with wheels, skis, or floats, and might carry one passenger or ten. Landings and take-offs on unusual surfaces, such as snow fields, beaches, gravel bars along rivers, and frozen lakes present situations not often covered in Lower 48 flight schools. Cold weather and high winds present potential dangers as well. Good pilots know how to deal with all of these conditions and how to read the weather and terrain which is no small task in Alaska.

The most difficult factor for Bush pilots to deal with is the unusual and temperamental Alaska weather. In the Lower 48, pilots usually have a variety of information sources to use, including regular updates from nearby airfields and other pilots in the area. Flying in Bush Alaska, however, presents complications. Most of the airfields are little more than gravel or dirt

basic services in the Bush. Supplies in Bush villages are also expensive, due to shipping costs. Everything, including food and gasoline, has to be flown in or brought in by barge if the village is on a large river. Expect prices exceeding US$6.00 a gallon for milk, for instance. Plan your budget accordingly, and bring as much of your own stuff as possible.

Backcountry Travel

The possibilities for places to go and things to do in the Alaskan Bush are absolutely overwhelming. There is more country to see and things to do than anyone could possibly undertake in several lifetimes. Do not make the mistake

strips carved out of the wilderness, and weather conditions are very localized. Mountains tend to create their own weather patterns, and flying through mountain passes is hazardous but necessary. Pilots are often left with only their own experience and instincts to guide them through tricky situations.

Besides having to deal with the above mentioned quirks of Bush flying, pilots often have to deal with unusual loads as well. Picking up hunting parties can be quite a challenge in itself. The hunters can have dead animals in varying states of disassembly to transport out, along with several sets of very unwieldy antlers. The pilot has to estimate the weight of people, gear, meat, and horns, arrange everything in such a way that things do not shift around in flight, and then take off from a rocky landing strip with no help from air traffic controllers.

Adding to the already complicated mix is the element of time. In many cases, pilots and passengers have the luxury of waiting for good flying conditions where safety is more important than time. Maybe the trip is a sightseeing flight or a casual fishing trip, and if it does not happen, or does not happen on time, it is no big deal. Other situations can be a good deal more critical, however, such as transporting an injured or seriously ill person to a hospital, rescuing the victims from an airplane accident, or retrieving a backcountry party that has been stranded long past their appointed pick-up time. These situations call for all the skill, courage, and ingenuity for which Alaska Bush pilots have become justifiably famous.

of trying to see and do it all - you simply cannot, and if you try, you will just wear yourself out in the attempt, and wind up glossing over a lot of things, and not really seeing the real things.

There are national parks, national wildlife refuges, national monuments, national preserves, national wild rivers, wilderness areas, state parks, state game

Eskimo whale bone sculpture blends into the Arctic.

refuges, and critical habitat areas scattered across Alaska's 586,000 sq miles (1,523,600 sq kms). Flying in to most of them demands lots of planning and the ability to exist self-sufficiently during your stay.

Gather information about the weather, terrain, wildlife, and potential hazards before you make your decision to visit. The public lands of the Bush are, with very few exceptions, undeveloped and primal. This is raw wilderness, just you, the wide expanse of land, the austere climate and the critters for company. That means no facilities of any kind for the traveler – no food, no telephones, no kindly rangers to take care of you – just your survival techniques. Exhilarating and profoundly moving if

Rawhide and furs out for sunning before they are made into winter clothes.

you are prepared, unforgiving and potentially deadly if you are not.

Once you are on the ground in the backcountry, travel is mostly limited to boats and feet in the summer. Numerous touring companies offer guided rafting trips down the rivers of the Bush, with a variety of types of experiences available for thrill-seekers.

You can take a short fishing trip down a mild little river or across interior lakes, or undertake a challenging, multi-week adventure through some of the most impressive white water ever found on the continent.

Luckily, backpackers can employ the services of a guide (if they wish to) or take to the Bush unaccompanied. Before walking into the wilderness, learn everything possible about the terrain, safety measures and the potential difficulties. Large expanses of wet tundra are virtually impassable most of the year, and stream crossings present potentially dangerous situations.

If you are planning to hike from point A and have a pilot pick you up at point B, allow plenty of time to make the trip, keeping in mind that severe weather can keep you pinned down in camp for days at a time. Weather can also delay your pick-up for days, so carry plenty of extra food and fuel.

When surveying potential hiking areas and making plans with a flight service, be especially wary of opinions of hiking terrain given by pilots. Although resourceful and knowledgeable

A family of baby seals at Kotzebue.

as most of them are about the area and about flying in it, if they have not actually walked an area, take their opinions with a grain of salt. What look like pleasant tundra meadows and gentle mountain streams from the air can turn into ankle-twisting tussocks or "uncrossable" torrents on the ground.

Wherever you travel in the Bush, or anywhere in Alaska for that matter, be prepared for bugs. Besides the ubiquitous and bothersome mosquito, there are black flies, 'no-see-ums', and an evil little creature called white socks to contend with, among others. Carry plenty of your favorite brand of mosquito repellent, and if you are going into the backcountry, a headnet can quite literally save your trip. Mosquito coils that give off repellent smoke can be very effective in banishing bugs from a small area, although some people find the smell offensive.

Traveling in areas not accessible by road opens up all kinds of possibilities unimaginable to the more casual visitor. Getting away from the clutter and crowds of highway Alaska and into the wild country demands courage, a commitment of time, planning, and expenses that most tourists are unable or unwilling to make.

However, for those who are willing to take up the challenge, the payoff for the determined traveler is a glimpse of the "real" Alaska, a trip to unique towns, villages, and wilderness that most people can only read or dream about.

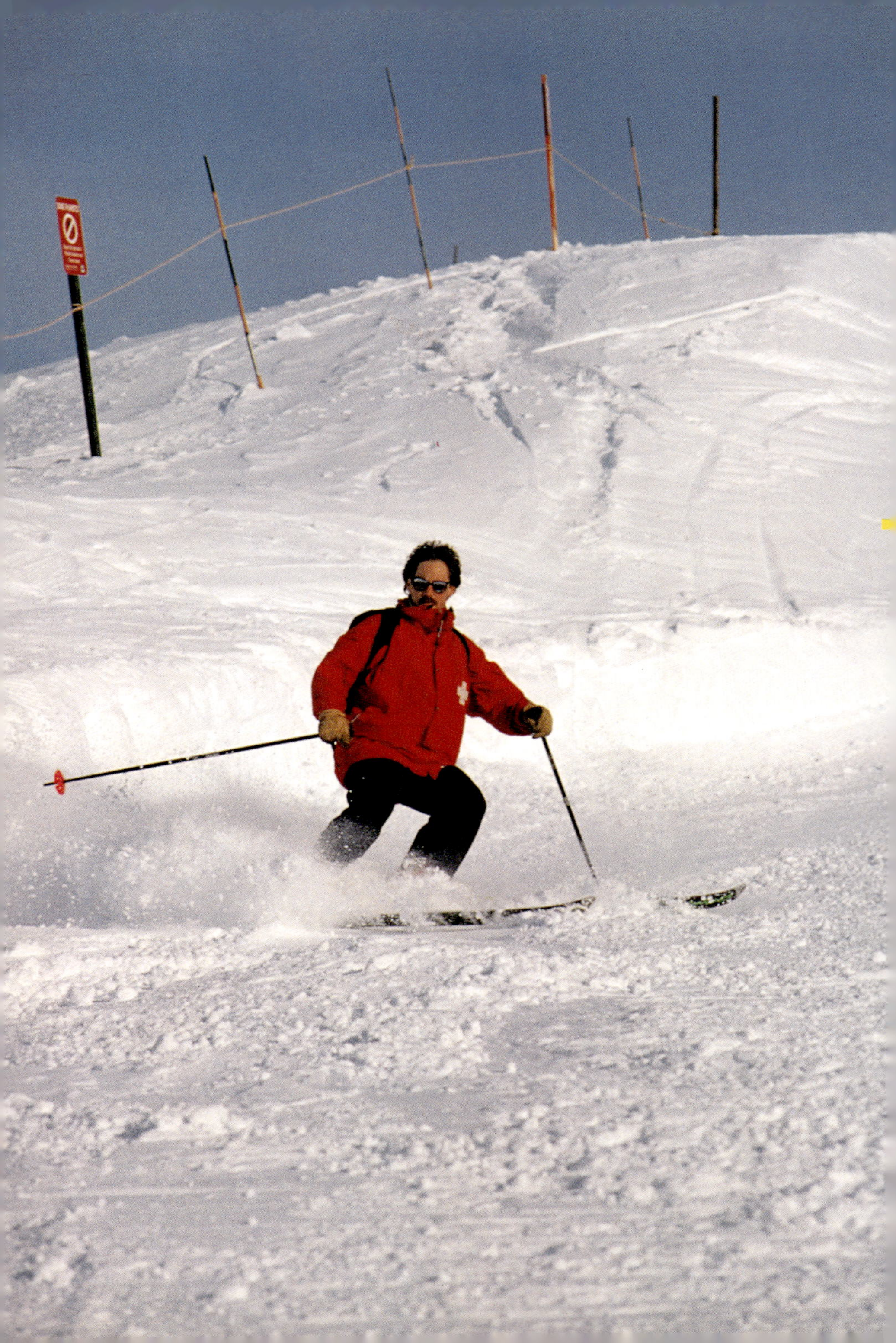

FAST & FUN

Sports & Recreation

Alaskan summertime activities tend to center around the water, for a couple of reasons. For one thing, there is just so much of it. Salt water bays and beaches and open ocean waters so turquoise against the sun, invite explorers, anglers, sea-kayakers, whale watchers, clam-diggers, and sightseers to sample the variety of adventures to be had. Fresh water lakes, rivers, and creeks offer a multitude of options to white water rafters, canoeists, avid anglers, and pleasure-boaters. And after a long, cold winter, Alaskans are glad just to see water in its liquid state again.

A skier unleashes his quest for speed down the Alyeska slopes.

River Sports

With literally thousands of rivers to choose from, float trips aboard rafts, canoes and kayaks are very popular. From short trips catering to day visitors to weeks-long expeditions in remote backcountry locations, there is something here to

Boating on the blue waters of Meyers Chuck.

SPORTS & RECREATION

253

The Iditarod: The Last Great Race

'Iditarod' – have sled dogs will travel.

Every year, 60 or 70 people get it into their minds that there is nothing they would rather do than to mush a team of about 20 dogs over 1,100 miles (1,771 kms) of frozen tundra between Anchorage and Nome. The Iditarod Trail Sled Dog Race is a test of endurance, dog handling, and survival in the harshest of environments. It is also the number one spectator sporting event in Alaska.

The race commemorates a dramatic piece of Alaska history. In 1925, word of a diphtheria epidemic in Nome reached the Territorial Governor's office in Juneau. A hastily organized relay system was improvised, and the necessary serum traveled to Seward by ship, and then by rail to Nenana. The only airplane in the district was in Fairbanks, and questions about the dependability of the plane and its pilot, coupled with the extreme cold at the time, -30 to -60°F (-34° to -51°C), made its use inadvisable. The

suit any taste of gravity-powered water trips for water-lovers.

One of the latest developments in water travel is sea kayaking. Paddling these stable and controllable craft gets you right down to the level of the sea creatures, and tales of close encounters with whales, sea otters and other marine animals are as impressive as it is awe-inspiring.

Kayakers usually carry all their gear inside the boat, and paddle from campsite to campsite as conditions and impulse dictate. The **Southeast** and **Prince**

only means of transport between Nenana and Nome was dog teams. A series of mushers carried the medication the final 700 miles (1,127 kms) to Nome in five and a half days.

Today the run starts in Anchorage, usually on the first Saturday in March, and the winner crosses the finish line on Front Street in Nome some 10 to 12 days later. The race attracts contestants from the Lower 48 and from several foreign countries. Every year the size of the winning purse grows as more mushers and more sponsors are attracted to the event.

The logistics behind the race are astonishing. Once the mushers leave the Matanuska Valley north of Anchorage, they are off the road system for the rest of the race. Checkpoints are established in a series of Bush villages along the way, and food and supplies for dogs and mushers have to be flown into the villages well ahead of time. An army of volunteers, an air force of pilots and planes and a medical corps of veterinarians work together to see that everything necessary for the health and safety of dogs and people is in the right place at the right time.

Transporting the food supply alone is a staggering task. Over 1,000 dogs running through an Alaskan winter pulling sleds burn up an unimaginable number of calories, and the tons of food necessary to sustain these world-class athletes are transported to the various villages and rest stops along the way. The total amount of gear and food exceeds 60 tons!

Even though these teams of dogs and mushers race through the Alaska interior in the winter, every precaution is taken to ensure a safe run. The mushers are required to carry certain safety equipment in their sleds, and enough food to sustain the team should they fail to reach a checkpoint. Along the way, the dogs are examined periodically by race veterinarians, and any dog that is injured or in any way not up to the task is removed from the team and flown back to Anchorage. Mandatory stops along the way help to keep the teams rested.

This grueling test of teamwork between musher and dog team keeps alive the Alaska tradition of sled dog teams, and has evolved from being more than just a sporting event – it is today an all Alaskan institution.

Spectators at Iditarod turn eagerly to their favorite sledder.

William Sound offer a combination of lots of shoreline and plenty of protected water for kayakers to enjoy.

While the more adventurous folks might prefer the thrill of whitewater rafting or sea kayaking in the company of whales, there is a lot to be said for canoeing on one of Alaska's more gentle streams or across a placid interior lake which can be quite a rejuvenating experience as well. A few outfits rent canoes by the day or week, and some of the fly-in camps and lodges have canoes available for their customers' use.

Safe and secure for a raft trip at Mendenhall.

Fishing Charters

While it's entirely possible to fish unguided anywhere in the state, most visitors find the sheer variety of kinds of fish available and the widely differing means and equipment required to catch them a bit daunting. It is usually easier to hire an experienced guide and skipper to take you to where the fishes are and show you how to catch them. Most charter outfits supply tackle, bait, and sometimes lunches as well. A knowledgeable captain can also point out wildlife and points of interest, and answer your questions about the area. If your stay is long enough, you can try some of the methods you have learned and strike off on your own.

Before paying your money to a charter company, make sure you know what you are paying for. Are bait and tackle furnished? Is lunch included, do you have to pay extra, or will you need to pack your own? How about cleaning the catch – is the service included in the price, available at an extra charge, or not available at all? Many companies charge by the pound, and if you catch a big halibut the cost of your charter can escalate quickly. It is helpful to keep these factors in mind when comparing prices, and make sure you are comparing similar levels of service.

The most popular, not to mention delicious, fishes are salmon and halibut. There are five species of Pacific

A quiet fishing trip at Kenai Peninsula.

salmon, and they can be caught either in salt or fresh water. Halibut live exclusively in salt water, and can weigh more than 400 lbs (180 kg). Fish that large are rare, but halibut in excess of 200 lbs (90 kg) are not at all unusual. If you are fishing from a port that runs a halibut derby, awarding prizes for the largest fish, by all means enter. Every year there are stories about people who spent thousands of dollars coming to Alaska, another hundred or more to go fishing, then decided to economize by not paying an additional five bucks for a derby ticket. Then, they go out and catch a huge fish, and miss out on a substantial cash prize. In the **Homer** derby, the biggest fish caught during the summer can win more than US$20,000.00! Not bad for a US$5.00 investment.

Whale-watching

The chances to see whales in coastal waters around the state are legion. In the summer, humpbacks and gray whales return to Alaska from the south to feed in the nutrient-laden environment. Killer whales, or orcas, patrol the coast year round, and beluga whales are frequently seen near Anchorage. Occasional and seldom seen visitors include fin, beaked, and Minke whales. The most famous of the whale watching spots is **Glacier Bay** in the Southeast. The humpbacks that return to this area every year have become such an attrac-

Alaskan waters are a great source of satisfaction for fishing enthusiasts.

tion that visiting ships and boats have had to be limited in number so that these amazing cetaceans can continue to go about their business unhindered by too many vessels. You can book visits to the bay out of **Juneau**, **Gustavus** or **Seattle**. **Glacier Bay** is not the only place in the Southeast to see humpbacks. The waters around **Sitka**, **Petersburg**, and **Ketchikan** also provide the chance to see these whales in action, and charter outfits that offer such packages abound. However, whale-watching trips are not the only chance to spot whales. Although trips specifically dedicated to finding and observing these huge sea mammals offer the best chances to do so, any time you are on salt water in Alaska there is a chance to get lucky. Whenever you are near the water, make it a habit to constantly scan the water's surface, looking for leaping whales, fins, flukes, or the telltale spout of misty air escaping from a whale's lungs when it surfaces. Traveling on cruise ships or ferries, fishing charters, even just driving along next to the coast all offer the potential for sightings. Killer whales and humpbacks are quite often seen in **Prince William Sound**, near Homer, out of Kodiak, and in the Seward area. Drivers along **Turnagain Arm** south of **Anchorage** and along the areas where the Sterling Highway offers a look at **Cook Inlet** on the **Kenai** often spot beluga whales during the summer. These white whales follow the schools of salmon as they head for their spawning

A pack of killer whales at Resurrection Bay.

grounds, and large pods of 50 or 60 animals are not at all uncommon. Be especially watchful along **Turnagain Arm** when the tide is high and the waters are smooth for the best chance of sighting whales. (It is best if the driver delegates this task to passengers, and keeps his eyes on the road!) Occasionally other whales are spotted in the Turnagain Arm as well, and recently a pod of orcas has been making regular appearances.

Camping

Camp sites in the Great Land are too numerous to mention. Besides the public camping areas on National Forest,

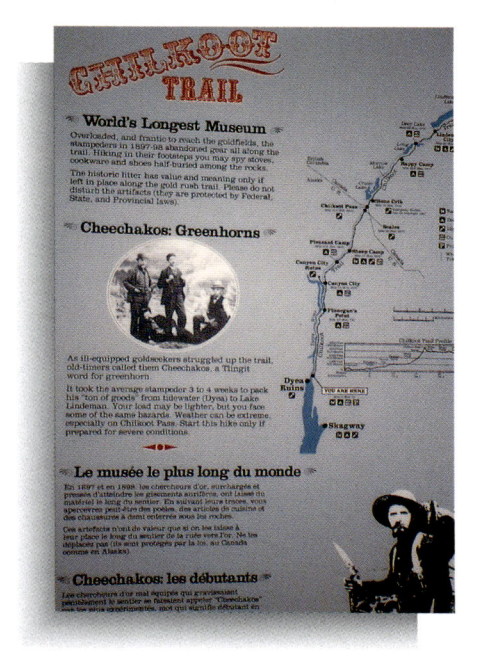

Chikoot Trail, the "world's longest Museum".

The World Eskimo Indian Olympics

An Eskimo demonstrates his kinetics at the kicking contest.

Every year Alaska Natives from all over the state meet for the World Eskimo Indian Olympics, (WEIO) in Fairbanks. Representatives from Bush villages meet with urban Natives to engage in games and contests to exhibit their prowess in activities handed down from times long before the coming of the Europeans.

These games have their roots in the survival skills necessary to live in the North. The ability to carry heavy loads, to endure pain, and to deal with the harshness of the environment were essential to life. Today, while many of these skills are still used on a daily basis, others endure mostly in the form of games. Participation is a way for Native Alaskans to come together as a community, to remind one another of their bonds, and to celebrate their heritage.

In the past, the only contests open to women were the Native Baby Contest, the Miss WEIO contest, and the seal skinning and fish cutting events.

Recently, with federal law mandating equal treatment for male and female athletics, the young women have been able to compete in the more physical events as well.

The greased pole walk replicates a slippery pole connecting a fish wheel to the shore. To check the catch, the person must walk out over the river and back. In the competition, a peeled (6 inch) 15 cms log is greased with Crisco, and the competitors see how far they can walk before falling off.

In the kicking contests, a seal skin ball is suspended above the floor. In the one- and two-foot high-kicking events, the competitors jump up and touch the ball with one or both feet. Balance and coordination are vital, and each athlete gets three kicks. With each successful touch, the ball is raised an inch until all but the winner are eliminated.

In the four man carry, the ability to carry heavy loads is tested. Each competitor carries four men at a time, a load of approximately 600 lbs (270 kgs). The distance walked is measured,

National Park, Bureau of Land Management and state park lands, many private camping areas provide RV facilities, tent sites, dump stations, etc. However, during the summer most of the roadside spots fill up quickly, so it pays to drop anchor early in the day, lest you be caught without a home for the night. Wherever you camp, do your best to keep your area clean, and always leave a campsite in better shape than you found it. In crowded areas, be considerate of your neighbors- just because it is still light out at midnight and you feel like having a party doesn't necessarily mean that everyone around you feels the same way. If you are in a motor home, be very conscious of when you're

with the world's record at this juncture in excess of 175 ft (53 meters).

The ear weight measures stamina and pain thresholds. 16 pounds (7.2 kgs) of lead is hung from the competitor's ear by a piece of twine, and he walks for as long as he can stand it. The present record is over a half mile!

In the ear pull, two men sit face to face, and a loop of sinew is placed over their opposing ears. A tug of war of heads ensues until the loop slips off the loser's ear.

The knuckle hop is always the last event due to the probability of injury to the participants. Assuming a push-up position on toes and knuckles, the athlete hops along the gymnasium floor until he can no longer stand the pain. The world record is over 165 ft (50 meters).

The big crowd pleaser of events is the blanket toss, or 'nalukatak'. The origins of the blanket toss are not known for sure, some maintain that it was used as a way to spot game or whales from flat terrain, while others say it was a way for the wives of whaling captains to celebrate the birth of a child. The blanket, made of seal skins stitched together, is grasped around its perimeter by 20 to 30 pullers, who must co-ordinate their efforts with one another and with the jumper. An experienced contestant with a good crew can jump 40 ft (12 meters), providing quite a thrill for the jumper, the pulling crew, and for spectators.

A dance competition rounds out the games, with awards given in Eskimo and Indian categories, the dancers judged by Elders on adherence to tradition in dance and costume.

running your generator- the noise from those things is a lot more noticeable to your neighbors than it is to you.

Clamming

If you "dig" clams, then Alaska is a great place to dig clams. Razor clams are available on the **Kenai Peninsula**, with the **Clam Gulch** and **Deep Creek** areas the most accessible and productive. The clams live buried in the sand below the high tide line, so an ebb tide is needed to gain access to them. A bucket, clam shovel, and a fishing license are all the equipment you need. The technique takes some practice, so watch your fellow clammers, and do not hesitate to ask for help. Most Alaskans are more than happy to share their knowledge of how to find, dig for, and clean clams. This last part is especially important, and the effort to clean the delicious bivalves is much more time-consuming than digging them. Check with the folks at the **Clam Shell Lodge**, Mile 118.3 of the Sterling Highway in Calm Gulch for equipment rentals, tips, and other facilities.

Ball Games

There is an active interest in baseball here. During a season lasting just over six weeks, two semi-pro leagues, including teams from Anchorage, Fairbanks, Kenai, and Palmer, play one another as well as teams from Hawaii, Canada, and the Lower 48. In Anchorage, free tickets to games can be picked up at the Tourist Information Center in the log cabin downtown. Basketball is also immensely popular in Bush villages, as it gives a community an indoor activity to engage in during the winter. And in Anchorage every November, the Great

A seaplane adds color to the blue skies and green forest.

Alaska Shootout is one of the few college pre-season tournaments approved by the NCAA. Seven teams from the Lower 48 get a trip to Alaska, and the Seawolves of the **University of Alaska-Anchorage** will test themselves against some of the finest college players in the country.

Winter Sports

Downhill skiing is available in Alaska, although with only one ski area in **Juneau**, a couple near Fairbanks, and three more in the **Anchorage** area, op-

Snow mobiles cover cross-country distances with speed and thrills.

portunities are somewhat limited. Cross-country skiing is much more popular, and with the state's long winters, heavy snowfalls, and huge expanses of skiable back country, it is easy to see why. Anchorage has a number of groomed and maintained ski trails in town, and local shops rent cross-country, downhill skis and snowboards.

Sled dog racing is Alaska's official state sport. Dog mushing skills important for a wide variety of sled dog racing, from short sprints with two dogs, up to and including the 1,100 mile (1,771 km) long **Iditarod Trail Sled Dog Race** that begins in **Anchorage** and ends in **Nome**. The **Yukon Quest** race from **Fairbanks** to **Whitehorse** is nearly as long as the Iditarod. According to many mushers, the Quest is the more grueling race, but it has not garnered the publicity of the Iditarod. Long distance races necessary for Iditarod qualification are held around the state, usually over distances of about 300 miles (483 km). World Championship sprint races are run in **Anchorage** during the **Fur Rendezvous** festival in February, and local races are run at the Tudor Road track in Anchorage on most winter weekends.

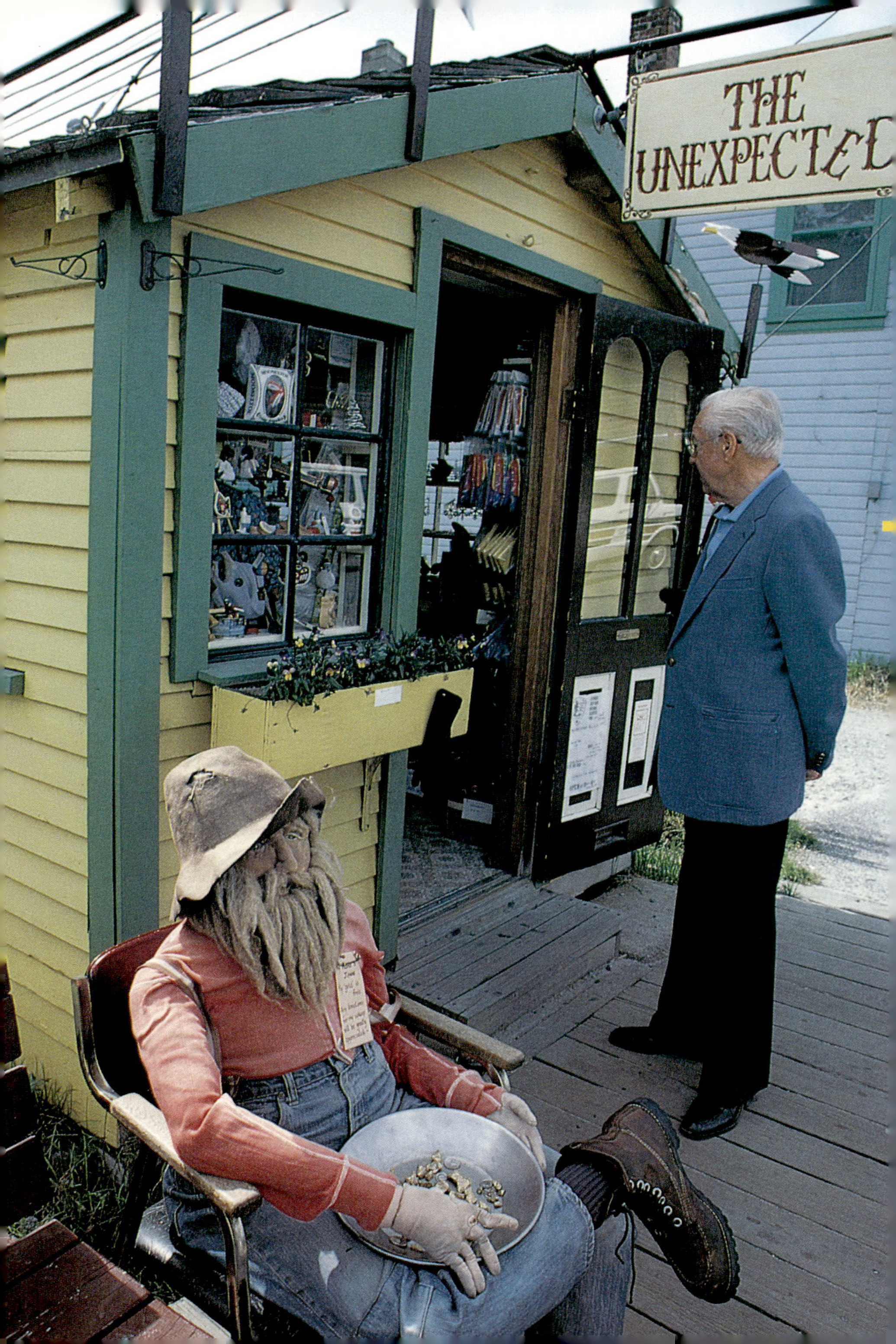
THE
UNEXPECTED

Shopping

The opportunities for going home after an Alaska vacation with a lot more in your luggage than you arrived with are stupendous. Tourism is one of Alaska's largest industries, and entrepreneurs take advantage of this large influx of capital that presents itself on the state's doorstep every year. If you are shopping for groceries or non-tourist kinds of things, the larger towns have a pretty good selection of retail establishments to choose from. National retailers such as Sears, and J.C. Penney have stores in Alaska, as do several West Coast chains, including Lamont's, Fred Meyer, and Grand Auto.

"The Unexpected" catches the eyes of a city gentleman.

The Price Spectrum

As a general rule, the prices will be the best in Anchorage, and as you move away from there in distance and in size of town, prices escalate. Retail prices are also a function of the item's weight, and in outlying areas, it is not unusual for grocery stores to charge upwards of US$6.00 a gallon for milk. Stores

"Tom Sawyer's" at Ketchikan, an Alaskan gift shop with the Mississippi spirit.

in the Southeast usually get their merchandise directly from wholesalers in Seattle, but for the rest of the state, Anchorage is the hub around which goods pivot. Container ships and barges dock and unload at the main Port of Anchorage, and the goods are dispersed via rail and truck from there. Some fresh produce arrives by air but the expence limits the amount of merchandise delivered in such a way.

If you are traveling around the state, especially if you are going to be traveling on your own as opposed to going with an organized tour group, try to anticipate your needs, and stock up to the best you can in the largest city on the itinerary.

If you are undertaking an extended backcountry trip and passing through Anchorage, Fairbanks, or Juneau, plan on spending some time stocking up on necessities. All of these cities have shopping malls, discount stores, and department stores, so just about anything you will need can be purchased somewhere in town. You would probably need to do some leg work to get what you want. There are several retailers specializing in clothing and outdoor gears, and for the most part the stores are staffed by knowledgeable sales people.

If you have any questions about whether or not the stuff you brought along is appropriate for Alaskan conditions, someone will be able to help you out. Prior to exploring the state in detail, stop by one of the many bookstores available to the visitor.

T-shirts, logos and souvenirs at Talkeetna Visitors Cabin.

Guide Books

Alaskans do a lot of reading, (probably has something to do with the long, dark winters) and support quite a number of bookstores, including good-sized book departments in drug, department, and even grocery stores. A wide range of titles concentrating on specialized aspects of the state are prominently displayed in most stores, with large sections devoted entirely to Alaskana. You can find guide books that go into detail on backcountry lodges, fishing, hunting, bed and breakfast establishments, wildflowers, rivers, animals, cooking, national parks- the list grows every year along with the increased interest.

"Two Bears and a Silver Hand" - Souvenir Shopping

Before buying any souvenirs, you should be aware that the state administers a program to award identifying emblems to manufacturers using Alaskan materials and artisans. This distinctive "Two Bears" emblem guarantees that your souvenirs and handicrafts are Alaska made. In addition, the "Silver Hand" emblem guarantees that your item was handcrafted by an Alaska Eskimo, Indian, or Aleut artisan. Look for these symbols on every craft item you buy to be sure that you are purchasing an authentic Alaskan handicraft.

As in any place that caters to visi-

Fur Shops

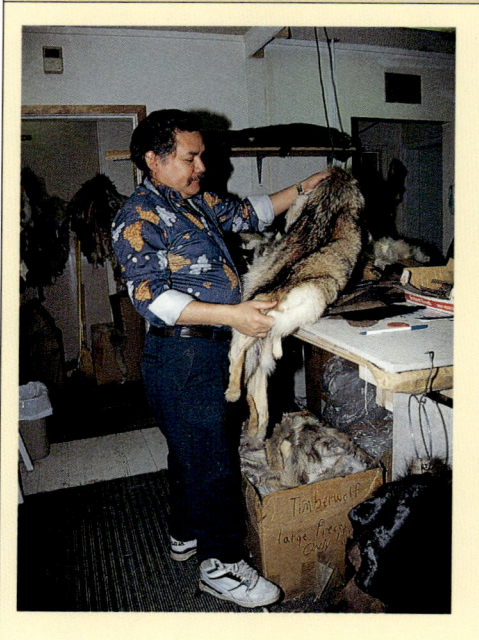

Retailers carry a wide range of fashionable and functional fur clothing.

The fur business is a small but important part of the state's economy. Economic recessions, the vagaries of fashion, and the outcry concerning "animal rights" have all affected the state's fur business, all of which are beyond the control of the locals. The fur clothing made and worn by Alaska Natives has always functioned well as a defense against the region's extreme cold. Fur insulates very well, and some furs such as wolverine and wolf, function especially well as ruffs around parka hoods, since they do not hold frost like others do. The variety of clothing made from furs is much larger than most people would imagine. Usually the thought of fur garments pretty much begins and ends with fashionable, full-length coats. However, there are lots of other items that are well suited to fur, including hats, mittens, gloves, mukluks, and slippers. The parkas made by Eskimo and Athabascan women (or "parkys") were originally worn strictly for function. Over the years, however, the design of these garments has evolved into some of the most beautiful clothing you are ever likely to see. Using a variety of furs and skins from different animals to achieve an artistic effect, the colors and patterns of furs in a Native-made parky can produce an astonishingly soothing blend of shades. This is done by alternating panels of very dark fur from wolves or seals, pure white fur from ermine or polar bear, brown patches of fur from lynx, mink, and marten, and elaborate ruffs of wolf or wolverine fur which are hand-sewn and offset with elaborate bead work to produce true works of art.

Mukluks too began as strictly functional footwear made from moose or caribou hide. Like parkys, mukluks can also be turned into a work af art by dedicated and skillful artisans. Beaver and moose fur are widely used both as

tors, there is no shortage of shirts, hats, coffee mugs, and other assorted knickknacks, ranging in quality from tacky to tasteful, from the ridiculous to the sublime. You will find many of the same kinds of items sold in other states, but since you have come all this way, why not buy something that really says "Alaska", literally and by way of its uniquely Alaskan character. Starting with the ridiculous, some novelty items show a somewhat unhealthy interest in moose poop. These "nuggets" left behind by the big, homely animal have spawned a kind of cottage industry, and you can buy "moose nugget jewelry" in stores all over the state. There are also coffee cups with ceramic nuggets inside, so your unsuspecting guest can get a glimpse of them as he drains his cup. It

ornamentation and for their functions in keeping the feet warm. Soles are often made of sealskin for durability and traction.

Fur shops that buy and work with hides can get furs from two main sources – from the trappers and hunters who harvest the animals in the wild, or from fur farms that raise animals such as fox and mink for their skins. There are very few fur farms left in Alaska, and most of the furs sold here come from the wild. Once the hides are cleaned up, they are then sent out of Alaska for tanning. The tanned hides are then either made into fur garments, or sold as it is. The hides are inspected and graded for size and quality. The hunting and trapping seasons take place mostly in the fall and winter, so the hides brought in are at their thickest and most luxurious. The highest grade of whole fur is "select". A select fur has all of its parts intact, and can be mounted by a taxidermist as a whole body mount. From there the grades go down to grades I through IV, depending on the overall quality of the hide. Length and thickness of the fur, absence of flaws, go into determining a fur's grade. Some furriers specialize in finished items such as coats, stoles, etc., while others deal more in whole furs. Many whole furs are sold to Alaskan Natives to make traditional garments, either for their own use or for sale to visitors. Besides the sale of traditional Native garments, Alaska furriers also cater to the high fashion industry across national borders. Retailers in the cities carry a wide variety of fashionable and functional fur clothing.

really does take all kinds of people, and all kinds of sense of humor, to make up a world.

Moving up the taste scale just a bit, T-shirts, coffee cups, or hats with Alaska themes are available absolutely everywhere. In tourist-intensive locations from Southeast to Nome, you can hardly swing a cat without hitting a T-shirt shop or a place selling hats proclaiming

Close-up view of hand-sewn Alaskan winter shoes.

"A Bad Day of Fishing Beats a Good Day of Working." When you get past the knick-knack category, there are still lots of retail establishments to choose from. As mentioned in the Handicrafts chapter, the range of traditional Native artworks covers baskets, ivory carvings, masks, needlecraft, dolls, blankets, etc. Some shops concentrate on the Native crafts of a certain region, while others handle items from all over the state.

The range of prices for authentic Native artwork is great, with simple carvings of soapstone and Alaska jade priced relatively low, progressing up through elaborate and labor-intensive artworks such as ornate baskets and intricate ivory carvings. Generally speaking you will pay the highest prices at

Artistically carved ivory geese.

posh hotels and gift shops that sit at a far remove, both physically and culturally, from the traditional Native artists.

Alaskan Art Galleries

Alaska also has an abundance of art galleries. Most tend to feature original artworks that reflect Alaskan wildlife and nature in paintings and photographs, while others specialize in contemporary Alaskan artists whose work is more stylized and a bit less representational. Contemporary Native artists are showcased as well, presenting artwork that marries their traditional cultures with modern interpretations of themes both ancient and current.

One form of handicraft that is not often seen in the Lower 48 but is Alaskan and not necessarily Native is carving done on antler and horn. Using moose antler or Dall sheep horn, these artists carve intricate scenes of wildlife on these natural materials, creating unusual and beautiful artifacts. Other natural art forms found in gift shops are diamond willow creations, and mineral and gemstones polished and presented for sale.

Diamond willow is a natural deformation of a willow branch made into distinctive walking sticks and other forms of handiwork. The many unusual rocks and gemstones found in Alaska's vast store of mineral resources make for interesting conversation pieces for the home. Especially unusual are geodes, large plain looking rocks that when split open reveal amazing crystalline structures inside.

Fish Taxidermy

Taxidermy is not often thought of as an art form, but people who know the trade can appreciate the attention to detail and the mastery of the craft that brings to life the remains of deceased animals. Mounting of fish and game is a widespread practice in Alaska, and exhibits are on display in hotels, airports, and private collections all over the state.

Beaded artwork on display at Sitka's National Historical Park.

One of the results of technical advances in fish taxidermy is that you no longer need the actual fish in hand to create a lifelike trophy suitable for hanging on the wall of your den.

The use of fiberglass casts and advanced coloring techniques has had a couple of interesting developments for fishermen. One side of the picture is that you no longer need to kill the fish in order to have a trophy. The popularity of catch-and-release fishing meshes nicely with this aspect of taxidermy, and anglers can measure and photograph their catch quickly, and then release the fish unharmed. (If you want your fish to swim away, able to fight another day, familiarize yourself with the techniques necessary for catch-and-release. It is important to minimize the stress placed on the fish.) Then, using the photos and measurements, the taxidermist can then recreate the fish.

On the other hand, no one is exactly bound by law to make sure that the fish you caught is every bit as big and ferocious looking as the trophy you bring home. High-tech taxidermy will ensure that your preserved 'souvenir' looks the size to put up quite a fight before succumbing to your fishing skills. As a matter of fact, you do not have to actually catch a fish in order to have a realistic mount made.

So if you are looking for something to put a stop to your buddy's constant bragging about that five pound bass he caught back in '86, here's your chance. All it takes is money and a taxidermist, and you can guarantee your own bragging rights for some time to come. Or at least until he decides to one-up on you and "catch" a bigger fish.

All the decoratives you need from an Anchorage gift shop.

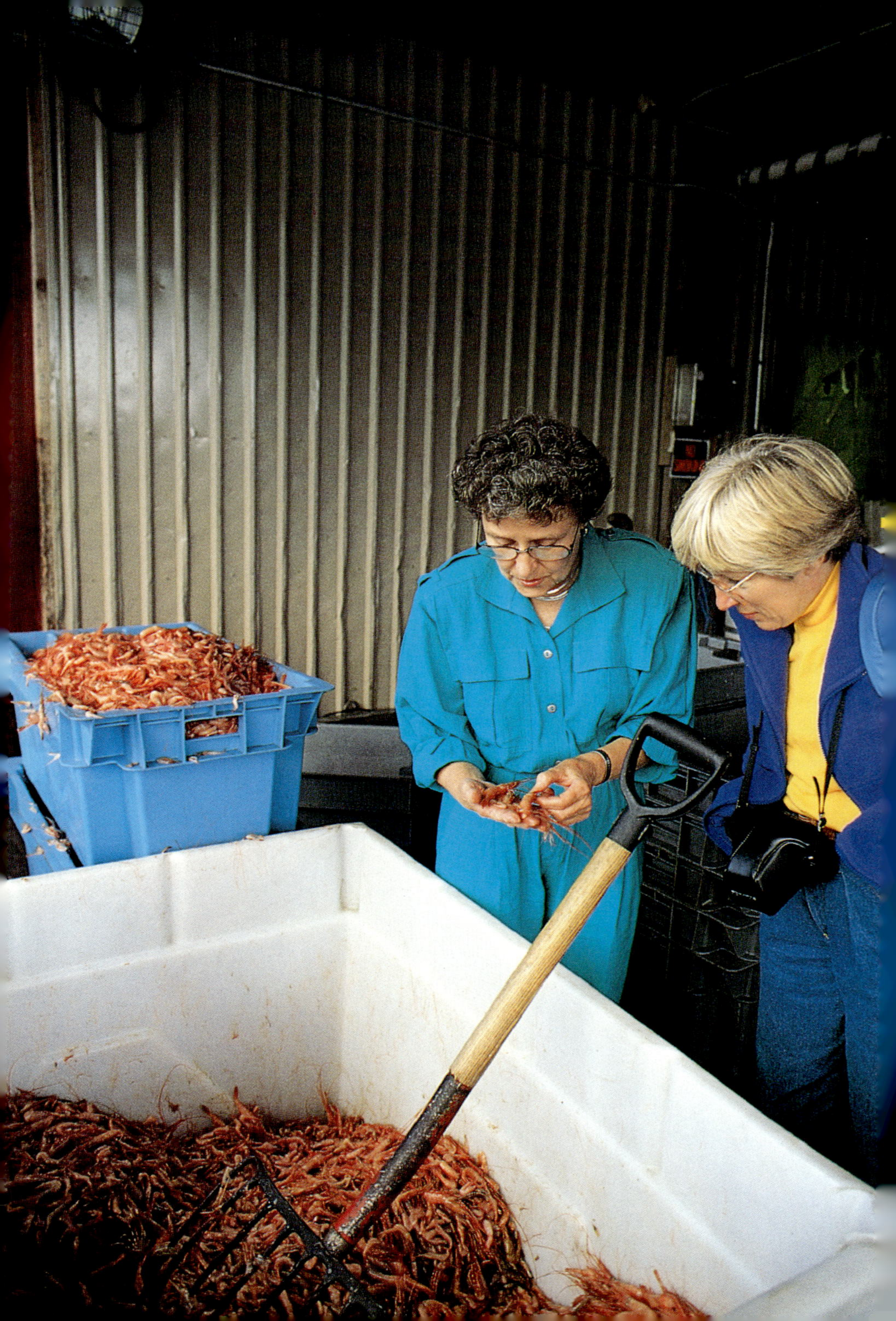

SUMPTUOUS SEAFOOD

Cuisine

Alaska cuisine means seafood, seafood, and more seafood. The opportunities for sampling the catch of the day, whether it is salmon, halibut, shrimp, crab or clams are legion. In addition, since most of the folks who live here came from somewhere else, and have often brought their own local or national specialties with them, there is quite a choice of restaurants. Most cities have a variety of types of eating experiences available, including continental, Asian, Mexican, meat 'n potatoes, barbecue, etc., so you probably will not go hungry. One of the unique forms of seafood indulgence is the salmon bake. Adapted from traditional Indian practices, the Alaska salmon bake most often takes the form of a very informal meal, usually held outdoors and consisting of an all-you-can-eat menu of barbecued salmon, ribs, halibut and other delicacies. Accompanying menu items usually include salads, corn on the cob, sourdough

At the shrimp cannery of Petersburg.

The mouth-watering aroma of salmon bakes fills the air at an outdoor gathering.

rolls, beverage service, and dessert. Most places have either an indoors eating area, or at least a roof for shelter in case of rain. By all means, give it a try. **Smoked salmon** is a local favourite. The finished product is well preserved and travels well, whether you decide to pack some along for snacking, or to take home to enjoy later or give as gifts. Recipes for different combinations of salmon species, pre-smoking marinades, smoking processes and types of wood used in smoking result in an infinite variety of tastes. You can buy the stuff almost anywhere in the state, and some smokehouses will either smoke the fish you catch for a fee, or trade you on a two-for-one basis. You bring in two fish, they will give you one smoked fish in exchange. Smoked halibut is less common, but every bit as tasty as the salmon. If smoked salmon is not to your liking, try taking home some canned salmon. Available in gift packs at most stores selling souvenirs and foodstuffs, canned salmon will keep indefinitely. Other variations on the salmon theme are quite numerous. Alaskans know their salmon, and restaurants tend to be very creative in coming up with new ways to appeal to their customers. They are also quite specific about just exactly what kind of salmon they are serving. Whereas restaurants in the Lower 48 can get away with referring to "Alaska salmon" on their menus, no such generalizations are tolerated by the locals here. They want to know what species of salmon

Clams Recipe

1 qt. tomato sauce:
1 medium onion
2 cloves garlic,
minced 1 green bell pepper
1/2 red bell pepper
1/2 yellow bell pepper
4 slices of sun-dried tomato,
in olive oil 1/2 cup sweet red wine
1- 10 oz. can of tomato puree
2- 15 oz. cans tomato sauce
1- 15 oz. can Italian-style stewed tomatoes
1- 6 oz. can tomato paste
1/3 cup chopped fresh basil
1/3 cup chopped fresh parsley
1/4 cup extra virgin olive oil sugar
1 lb. razor clams, chopped seasoned bread crumbs
4 Tb. olive oil
1 small onion
1 lb. tortellini

For the sauce, chop the onion, peppers, and sun-dried tomato, and saute them slowly together in the olive oil until soft. Add and saute the garlic, be careful not to burn it. Add the canned sauce, tomatoes, puree, and paste, stir in the basil and parsley, and stir together. Add the wine, and sugar to taste. Simmer everything together slowly for two hours, tasting occasionally and adjusting wine and sugar. Dredge the chopped clams in the seasoned bread crumbs to coat. Saute the onion slowly in the olive oil until translucent. Add the clams coated with bread crumbs, and saute slowly for 5 minutes. Add the clams and onion mixture to the tomato sauce. Deglaze the pan with red wine, and scrape this mixture into the tomato sauce as well. Boil the tortellini according to package instructions, cover with the clams and sauce mixture, and sprinkle each serving with grated Romano or Parmesan cheese.

they are being served, where it came from, and in some instances, exactly how it was caught!

You will see references on menus to "Copper River Red Salmon", or "Troll-caught Southeast King Salmon", and woe to the restaurateur who would try to serve the lowly pink salmon in an Alaska eating establishment.

Shellfish from Alaska waters is usually available, and it is prepared in a nearly infinite number of ways. Crab is sold fresh in seafood stores, and even the local supermarkets have a surprisingly good selection of fresh, local items. King crab legs, "snow" crab, (snow crab is a marketers term for tanner crab), and Dungeness are all caught in Alaska, although seasonal variations will determine which varieties are available fresh.

Razor clams are served in chowders, and there is a fledgling oyster-raising industry underway as well. Many visitors are surprised to find fresh-caught shrimp available in Alaska, associating these delicious crustaceans more with the Gulf of Mexico than with the Gulf of Alaska. However, several varieties of shrimp are native to local waters, and although the shrimping fleet is not large, they do furnish the local restaurants and seafood stores with a steady supply. Often the small-scale shrimpers who fish Prince William Sound or off the Kenai will sell their catch from roadside stands. This is a good opportunity to buy a lot of fresh seafood at a relative bargain, and to indulge in a large-scale shrimp boil at your next camp site. Examine the shrimp carefully and if

Whale blubber – keeping young Eskimos nourished and warm.

things do not smell super fresh, it is probably best to pass up that particular seller. If you cannot find several varieties of Alaska seafood to your liking, then you just do not like seafood.

Sourdough is inextricably tied in with the Alaska mystique. When the gold prospectors came to Alaska in the 1890s, many of them carried a bit of sourdough starter, a yeast culture the consistency of pancake dough, to use in making breads, hotcakes, and other baked goods. It contains living yeast organisms, and the starter is used to make a batch of dough for baking, with a small portion reserved for starting the next batch. The yeast culture is kept alive and perpetuated by careful tending. Sourdough starters are passed on from person to person, and sometimes from generation to generation, their lineages traced and followed like the genealogy of royal families. Today, there is hardly a restaurant in Alaska that does not serve sourdough bread with their meals, and the finer establishments make it a point to have fresh rolls or loaves of bread available for diners. Sourdough bakeries pride themselves on the quality and taste of their particular strain of yeast culture. Entire cookbooks devoted to sourdough are available, complete with detailed instructions on the creation, care, and feeding of this delicious yeast culture. Some restaurants and bakeries will even part with a small bit of starter upon request,

Fresh green cabbages at Matanuska attest to the Great Land's fertility.

Salmon Recipe

1-inch thick fresh salmon steaks (can use canned salmon or fresh fillets, if available)
4 tablespoons extra-virgin olive oil
1 large sweet onion, chopped
1/4 cup finely chopped fresh basil
12 oz. pasta, vegetable spirelli recommended

Pre-cook salmon carefully until it just barely flakes.
The steaks microwave well if done on high for about three minutes. Remove the skin and bones, and separate the fish into small pieces. Boil the pasta for 8-10 minutes. Saute the onions in the olive oil until translucent. Add the salmon, pasta and basil, and toss together over medium heat. Serve hot with ground romano or parmesan cheese. Serves 4.

---

so if you taste a version that especially appeals to you, it does not hurt to ask for a sample. That way you can take home a living souvenir of Alaska, something to rekindle your memories every time you taste it.

The sale of **wild game meat** is illegal, so you cannot buy moose burgers or caribou steaks. However reindeer, even though it is the same genus and species as the caribou, is a domesticated animal, so the sale of reindeer meat is allowed. It is usually sold as sausage, and reindeer sausage and eggs make for a hearty Alaskan breakfast. Retail markets also sell reindeer sausage, and many of the gift packages of samples of Alaska food will have some form of reindeer meat included, often for its novelty value as much as for its taste. All you have to do is to convince the youngsters that they are not eating 'Rudolph'.

Other local specialties include **birch syrup**, made from the sap of birch trees in the same way that New Englanders make maple syrup, various berry products including jams and jellies, and honey produced from bees gathering pollen from the blossoms of the fireweed plant found in abundance in Alaska.

Dining in Alaska is very informal, and with the exception of a small handful of the most expensive restaurants in Anchorage and Juneau, "dressing" for dinner is not required. It is a lot easier to be overdressed than underdressed in most places, and the eclectic mix of locals and visitors makes for interesting people watching opportunities. It is not at all uncommon to see a group of

Halibut in Cheese Sauce

Ingredients:
1/4 cup butter
4 tablespoons flour
1 small can (5 oz.) evaporated milk
3 oz. white wine
1 teaspoon salt
1 1/2 cups grated cheddar cheese
1/8 teaspoon cayenne pepper
1/2 teaspoon dry mustard
2 pounds halibut in 1/2 inch-thick fillets Paprika

Make a white sauce by melting the butter over low heat and gradually adding the flour, stirring continuously to keep the flour from forming lumps. Combine the evaporated milk with the white wine and stir the mixture slowly into the sauce, blending until smooth. Add the cheddar cheese, and warm slowly. Add the salt, cayenne, and dry mustard. When the sauce is thoroughly blended, place the halibut in a greased ovenproof dish, and pour the sauce over it. Sprinkle with paprika, and bake at 177°C (350°F) for 20-25 minutes. Serves four.

Restaurant alfresco by the scenic Chena River.

diners wearing dresses and sport coats sitting next to a bunch of folks wearing waders and coveralls. You can be pretty sure in such a situation that the people in the "Sunday" clothes are the visitors, and the folks in hip boots and baseball caps are locals. Alaskans in general tend to eschew the trappings of formality, and they are perfectly comfortable walking into some of the state's finest restaurants in jeans, sneakers, and t-shirts. The problem that visitors sometimes have of finding restaurants serving sophisticated menus and catering to a more upscale clientele is simplified in Alaska. Any such restaurants that exist in the state will invariably be found in the handful of larger cities. Anchorage, Juneau, Fairbanks - the list of towns of sufficient size to sustain these kinds of establishments is a short one. It takes a certain critical mass of potential year-round customers to keep an eating establishment in business. Once you get away from the cities, and once the tourists go home for the winter, it is all a lot of places can do then is to keep their heads above water and stay solvent from year to year. Another problem with keeping restaurants in business in out-of-the-way places, even on the few heavily traveled highways, is the changing nature of tourism. A large percentage of travelers visit the state by taking advantage of package deals. They do not travel independently, but are shuttled from point to point in airplanes, ships, and buses. This does not give

A chef shows off his smoked salmon.

them the chance to stop at interesting looking little roadhouses, or to explore any areas in much depth. Further complicating the picture is the emergence of the motor home for the people who do travel independently. The occupants of these self-contained vehicles, often referred to as "road barns" by drivers unfortunate enough to be caught behind them on twisty roads, tend to stock up on groceries in the big cities, and to bypass restaurants along the way. However, even under these adverse conditions, the Alaska roadhouse is surviving although in diminishing numbers. Historically, these places served as waypoints for travelers, providing hearty meals and a place to bed down for the night. With the coming of the automobile, they evolved into combination restaurants, motels, gas stations, and general merchandise stores. And while you will not find any of these places serving Beef Wellington or Oysters Rockefeller, for the most part you will find hearty, honest, meat and potatoes meals, served with a minimum of fuss in an unpretentious atmosphere. Although there are some bargains to be had, do not expect food prices to parallel those in the Lower 48. Almost all of the foodstuffs served in restaurants, with the exception of the local seafood, vegetables, and baked goods, are shipped up here from outside. Additional shipping expense is required for food outside of the larger cities, so be prepared to pay higher than average food costs.

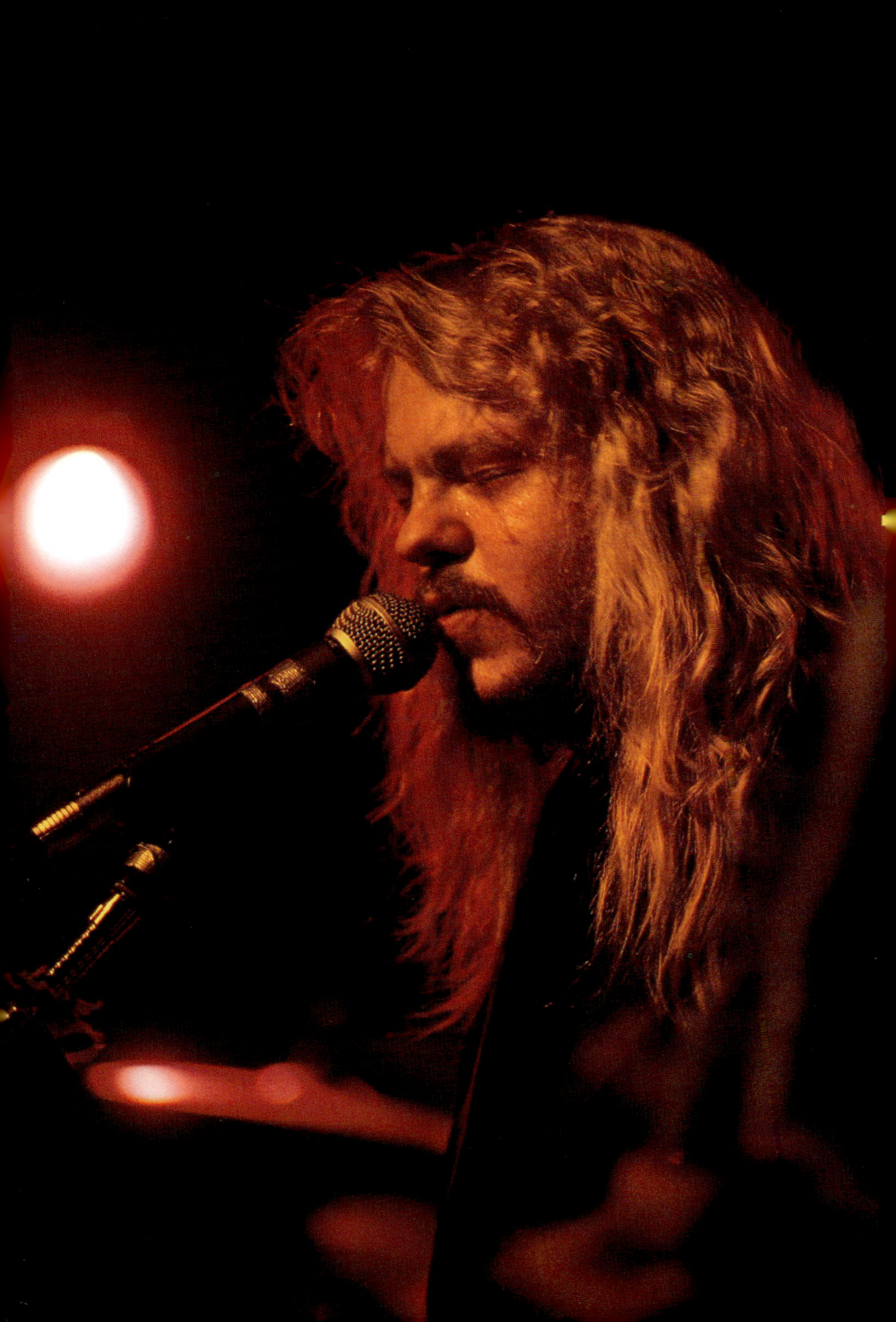

Entertainment

When it comes to entertainment, a lot depends on your personal definition of what exactly constitutes a good time when on vacation. Some travelers like to maintain contact with the familiar, doing the sorts of things they do at home, albeit in a different setting. That way they can compare the local way of doing things with their home towns. Do the bingo parlors play the same games they do at home, and how do the callers compare? What kinds of local or exotic beers are available in the new place, and how do the prices compare? How does the zoo stack up against the one at home? Other folks prefer to branch out a bit more when they travel, to see the sorts of things that they do not see at home. People who would not be caught dead in their hometown museums suddenly become history buffs, drawn to study the past in locations that just seem more interesting than the familiar old buildings they grew up around. Still others undergo complete

Nightlife in Ketchikan is like elsewhere in the world.

A horse-drawn 'taxi' for the romantic in Skagway.

personality changes when they leave home. Visiting new and interesting locations can draw some people out of their shells, shatter their routines and open up new and interesting possibilities. Whichever category you fall into, Alaska has something to offer you, from the safe and familiar up to the exotic and dangerous. Whether you choose to follow your old routines, or just go nuts and throw caution to the wind, what you decide to tell the folks back home is really up to you.

One thing you will find no shortage of in Alaska is bars. The rough-and-tumble, Last Frontier nature of the place pretty much guarantees a lively interest in beverage alcohol. There are waterfront bars, touristy bars, yuppie bars, roadside pick-up truck type bars and singles bars, sand bars. Liquor laws are not quite as free wheeling as you might expect, nor are they the Byzantine mess you will find in some other states. Most restaurants sell alcohol with meals, and many of the larger ones catering to tourists have lounges as well. Privately owned liquor stores sell liquor, beer, and wine, but no alcohol is sold in grocery stores. Sunday sales are allowed, and you would not have a hard time finding a drink anywhere along the road system in Alaska. Bush villages are totally different, and most have very severe restrictions on import, sale and possession of alcohol. Before traveling to any Bush village, make sure you are familiar with their laws before you leave.

A stylish way around Skagway town.

Airborne entertainment is available everywhere. Alaska's long-time association with and dependence upon the airplane as a major form of transportation has fostered a culture closely associated with flight. Alaska has the highest number of pilots and airplane owners per capita of any state in the Union, and the Lake Hood-Lake Spenard floatplane base is the busiest facility of its kind in the world.

To get a glimpse of the sights and wonders of the 49th state, you can charter flightseeing trips no matter where you are – aboard fixed-wing aircraft on wheels, floats and/or skis. Helicopters are ready to take you on a pre-arranged tour of the local highlights, or any place your schedule and budget will allow.

Glacier landings are popular in Juneau, and the flight services in Talkeetna routinely land on the glaciers of Mt. McKinley when ferrying climbers back and forth to the mountain attractions.

Arctic Escapades – Juneau

Juneau, being the largest town in Southeast, provides the most options for entertainment. One type of show not often seen in the Lower 48 but fairly common in Alaska is the **Gold Rush Revue**. These shows, available in Juneau, Skagway, and Fairbanks combine dancers and storytellers to recreate a modern version of the kinds of entertainment supposedly preferred by the gold rush prospec-

The Fly by Night Club

A friendly and down-to-earth skit at the 'Fly by Night Club'.

Before the Municipality of Anchorage was incorporated to swallow up the entire bowl area, Spenard was a separate city, a city with an independent attitude. Being the location of a multitude of after hours bars, massage parlors, and strip joints, Spenard acquired a reputation as a wrong-side-of-the-tracks kind of place. Today Spenard has been relegated to being just another neighborhood in Anchorage, but much of the old attitude survives and is relived. And the keeper of the flame in Spenard is a guy who calls himself Mr. Whitekeys, the owner of the 'Fly By Night Club'.

From spring time until after Christmas, Mr. Whitekeys hosts a hilarious "multi-media extravaganza", featuring his troupe of performers, music, dancing, a slide show, skits and other thrillers. He has taken the idea of the old time gold rush revue and turned it on its ear, bringing it up to date and adding more than a little spice to the concept. Operating in an unassuming little building at 3300 Spenard Rd., (you can't miss it- it's the one that has the tail end of an airplane protruding from its side), "Keys" presents his show every night from Tuesday through Saturday. Combining a slide show with live entertainment, he pokes fun at every aspect of Alaskana that strikes him as being absurd, ridiculous, or just a bit out of the mainstream. Billing his "Hilarious, outrageous, tasteless,"

tors. Juneau also has a collection of bars providing night time live entertainment.

The **New Archangel Russian Danc-** ers schedule performances to coincide with cruise ship arrivals in Sitka. Check at the Centennial Building on Harbor

show as "The one the Chamber of Commerce does not want you to see," he skewers local politicians and public figures, and Alaska life in general. His talented entourage of entertainers assist in the festivities with a succession of original parodies, popular songs and skits tailored for the local audiences. One thread that weaved its way through eveything in the show is spam, served in his kitchen, among other tasty items, with as wide a range of hors d'oeuvres and munchies based on Spam as you are ever likely to find in the civilized world. Friends of the club also carry cans of Spam with them to the far corners of the earth and have their pictures taken standing near famous landmarks holding the familiar blue cans. "Keys" then features these photos in his slide show, weird Alaskans smiling and holding up cans of Spam in some very unlikely locations. He even features the mystery meat in his phone number, 279-SPAM (279- 7726), making it easy to remember. The club carries a very nice selection of beers from around the country, and an inviting menu that does have non-Spam items on it.

On Friday and Saturday nights, there is dancing after the show to the house band called, what else, the Spamtones. The club also features visits by non-Alaskan artists such as the Mississippi blues performers, and he has had a very distinguished list of performers come up to visit. The Fly By Night Club offers a succession of slightly different shows, starting with Springtime in Spenard, "A Break-up Extravaganza", the Whale Fat Follies during the summer months, and ending the year with Christmas in Spenard. Some of the material carries over from show to show, some is tailored to the season, and the troupe adds new bits often, keeping the entertainment fresh and topical. If you are easily offended by the slightest bit of off-color humor, be forewarned. The material is adult and risque, but not raunchy. Reservations are necessary most nights, as the show is very popular with residents and tourists.

Drive near the Crescent Boat Harbor for show times and location. If you are looking for something a bit less sedate, try the Pioneer Bar on Katlian St., where you can mingle with local fishermen.

Ketchikan

Ketchikan is a great town for waterfront bars, boaters of the Inside Passage frequent the place, so do cruise ship passengers – quite a mixture to thrill the compulsive people-watcher. A trip down Front Street presents a multitude of establishments to drop into for a quick nip. Several places also provide live entertainment in the evenings. While you are wandering around Ketchikan, meander on over to the Creek St. boardwalk area. Formerly the location of Ketchikan's red light district and Prohibition-era speakeasies, it serves as a reminder that this pretty little tourist town at one time was a fairly seamy place. Because of the quirks in Territorial Laws, the distance from the reach of federal laws, and the nature of the prospectors, fishermen and adventurers who first headed up here, many Alaska towns have had colorful histories of bawdy houses and free-flowing liquor. Here in Ketchikan, brothels once flourished until the 1950s, before a series of scandals and the changing nature of the town finally brought this era to a close.

Fairbanks

Fairbanks is the hub of all activity of the Interior, and there is certainly no short-

A rock band spellbinds the audience into the night.

age of bars there. However, visitors might be advised to stick to the more touristy spots in Fairbanks and keep away from some of the local downtown hangouts. Mike Doogan, a columnist with the Anchorage Daily News, has described Fairbanks, his home town, as being a city with the motto, "You wanna step outside and say that?" Most of the local places are perfectly friendly, but if your instincts tell you to avoid a certain spot, listen to them.

There is a Gold Rush Revue at the **Ester Gold Camp** just south of town, and **Alaskaland** offers the chance to see the state's only theme park. Gold Dredge Number 8 at Mile 9 of the **Old Steese Highway** has guided tours, gold panning, and the chance to watch a working gold dredge in action.

Anchorage

Southcentral Anchorage, being the state's largest city, also has the largest selection of entertainment options – live music, theater, dancing, first-run movie theaters. For the more culturally inclined, check the daily paper for activities at the **Performing Arts Center** downtown. Besides nationally known artists, the PAC has a constant series of locally produced and performed features in theater, dance, and music. Bars are plentiful as well, although some of the seedier establishments on 4th Ave. are best avoided. Live music is available every

Sitka's famous New Archangel Dancers never fail to entertain.

night in local drinking establishments, as well as in the thriving coffee house scene, a non-alcoholic entertainment alternative. The Friday paper carries a supplement called Weekend with movie reviews and listings, cultural events, and other goings-on about town. Anchorage also has a comedy club, the **Pierce Street Annex**, featuring weekend appearances by an ever-changing cast of touring comics.

On the Kenai, nightlife options tend to be a bit limited. However, Seward has some interesting waterfront bars, a couple of which feature live music, especially on weekends. Homer has a very few nightspots as well, and live theater presented on week-ends at the **Pier One Theater** on the Spit.

Meet the "Keystone Kops", at the Fur Rondy, Anchorage.

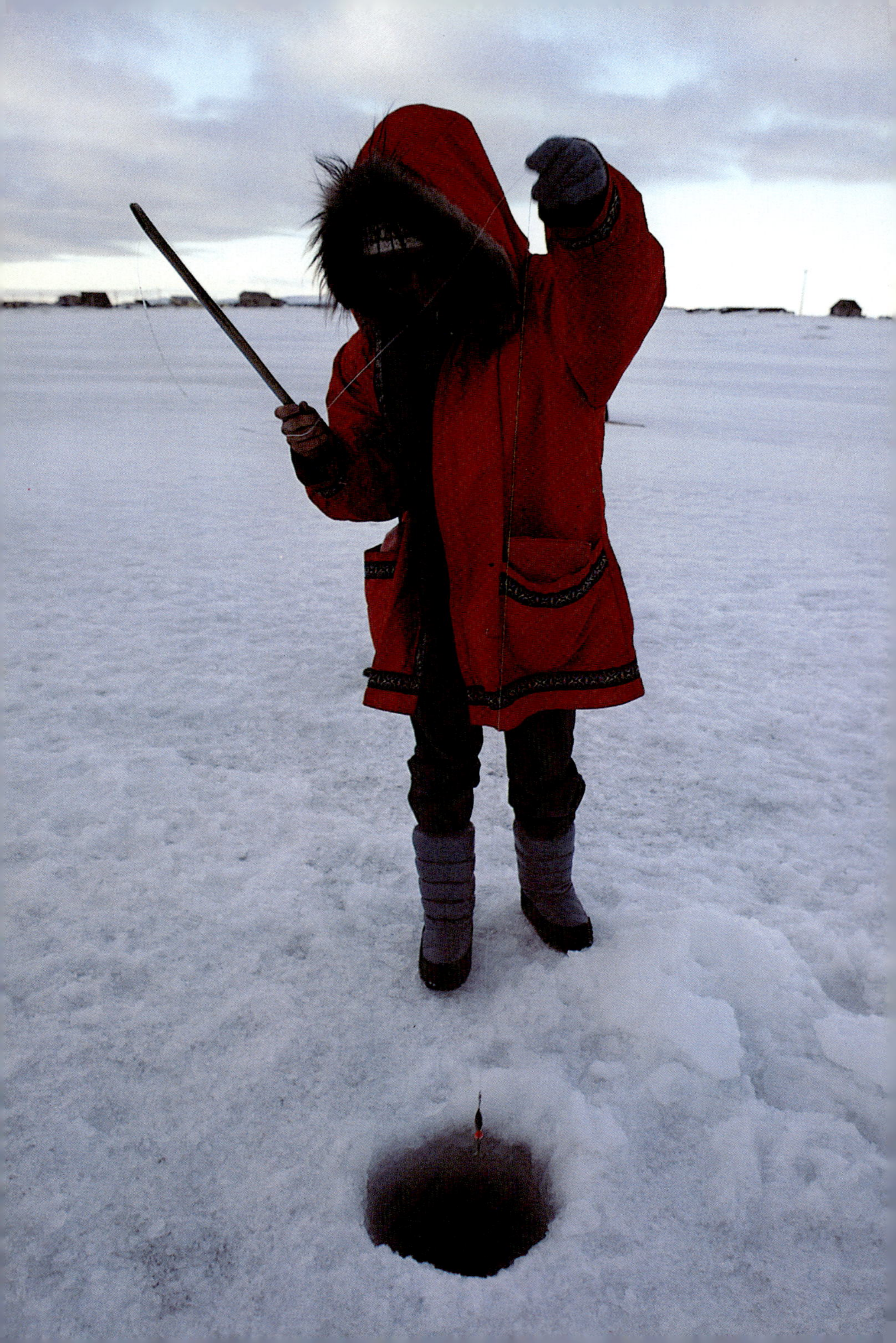

TRAVEL TIPS

BUSINESS HOURS
Most retail establishments are open from 10:00 AM to 5:00 or 6:00 PM. Stores in shopping malls frequently stay open until 9:00 PM Monday through Friday. Weekend hours vary, many retailers closing at 6:00 on Saturday and Sunday, and others do not open at all on those days, depending on the nature of the business. Government offices usually open at 9:00 and close at 5:00, and most are closed on week-ends. Towns visited by cruise ships frequently tailor their hours to coincide with the ships' comings and goings. In Anchorage, several of the larger grocery stores are open 24 hours a day.

CAR RENTAL COMPANIES:
ANCHORAGE:
Rent-A-Wreck
Tel: 562-5499 or
800-478-5499 in Alaska.

Avis Rent-A-Car
Tel: 277-4567 or
800-331-1212

Denali Car Rental
Tel: 276-1230

Dollar Rent A Car
Tel: 248-5338 or
800-800-4000

FAIRBANKS:
Allstar Rent-A-Car
Tel: 479-4229

Budget Rent A Car
Tel: 474-0855 or
800-248-0150 (Ak) or
800-527-0700

Avis
Tel: 474-0900

Rent-A-Wreck
Tel: 452-1606

Affordable Car Rental
Tel: 452-1701

JUNEAU:
Allstar Rent-A-Car
Tel: 790-2414 or
800-722-0741

Hertz Rent-A-Car
Tel: 789-9494 or
800-654-3131

Budget Rent A Car
Tel: 789-5186

KETCHIKAN:
Alaska Car Rental
Tel: 225-5000 or
800-662-0007

Avis
Tel: 225-4515

Practical Rent-A-Car
Tel: 225-8778

WRANGELL:
Practical Rent-A-Car
Tel: 874-3975

HAINES:
Eagle's Nest Car Rental
Tel: 800-354-6009

KODIAK:
Budget Rent-A-Car
Tel: 487-2220

Rent A Heap
Tel: 487-4001

KENAI PENINSULA:
Avis- Kenai Airport
Tel: 283-7900

Crazy Gary's- Soldotna
Tel: 262-2999

National Car Rental- Homer
Tel: 235-5515

Allstar Rent-A-Car- Kenai
Tel: 283-5005

BICYCLES
ANCHORAGE:
Anchorage Coastal Bicycle Rentals
414 K St.
Tel: 279-1999

Downtown Bicycle Rental
6th & B
Tel: 279-5293

Saga-Alaskan Bicycle Adventures
2734 Illiamna Ave. Anchorage area day tours
Tel: 243-2329

Sunshine Sports
1231 W. Northern Lights
Tel: 272-6444

FAIRBANKS:
7 Bridges Boats & Bikes
Tel: 479-0751

HAINES:
Sockeye Cycle/Alaska Bicycle Tours
Box 829 Haines
Tel: 99827 766-2869

HOMER:
Quiet Sports
144 W. Pioneer Ave.
Tel: 235-8620

Homer Rental Homer Spit
Tel: 235-2617

SITKA:
J&B Bike Rentals Southeast Diving & Sports
203 Lincoln St.
Tel: 747-8279

CLIMATE & TEMPERATURE
As detailed in the Geography & Climate chapter, temperatures from -80°F – +100°F (-62°C – +38°C) can occur. However, exactly where along that very large spectrum you can expect the temperatures to fall varies by location and season. The Interior is both the hottest region in the state during the summer and the coldest in the winter. The North Slope is cold all year round, although summer temperatures can get into the 60s. The coastal regions of Southeast, Kodiak, and the Aleutians do not get as hot in the summer or as cold in the winter as the landlocked areas, although frequent wind and rain can make them seem colder. The Southcentral region has relatively low precipitation and moderate temperatures, summer daytime temperatures seldom exceeding the 70s°F (180°C), and winter temps not usually colder than +10°F (-12°C).

CUSTOMS REQUIREMENTS
Customs requirements for visitors are lengthy and detailed. Before you pack your belongings for your visit, review the regulations, and direct any questions to your American embassy or consulate, or the appropriate U.S. government office. The publication, "United States Customs Hints for Visitors", number 511-A, summarizes the rules nicely. You can obtain a copy from Department of the Treasury, U.S. Customs Service, Washington, D.C., 20229.

Before entering the country, you will be required to fill out a Customs Declaration form. Personal effects are exempt from any duty costs as long as they are appropriate for your use while visiting. Also, your personal exemption from duty costs includes one liter of alcoholic beverage, 200 cigarettes or 50 cigars, and US$100.00 worth of gift items if you will remain in the country for 72 hours.

If you transport more than US$10,000.00 in "monetary instruments" into or out of the country, you must file form 4790 with the Customs service. Monetary instruments include currency, coin, traveler's checks, money orders, and negotiable instruments or investment securities in bearer form. Transporting large amounts of money is legal as long as the proper forms are filed. Certain animal products cannot be brought into the U.S. due to restrictions on the traffic in endangered species. Some products made from ivory, tortoise shell, coral, reptile skins, and items made from the skins of most spotted cats and all marine mammals are prohibited. For further information, contact TRAFFIC(USA), World Wildlife Fund, 1250 24th St. N.W., Washington D.C. 20037, or the Division of Law Enforcement, U.S. Fish & Wildlife Service, Box 3247, Arlington VA 22203.

Bringing pets into the country presents potential complications, as vaccination and quarantine requirement vary from species to species. Request Customs Publication No. 509 from the U.S. Customs Service for details.

ELECTRICITY

Wall sockets in the U.S. connect to 15 amp, 120 Volt, 60 Hz alternating current. Most modern wall sockets use a three-prong connection, but you may find occasional two-prong outlets. Conversion adapters for foreign-made appliances are available in electronics supply stores. If you are bringing electrical devices to the U.S., it might be easier to find the appropriate adapters in your home country.

GETTING THERE

By Air

The only Alaska airport you can fly into from international locations is Anchorage. Anchorage serves as an airline hub, and from there you can catch jet flights to all the sizeable towns in the state and then take commuter airlines to many of the smaller ones. Outlying cities act as regional hubs, offering scheduled flights in propeller-driven planes to bush villages in the area. Charter service is available to anyplace with a sandbar, river, primitive airstrip, or lake big enough to land a Super Cub.

By Sea

Cruise ship traffic has been increasing steadily, and numerous ships visit port cities in Southeast, Anchorage, Prince William Sound, the Kenai Peninsula, Kodiak, and the Aleutians. Cruises originate in Seattle, Vancouver B.C., and other West Coast port cities. Many of the lines offer cruise/fly packages, taking you to a port city by ship, then flying to Anchorage or Fairbanks. From there, flights, bus trips, and rail connections branch out to various locations. Princess Tours (800-568-3262) and Holland America Line (800-426-0327) offer a variety of travel options.

The Alaska Marine Highway transports passengers and vehicles from Bellingham, Washington and Prince Rupert B.C. to all of the towns in Southeast Alaska. Their ferries also connect the towns in Prince William Sound with one another, with the Kenai Peninsula, Kodiak, and the Aleutians, but not with Southeast. For more information contact them at Box 25535, Juneau 99802, or call 800-642-0066 from the U.S.,or 800-665-6414 from Canada. FAX number is 907-277-4829 for reservations.

By Rail

You cannot get to Alaska by rail, but you can travel within the state by the railroad connecting Seward, Whittier, Anchorage, Denali National Park, and Fairbanks. On "local" runs between Anchorage and Fairbanks, the train will stop and let you off if you want to start a backcountry trip from anywhere along the route. This run provides people in remote communities along the railbelt with access to the cities. To pre-arrange for a drop-off, or for passenger information, contact the Alaska Railroad Corporation at Box 107500, Anchorage 99510, or call 907-265-2494, 800-544-0552, or 907-265-2323 (FAX).

From Skagway, you can take the White Pass and Yukon Route to Fraser B.C., and from there connect by bus to Whitehorse, Yukon. This train also serves as a shuttle for hikers on the Chilkoot Trail. For information, write: White Pass & Yukon Route, Box 435, Skagway AK 99840, or call 800-343-7373 in the U.S., or 907-983-2217 in Skagway.

By Road

There is only one road into Alaska, so the choice of routes is an easy one. The Alaska Highway, (formerly referred to as the Alcan, the Alaska-Canada Highway), has long had a reputation for devouring vehicles due to rough road conditions. Much of the road is now paved, with more paved miles added every year. Any highway vehicle in decent condition should have no trouble making the trip- four-wheel drive and bumper-mounted winches are no longer a necessity. Every year, vehicles ranging in size from motorcycles and sub-compact cars up to the largest motorhomes make the trip without incident.

However, in many places the distances between civilized outposts can be great. A certain amount of self-sufficiency is wise, including a full-sized spare tire, some food and water in case of breakdown, warm clothing, highway flares, etc. Do not travel without a copy of the Milepost, the 'Bible' for road travel along the Alaska Highway and within the state. Call Vernon Publications at 800-726-4707, or write to them at: Vernon Publications, Box 96043, Bellevue WA 98009. Keep an eye on your fuel gauge, and do not try to stretch your miles between fill-ups. Running out of gas is inconvenient, and very avoidable.

Keep your eyes open for wildlife on the highway for two reasons – one, it is always a joy to see wild animals in their natural environment, and two, it is never a joy to hit one with your car. The animal, your vehicle, or both, could be mortally wounded. There have even been human fatalities resulting from collisions with moose and bears- be careful out there!

HEALTH

Medical care is very expensive in the U.S. Before leaving home, arrange for your health care insurance needs. Check with a travel agent experienced in U.S. travel, and keep careful track of the paperwork.

Travelers visiting Alaska should be aware of some aspects of the health care system peculiar to the state. In the cities, the system functions as it does in the Lower 48. Private physicians and dentists serve as independent providers, treating patients covered, for the most part, by health insurance policies. Before providing any service the health care practitioner will want to know how you plan on paying for the care. Proof of insurance or other ability to pay will be required. If a hospital stay is necessary, you must meet the same set of requirements, even for emergency care. In extreme cases, where life and death hang in the balance, care will be given and discussion of the financial aspects will be delayed, but not for long.

Away from the larger cities, a different sort of system prevails. In the larger towns and villages such as Nome, Kotzebue, Barrow, Dillingham, Bethel, etc., the hospitals are run by the Native Health Service, an agency of the federal government. The physicians work for the government and provide health care to Alaska Natives free of charge. However, since they are the only health care facilities in the area, they will also treat non- Natives. However, this care must be paid for, again by your own health insurance or in cash. Alternatives for care simply do not exist in most of these communities.

In the smaller villages, no health care facilities exist. Many villages use the services of a local resident serving as a Health Aide, but their training does not prepare them for complex health care situations. Often they can establish radio or telephone contact with a physician at the nearest Native Health hospital, but this is far from an ideal situation.

If you are struck by a medical emergency away from the road system, you are really on your own. If you break a leg or suffer an attack of appendicitis, you cannot just pick up a phone and call an ambulance when you are deep in the Brooks Range. Rescue by aircraft is hard to arrange, not to mention very expensive. Be careful, and do not do anything reckless or dangerous in the backcountry. Or anywhere else, for that matter.

Before leaving home, make sure you are in good health, and carry any necessary prescription drugs with you. Also, you should be aware that many drugs sold over the counter in other countries are sold only by a physician's prescription in the U.S. If you depend on any such medications at home, be advised that they may not be available for purchase here. No amount of pleading on your part will persuade a pharmacist to dispense drugs without the proper prescription.

A common ailment among travelers in Alaska is giardiasis. This ailment is contracted by drinking untreated water from streams and lakes. Too often, people think that since the Alaskan wilderness looks so pristine that all the water is safe to drink. Not so. Giardia is a waterborne parasite passed along through human and animal wastes, and the symptoms can be debilitating. All surface water should be treated by filtration, chemical means, or by boiling. Water should be boiled for at least five minutes before drinking. Filters to remove giardia organisms from the water are sold at camping and sporting good stores. Hepatitis is a recurring problem in some villages, so a filter that removes viruses should be considered if you are spending time in the Bush. Should anyone in your party ingest a poisonous substance, or take an overdose of a drug, the state-wide Poison Control Center number is 800-478-3193.

HOLIDAYS

National holidays include; New Years Day, (January 1), Martin Luther King Jr.'s Birthday (Monday closest to January 15), President's Day (Monday closest to February 22), Memorial Day, (May 30),

Independence Day, (July 4), Labor Day, (First Monday in September), Columbus Day, (Monday closest to October 12), Veteran's Day, (November 11), Thanksgiving Day, (Fourth Thursday in November), and Christmas Day, (December 25). Government offices and banks close on all of those days, and many retail businesses close on many of them, depending on the nature of the business and the nature of the holiday.

MEDIA – RADIO AND TELEVISION

The larger the city, the more media outlets you will find. Anchorage has numerous AM and FM radio stations, and TV stations representing all of the U.S. networks. In addition, many parts of the city are wired for cable TV. As the towns become smaller, so do the media opportunities. Most villages receive one TV station, RATNET (Rural Alaska Television Network), a service operated by the state. Most can also receive at least one radio station as well.

MONEY

Foreign currency will not be accepted for payment. Currency exchange should be taken care of before leaving Anchorage. Thomas Cook Foreign Exchange (907-278-2822) has an office in the Anchorage Hilton at 500 W. 3rd. Ave. Traveler's checks payable in U.S. dollars are accepted in many places, as are major credit cards such as MasterCard, Visa, and American Express. However, once you venture away from the tourist centers and into small towns and villages, it's likely that only cold, hard American cash will be accepted.

There is no state sales tax added to the prices of goods, but some towns levy local taxes on items purchased. This price will not appear on the price tags, so if you are unsure about local practices, ask about sales taxes.

PASSPORTS & VISAS

Visitors from foreign countries must inquire at the American embassy or consulate in their home countries concerning passport and visa requirements for visiting the U.S. When contacting these officials, ask questions about the process and have everything explained to you in detail if you are at all uncertain about the facts. International travel is usually not complicated, but also not to be undertaken with the same blithe spirit under which you travel within your home country. Mistakes happen, misunderstandings can occur, assumptions prove to be unfounded in reality, and the consequences of these problems can ruin your trip.

Do not put off applications for passports and visas until the last minute. Paperwork takes time, bureaucracies have been known to operate at glacial speeds, and unforeseen glitches can slow the process down even more than usual. As soon as you know where you want to go, start the process in motion.

Citizens of some countries, mostly European nations and Japan, can enter the U.S. for 90 days without a visa under the visa waiver plan. However, in doing so you waive all rights to due process while you remain in the country- if you fall afoul of the law or immigration authorities for any reason, you can be summarily deported without recourse to a hearing of any kind. Waiving the visa requirement may simplify your paperwork, but be advised that by doing so, you relinquish all rights normally afforded immigrants and tourists.

Upon entering the country, foreign nationals are supplied with a landing permit granting permission to stay in the country for 6 months. During that time, they may visit countries contiguous to the U.S., (Canada and Mexico), for periods of less than 30 days and re-enter without penalty. Extensions of the 6 month limit are possible, but difficult to obtain- you need a real good reason to be on vacation for more than 6 months at a time.

PHOTOGRAPHY

Figure out a reasonable amount of film for your camera, then double it. Buy large quantities of the film you like before leaving home, or shop for it in Anchorage, Juneau or Fairbanks. Once you get away from the cities, the only kind of film you are likely to find is Kodak color print film, and it will be far from cheap. Be prepared! Likewise, video tape and batteries are best purchased in quantity before you leave home or in the cities. You probably will not need fast film- if you visit in the summer, chances are you will never see anything resembling night time. Traveling into the mountains means you can encounter snow and glare, and sunlight reflecting off the water can be brutal, so come prepared with the appropriate filters.

POSTAL SERVICES

City post offices are usually open from 10:00 A.M. until 5:00 P.M. Village hours may vary. In Anchorage, the main office near the airport at

4141 Postmark Dr. is open 24 hours a day.

PRIVATE TRANSPORT:

Because so many tourists arrive in Alaska by plane and ship, car rental service is in much demand. All of the national chains are well-represented in the cities, as are several smaller franchises and some independent outfits. Standard late-model sedans are available, and quite a few companies also offer specialized vehicles appropriate to Alaska's terrain and the needs of adventurous travelers. Large capacity vans capable of carrying lots of people and mountains of camping gear are widely available, as are station wagons, four-wheel drive vehicles, mini-vans, and even motor homes. Quite a few companies offer older model cars at reduced rates.

The car rental business is very competitive, and rates vary considerably between companies. Before signing an agreement to rent a vehicle, check around and compare prices.

One wrinkle in the rental business is the "unlimited free mileage" option. Some companies quote a daily or weekly rate that covers a certain number of miles per day allowed. Any miles over that total have to be paid for at a set rate, usually 10 or 15 cents per mile. Unless you are sure you will be doing your driving in town, or only traveling between two points of a known distance, be very careful before agreeing to this sort of arrangement. Alaska is a huge state, and points of interest are separated by long stretches of highway. Once you exceed the daily mileage allowance, racking up miles at 15 cents each gets very expensive fairly quickly. The rates quoted with unlimited mileage allowed will usually be a bit higher than those including a pre-set number of miles, but in the long run it can save money. Check the distances you intend to travel, adding a certain amount for unplanned side trips, before agreeing to a contract.

Before hitting the road, check over the vehicle and make sure that the owner's manual and spare tire and jack are aboard. If at all possible, try to arrange for a real spare tire- those cheesy little space-saver spares do not hold up well to some of the rougher roads you may encounter along the way.

Most companies require a major credit card before they will rent a car to you. If you do not carry one, check with the company beforehand to see if they will accept a cash deposit instead. Because there is such as demand for rental cars, reserve a vehicle before you get here. Demand is high, and although you can usually find something to rent at the last minute, it may not be the vehicle best suited to you. You will wind up paying more than if you had checked out the competition ahead of time and compared rates and services.

Check out your car insurance policy before leaving home, and if necessary ask your agent if you need to purchase additional insurance when you rent a car. Insurance charges can jack up the price of a rental agreement, and there is no sense paying for it if you are already covered. On the other hand, if your own policy does not cover you, you are taking a real chance and exposing yourself unnecessarily to considerable liability if you drive uninsured.

PUBLIC TRANSPORT

Anchorage, Fairbanks, and Juneau operate municipal bus systems. For route and schedule information call:

ANCHORAGE
Tel: 343-6543

FAIRBANKS
Tel: 459-1011

JUNEAU
Tel: 789-6901

The following bus lines operate scheduled service between Alaska cities:

Seward Bus Lines – serving Homer, Seward, Kenai, Soldotna, Anchorage, and points in between. Call 278-0800
Caribou Express – serving Anchorage, Fairbanks, Valdez, Denali, Homer, Seward, Whittier, Tok, Talkeetna, and points in between. Call 278-5776
Moon Bay Express – service between Anchorage and Denali National Park. Call 274-6454
Alaskan Express – service to Skagway, Haines, Tok, Fairbanks, Anchorage, Valdez, Whitehorse, Seward, Whittier, Beaver Creek, and points in between. Call 277-5581.
Alaska Direct Bus Line – Anchorage, Fairbanks, Whitehorse, Skagway, Haines, and points in between. Call 277-6652.

TELEPHONE

Telephone service is available in all but a few of the very tiniest and most remote villages. Public phones are widely available for local, long distance, and international calls. All of Alaska is covered by the 907 area code. Detailed instructions for making international calls are printed in the front of the telephone books. If you have any questions, or the instructions are unclear, dial '0' for operator assistance. No charge is made for dialing the operator from pay phones.

In case of emergency, dial 911 from any pay phone, no payment required. This service connects you to an operator who can dispatch police, fire, and ambulance service.

TAXI SERVICES
ANCHORAGE:
Anchorage Taxicab
Tel: 278-8000

Yellow Cab
Tel: 272-2422

Alaska Cab
Tel: 563-5353

FAIRBANKS:
Alaska Cab
Tel: 456-3355

Fairbanks Taxi
Tel: 452-3555

United Cab
Tel: 451-0001

JUNEAU:
Taku Glacier Cab
Tel: 586-2121

Capital Cab
Tel: 586-2772

KETCHIKAN:
Alaska Cab
Tel: 225-3133

Sourdough Cab
Tel: 225-5544

KODIAK:
AAA Ace Mecca Taxi
Tel: 486-3211

A&B Taxi
Tel: 486-4343

TIME ZONES
Except for the islands near the end of the Aleutian chain, the state is on Alaska-Yukon time, one hour behind Pacific (West coast) time and four hours behind Eastern time. In the summer, the state switches to Daylight Saving Time, (although it hardly seems necessary) with the rest of the country.

TIPPING
In restaurants providing good service, 15 percent of the total bill is the normal tip, 20 percent for very good service. If your waiter or waitress ignores your needs, makes too many mistakes on the order, or gets snotty with you, feel free to leave nothing. Providing tips for bad service only encourages more of the same.

Skycaps helping with luggage at airports expect US$1.00 or US$2.00 per bag. If you are on a package tour, a commensurate fee for the kid muscling those mounds of bags is also a nice thought. A five dollar tip for an especially attentive and cheerful tour guide is generous, but not required. Taxi drivers usually receive 15 percent of the fare, with a bit more for helpfulness or cheerfulness beyond the call of duty.

If you go on a fishing charter, a five or ten dollar tip for the skipper is appropriate, if he does not own the boat. A rule of thumb in America is that you do not tip owners, whether it is a charter boat, barber shop, or hairdresser. Crew members appreciate five or ten bucks after a full day, especially if they clean your catch as part of the charge for the trip. Again, do not feel obligated to reward sub-standard service.

TOURS
Tours of every imaginable configuration are widely available in Alaska, from short one-hour drives around town to major expeditions into the most remote backcountry locations. Towns on the water provide the opportunity to take a short sightseeing cruise, go fishing for a half-day or full day trip, or charter a boat for as long as your heart, and pocketbook, desires.

Flightseeing is a great way to look over large pieces of Alaska in a fairly short time. Pilots provide trips in helicopters or fixed-wing aircraft of varying sizes, usually adding commentary and local knowledge as you fly. Prices vary according to time aloft, number of passengers, and size of the aircraft.

WEIGHTS & MEASURES

The United States is one of the few countries in the civilized world that has not embraced the metric system. Although some highway mileages will be given in kilometers, and the speedometers of American cars are marked in kilometers as well as miles per hour, no one here pays much attention to these things.

Some of the most frequently used weights and measures are:

Multiply	By	To obtain
Acres	4047	Square meters
Centimeters	0.3937	Inches
Feet	0.3048	Meters
Gallons	3.785	Liters
Gallons	4	Quarts (liq.)
Inches	2.54	Centimeters
Kilograms	2.2046	Pounds
Kilometers	3,281	Feet
Kilometers	0.6214	Miles
Miles	1.6093	Kilometers
Miles	5,280	Feet
Ounces	28.35	Grams
Pounds	453.6	Grams
Pounds	16	Ounces
Square miles	640	Acres
Square miles	2.59	Square kilometers
Temp. (degs. C)	+17.8	1.8 Degrees F
Temp. (degs. F)	-32	5/9 Degrees C

WHAT TO WEAR

Informality is the ticket in Alaska. Besides some of the more expensive restaurants in Anchorage and Juneau, coats and ties for gentlemen and dresses for ladies are not required. Once you get away from the cities, hiking boots, jeans, and t-shirts are far more common than sport coats.

For comfort, bring clothing that will keep you warm and dry. A good Gore-Tex parka is one of the most utilitarian garments you can bring along. It will keep you dry in rainy weather, keep the spray off if you are aboard a boat, serves as an excellent windbreaker, and can be worn around town for shopping, and to all but the snootiest eating establishments. For travel into the backcountry a pair of rain pants will help keep you dry.

Synthetic fabrics such as polypropylene long underwear, polyester fleece jackets, hats and mittens, and poly/cotton or light wool blend pants and shirts will keep you comfortable in all but the most extreme situations. Dress in layers so you can juggle garments to adapt to the very changeable weather.

Comfortable footwear is essential, and for "civilized" pursuits, sneakers or walking shoes are ideal. For hiking, waterproof boots work best, lightweight trail boots will suffice unless you carry a backpack. Winter visits require insulated boots, and heavier-duty outerwear.

DIRECTORY

ACCOMMODATIONS
Travelers may have to adjust their expectations when it comes to accommodations in Alaska. While there are a few truly deluxe establishments here and there, for the most part the rooms lean more toward the basic than the palatial. Most of the places are clean and secure, and as long as you are not expecting world-class, gold plated digs, you probably would not be disappointed. On the "budget" end of the scale, however, things can be, shall we say, rustic.

ANCHORAGE:
Expensive
Regal Alaskan Hotel
4800 Spenard Rd.
Anchorage 99517
Tel: 243-2000 or
    800-544-0533

Hotel Captain Cook
5th & K
Anchorage 99501
Tel: 276-6000 or
    800-478-3100 (in AK)

The Hilton
500 W. 3rd Ave.
Anchorage 99501
Tel: 272-7411 or
    800-445-8667

Sheraton Anchorage Hotel
401 E. 6th Ave.
Anchorage 99501
Tel: 276-8700

Moderate
Days Inn
321 E. 5th Ave.
Anchorage 99501
Tel: 276-7226 or
    800-325-2525

Ramada Northern Lights Inn
598 W. Northern Lights
Anchorage 99503
Tel: 561-5200 or
    800-235-6546

Puffin Inn
4400 Spenard Rd.
Anchorage 99517
Tel: 243-4044 or
    800-478-3346 (in AK)
Fax: 907-248-6853

Budget
Kobuk Motel
1104 E. 5th Ave.
Anchorage 99501
Tel: 274-1650

Alaska Budget Motel
545 E. 4th Ave.
Anchorage 99501
Tel: 277-0088
Fax: 277-1517

Thrift Motel
606 W. Northern Lights
Anchorage 99503
Tel: 561-3005

FAIRBANKS:
Expensive
Fairbanks Princess Hotel
4477 Pikes Landing Rd.
Fairbanks 99709
Tel: 455-4477
Fax: 455-4476

Westmark Fairbanks Hotel
813 Noble St.
Fairbanks 99701
Tel: 456-7722

Moderate
Super 8 Motel
1909 Airport Way
Fairbanks 99709
Tel: 451-8888 or
    800-800-8000

Alaskan Motor Inn
419 4th Ave.
Fairbanks 99701
Tel: 452-4800

Klondike Inn
1316 Bedrock St.
Fairbanks 99709
Tel: 479-6241
Fax: 479-6254

Budget
Noah's Rainbow Inn
700 Fairbanks St.
Fairbanks 99709
Tel: 474-3666

Monson Motel
1321 Karen Way
Fairbanks 99709
Tel: 479-6770

JUNEAU:
(Zip 99801)
Expensive
Westmark
Juneau 51 W. Egan Dr.
Tel: 586-6900 or
    800-544-0970
Fax: 907-463-3567

Baranof Hotel
127 N. Franklin St.
Tel: 586-2660 or
    800-544-0970
Fax: 586-8315

Moderate
Breakwater Inn
1711 Glacier Ave.
Tel: 586-6303 or
    800-544-2250
Fax: 463-4820

The Prospector Hotel
375 Whittier St.
Tel: 586-3737
Fax: 586-1204

Silverbow Inn
120 2nd St.
Tel: 586-4146
Fax: 586-4242

Budget
Inn at the Waterfront
455 S. Franklin St.
Tel: 586-2050
Fax: 586-2999

Driftwood Lodge
435 Willoughby Ave.
Tel: 586-2280 or
    800-544-2239
Fax: 586-1034

The Alaskan Hotel & Bar
176 S. Franklin St.
Tel: 586-1000 or
    800-327-9347
Fax: 463-3775

KENAI PENINSULA:
Expensive
Kenai Princess Lodge
Cooper Landing 99572
For information write:

Princess Tours
2815 2nd Ave.
Seattle WA 98121
Tel: 800-426-0500

Soldotna Inn
35041 Kenai Spur Highway
Soldotna 99669
Tel: 262-9169

**Best Western
Bidarka Inn**
575 Sterling Hwy.
Homer 99603
Tel: 235-8148

Moderate
Vinton's Alpine Inn Motel
Box 801
Cooper Landing 99572
Tel: 595-1212
Fax: 595-1227

Merit Inn
206 S. Willow St.
Kenai 99611
Tel: 283-6131

Van Gilder Hotel
308 Adams St.
Seward 99664
Tel: 224-3079

Budget
Anchor River Inn
Milepost 157, Sterling Highway
Anchor Point
Tel: 235-8531

North Star Lodge & Restaurant
54656 Industrial Ave. North
Kenai
Tel: 776-5259

Tustumena Lodge Mile
111 Sterling Highway
Kasilof 99610
Tel: 262-4216

The Place Mile
17.5 Kenai Spur Highway
Kenai 99611
Tel: 283-9915

AIRLINES
The following domestic airlines provide service to Alaska airports from the Lower 48. Letters in parentheses indicate Anchorage, Fairbanks, Juneau, and Kodiak.

Alaska Airlines
Tel: 800-426-0333 (A, F, J)

Continental Airlines
Tel: 800-525-0280 (A)

Delta Airlines
Tel: 800-221-1212 (A, F, J)

MarkAir
Tel: 800-478-0800 (A, F, J, K)

Morris Air
Tel: 800-444-5660 (A)

Northwest Airlines
Tel: 800-225-2525 (A)

United Airlines
Tel: 800-241-6522 (A, F)

**FROM HAWAII:
Hawaiian Airlines**
Tel: 800-367-5320

Scheduled intrastate service through Anchorage is provided by:

ERA Aviation
Tel: 800-426-0333

PenAir
Tel: 800-448-4226 or
907-243-2323

Reeve Aleutian Airways
Tel: 907-243-4700

FAIRBANKS:
Wright Air
Tel: 474-0502

Larry's Flying Service
Tel: 474-9169

Warbelow's Air Ventures
Tel: 474-0518

KENAI PENINSULA:
ERA Aviation-Homer
Tel: 235-5205

Kenai
Tel: 283-3168

Southcentral Air-Kenai
Tel: 283-7676

KETCHIKAN:
Ketchikan Air Service
Tel: 225-6608

Taquan Air
Tel: 225-8800

KODIAK:
Penair
Tel: 487-4014

ERA Aviation
Tel: 487-4363

MarkAir
Tel: 487-9798 or
800-627-5247

JUNEAU:
ERA Aviation
Tel: 586-2030

Wings of Alaska
Tel: 789-9863

Foreign carriers providing passenger service to Anchorage:

Aeroflot
Tel: 907-248-8400

China Airlines
Tel: 800-227-5118 or
907-248-3603

Korean Air
Tel: 907-243-3329

BANKS
National Bank of Alaska (NBA) is the bank most widely represented in towns large and small across the state. Banks based in the Lower 48 with branches or franchises in Alaska include Bank of America, Key Bank of Alaska, and First Interstate Bank of Alaska.

CAMPGROUNDS
Scenic View RV Park
P.O. Box 202553-VG,
Anchorage, AK 99520-2553
Tel: 907-349-7410
907-567-3909

Land's End RV Park
P.O. Box 273-VG,
Homer, AK 99603-0273
(4799 Homer Spit Rd)
Tel: 907-235-2525
Fax: 907-235-6695

Ocean View RV Park
1901 Commodore Dr-VG,
Anchorage, AK 99520-2553
Tel: 907-349-7410
907-567-3909

Campgrounds & Services
P.O. Box 2408669-VG,
Anchorage, AK 99524-0866

CINEMA
First run movie theaters are available in Anchorage, Fairbanks, Juneau, Ketchikan, on the Kenai, and Kodiak.

ANCHORAGE:
Fireweed Cinemas Fireweed and Gambell Sts.
Tel: 275-3139

Totem Cinemas
3131 Muldoon Rd.
Tel: 275-3188

Denali Theater
4230 W. 27th Ave.
Tel: 275-3106

FAIRBANKS:
Goldstream Cinemas
1855 Airport Way
Tel: 456-5113

JUNEAU:
20th Century Twin Theater
222 Front St.
Tel: 463-3549

KETCHIKAN:
Coliseum Twin Theater
405 Mission St.
Tel: 225-2294

KODIAK:
Orpheum Theater
102 Center St.
Tel: 486-5449

KENAI PENINSULA:
Homer Family Theater Main & Pioneer
Tel: 235-6728

Liberty Theater
305 Adams St. Seward
Tel: 224-5418

Orca Theater Red Diamond Center,
Soldotna
Tel: 262-7003

CONSULATES
ANCHORAGE:
Consulate General of Japan
550 W. 7th Ave.
Tel: 279-8428

Consulate of Finland
550 W. 64th Ave.
Tel: 562-3326

Consulate of France
501 W. Northern Lights
Tel: 278-3535

German Consul- Honorary
425 G St.
Tel: 274-6537

Korean Consulate General
101 W. Benson Blvd.
Tel: 561-5488

Norway Vice Consul
203 W. 15th Ave.
Tel: 279-6942

COURIER SERVICE
Federal Express:
Tel: 800-238-5255 (A, F, J)

United Parcel Service
Tel: 800-222-8333 (A, F, J)

DHL Worldwide Express
Tel: 800-345-2727 or
     907-243-1503 (A)
     907-474-0707 (F)

DEPARTMENT STORES
ANCHORAGE:
Sears Roebuck & Co.
700 E. Northern Lights Blvd.
Tel: 279-4442

JC Penney Co.
5th & D Sts.
Tel: 279-5656

Fred Meyer One Stop Shopping
1000 E. Northern Lights Blvd.
Tel: 264-9600 or
2000 W. Dimond Blvd.
Tel: 267-6700

Nordstrom's Apparel & Shoes
603 D St.
Tel: 279-7622

FAIRBANKS:
JC Penney
610 Cushman
Tel: 452-5131

Fred Meyer
19 College Rd.
Tel: 459-4200

Lamont's
1255 Airport Way
Tel: 456-2550

JUNEAU:
JC Penney
9105 Mendenhall Mall Rd.
Tel: 790-2610

Lamont's
8745 Glacier Highway
Tel: 789-2243

Fred Meyer's
8181 Old Glacier Highway
Tel: 789-6523

KETCHIKAN:
Bon Marche
2417 Tongass
Tel: 225-2165

Tongass Trading Co.
201 Dock St.
Tel: 225-5101

KODIAK:
Kraft's Department Store
111 Rezanof Dr.
Tel: 486-5761

KENAI PENINSULA:
K-Mart
10480 Spur Highway,
Kenai
Tel: 283-7616

Lamont's
35249 Spur Highway,
Soldotna
Tel: 262-7000

Sears Roebuck & Co.
44455 Sterling Highway,
Soldotna
Tel: 262-5841

HIKING
Crow Pass Trail
25 mile (40 km), formerly a part of Iditarod Trail, access at Eagle River Visitor Information Center, 12 mile (19.2 km) Eagle River Rd, Eagle River or Crow Creek Rd, Girdwood. Eagle and Raven glaciers viewable from trail.

Arctic to Indian territory
A 22 mile (35 km) trail, accessible from Arctic Valley. Height: 1,000 ft (300 m) to Indian Creek Pass. Wildlife & Nordic skiing available.

Twin Peaks
5 mile (8 km); accessible from Eklutna Campground. Great view of Eklutna Lake. Climb is steep.

River Trail
3 mile (4.8 km) round trip. Accessible from Chugach State Park through glacial river

FISHING FACILITIES
Fishing seasons of the years:
King Salmon: January-May
Halibut, Rainbow & Lake Trout, Dolly Varden, Grayling: (Year-round)
Cod: May-Oct
Red Salmon: June-July
Pink & Chum Salmon: July- August
Silver Salmon: July-November
Steelhead: Sept-Nov

ANCHORAGE FISHING CHARTERS
Alaska Fishing Expenses
6311 DeBarr Road, #102-VG,
Anchorage, AK 99504-1799
Tel: 907-346-1018

Rust's Fishing Service, Inc.
P.O. Box 190325-VG,
Anchorage, AK 99519-0325
Tel: 907-243-1595
Fax: 907-248-0552

GUIDES
Alaska River Adventures
1831 Kuskokurim St,
Ste D-VG,
Anchorage, AK 99508-3229
Tel: 907-276-3418
Fax: 907-272-9839

Chassalaska
P.O. Box 10-2326-VG,
Anchorage, AK 99510-2326
Tel: 907-563-6293
Fax: 907-345-9599

MAT-SU FISHING CHARTERS
Gabbert's Fish Camp
Alexander Creek
P.O. Box ACR-VG
Anchorage, AK 99695-0020
Tel: 907-733-2371

PWS FISHING CHARTERS
Choice Marine Charters
P.O. Box 200592-VG,
Anchorage, AK 99520-0592
Tel: 907-243-0069

Natchik Customs Charters
P.O. Box 3243-VG,
Valdez, AK 99686-3243
Tel: 907-835-5042
Fax: 907-835-4845

SEWARD FISHING CHARTERS
Admiral Halibut Charters
11437 Echo St-VG,
Eagle River, AK 99577-7865
Tel: 907-694-4940

Artic Wilderness Charters, Inc.
9760 Old Seward Hwy-VG,
Anchorage, AK 99515-2189
Tel: 907-344-2845
Fax: 907-348-9683

Save & MArie's Excellent Adventures
1730 Commodore Dr-VG,
Anchorage, AK 99507-4513
Tel: 907-344-9468

GUIDES
Alaskan Fishing Adventures
2498 Trower Ave-VG,
Napa, CA 94558
Tel: 707-257-8092

KENAI/SOLDOTNA FISHING CHARTERS
Anglers Lodge & Fish Camp
P.O. Box 508-VG,
Sterling, AK 99672-0508
Tel: 907-262-1747

Alaska Wildland Adventures
P.O. Box 389-VG,
Girdwood, AK 99587-0389
(Milepost 50.1 Sterling Highway)
Tel: 907-595-1279
Fax: 907-595-1428

GUIDES
Alaska Wildland Adventures
P.O. Box 389-VG,
Girdwood, AK 99587-0389
(Milepost 50.1 Sterling Hwy)
Tel: 907-595-1279
Fax: 907-595-1428

Bo's Fishing Guide Service
P.O. Box 1728-VG,
Soldotna, AK 99669-1728
Tel: 907-262-5154

HOMER FISHING CHARTERS
A & A Fishing Charters
P.O. Box 1487-VG,
Homer, AK 99663-1487
Tel: 907-235-2524

Alaska Fishing Charters
P.O. Box 2807-VG,
Homer, AK 99603-2807
Tel: 907-235-6468

Aurora Sportfishing
P.O. Box 2824-VG,
Homer, AK 99603
Tel: 907-235-7765

GUIDES
Viking Brothers Halibut Charters
P.O. Box 3056-VG,
Homer, AK 99603-3056
Tel: 907-235-6155

OTHER AREAS
Kodiak Western Charters
P.O. Box 4123-VG,
Kodiak, AK 99615-4123
Tel: 907-486-2200
Fax: 907-486-4084

GUIDES
Sport Fishing Alaska
1401 Shore Dr-VG,
Anchorage, AK 99515-3206
Tel: 907-344-8674
Fax: 907-349-4330

GOLD PANNING
ANCHORAGE
Crow Creek Mine
P.O. Box 113-VG,
Girdwood, AK 99587-0113
(Mile 3.1 Crow Creek Rd)
Tel: 907-278-8060

Indian Valley Mine
6470 Village Pkey-VG,
Anchorage, AK 99504-3903
Tel: 907-337-7749
    907-653-1120

MAT-SU
Thirsty Creek Outfitter, Ltd
2609 Arctic Blvd-VG,
Anchorage, AK 99503-2517
Tel: 907-279-1934

GOVERNMENT OFFICES
Extensive listings of government offices are given in the front of local telephone directories. These pages are usually highlighted or edged in blue. Separate listings are given to local municipal, state, and federal government offices.

HOSPITALS
Alaska Regional Hospital
2801 DeBarr Rd.
Anchorage
Tel: 276-1131

Alaska Native Medical Center
255 Gambell Rd.
Anchorage
Tel: 279-6661

Providence Hospital
3200 Providence Dr.
Anchorage
Tel: 562-2211

Fairbanks Memorial Hospital
1650 Cowles
Fairbanks
Tel: 452-8181

Valley Hospital
515 E. Dahlia Palmer
Tel: 745-4813

Bartlett Memorial Hospital
3260 Hospital Dr.,
Juneau
Tel: 586-2611

Ketchikan General Hospital
3100 Tongass
Tel: 225-5171

Kodiak Island Hospital
1915 E. Rezanof Dr.
Tel: 486-3281

Central Peninsula General Hospital
250 Hospital Pl.,
Soldotna
Tel: 262-4404

Seward General Hospital
417 1st Ave.,
Seward
Tel: 224-5205

South Peninsula Hospital
4300 Bartlett St.,
Homer
Tel: 235-8101

LIBRARIES
Z.J. Loussac Library
3600 Denali St.
Anchorage
Tel: 261-2975

UAA Consortium Library
3211 Providence Dr.
Anchorage
Tel: 786-1871

Noel Wein Public Library
1215 Cowles St.,
Fairbanks
Tel: 459-1020

Juneau Public Library
392 Marine Way,
Juneau
Tel: 586-5324

Douglas Public Library
1016 3rd St.,
Douglas
Tel: 364-2378

Mendenhall Public Library
Mendenhall Mall,
Juneau
Tel: 789-0215

Ketchikan Library
629 Dock St.,
Ketchikan
Tel: 225-3331

Kodiak Public Library
319 Lower Mill Bay Rd.,
Kodiak
Tel: 486-8686

MUSEUMS
Anchorage Museum of History & Art
121 W. 7th Ave.
Anchorage 99501
Tel: 343-6173
    (recorded message)
    343-4326
Fax: 343-6149

Alaska State Museum
395 Whittier St.
Juneau 99801
Tel: 465-2901
Fax: 465-2976

Alaska Natural History Association
250 Cushman St.
Fairbanks 99701
Tel: 451-7352
Fax: 452-7286

Juneau Douglas City Museum
155 S. Seward
Juneau 99801
Tel: 586-3572

Oscar Anderson House Museum
420 M St.
Anchorage 99501
Tel: 274-2336
Fax: 274-3600

Alaska Aviation Heritage Museum
4721 Aircraft Dr.
Anchorage 99502
Tel: 248-5325

Sheldon Jackson Museum
104 College Dr.
Sitka 99835
Tel: 747-8981
Fax: 747-3004

University of Alaska Museum
907 Yukon Dr. UAF Campus
Fairbanks 99775
Tel: 474-7505

Tongass Historical Museum
629 Dock St.
Ketchikan 99901
Tel: 225-5600
Fax: 225-5602

Valdez Museum
Box 8
Valdez 99686
Tel: 835-2764
Fax: 835-4597

NIGHTSPOTS
SOUTHEAST:
Sourdough Bar & Liquor Store
301 Front St. Ketchikan
Tel: 225-2217

Bar, CD juke box, video games, and large collection of historical Ketchikan photographs.

Jeremiah's
(In the Best Western Landing Hotel)
3434 Tongass Ave.
Tel: 225-6530

Quiet lounge, across from the ferry terminal.

Totem Bar
314 Front St.
Tel: 225-9521

Advertises the friendliest bartenders in town.

Arctic Bar & Liquor Store
509 Water St.
Tel: 225-4709

Great view of the harbor from the patio.

JUNEAU:
Gold Nugget Revue Thane Ore House
4400 Thane Rd.
Tel: 586-1463

Cancan dancers, musical revue, all-you-can-eat salmon, halibut, and beef ribs buffet, beer and wine.

Red Dog Saloon
278 S. Franklin St.
Tel: 463-3658

Live entertainment, sawdust floors, raucous party atmosphere.

Lady Lou Revue Merchant's Wharf Mall
Tel: 586-3686

Musical revue based on the work of Robert Service, presented by the Perseverance Theatre. Performance times vary according to cruise ship arrivals- call for details.

SKAGWAY:
The Red Onion Saloon
Broadway at 2nd

Ragtime piano, occasional local bands, pizza and sandwiches, more tourist than local.

Moe's Frontier Bar Broadway
between 4th & 5th

Calls itself "Skagway's oldest operating bar", more local than tourist.

FAIRBANKS & THE INTERIOR
The Pump House
796 Chena Pump Rd.
Tel: 479-8452

Great bar, karaoke, large selection of beers from breweries large and small, entertainment, and if you work up an appetite, an excellent restaurant.

Malemute Saloon Mile
351.7 Parks Highway Ester
Tel: 479-2500
       1-800-676-6925

Music, dancing, readings of Robert Service poetry.

Howling Dog Saloon Mill
11 Old Steese Highway
Tel: 457-8780

Live rock and roll, rowdy atmosphere.

ANCHORAGE:
Chilkoot Charlie's
2435 Spenard Rd.
Tel: 272-1010

No trip through Anchorage's nightlife is complete without a trip to 'Koot's. Live music, dancing, party atmosphere, and their motto is, "We cheat the other guy and pass the savings on to you."

The Fly-By-Night Club
3300 Spenard Rd.
Tel: 279-7726

Another must-see on the Anchorage scene. Mr. Whitekeys troupe of performers puts on a show advertised as "Hilarious, outrageous, tasteless". Live entertainment at its best, along with an outstanding menu of beers and concoctions featuring Spam.

Gaslight Lounge
721 W. 4th Ave.
Tel: 277-0722

Live music and dancing.

The Pines Club
2421 E. Tudor Rd.
Tel: 563-0001

Live country-rock music, dancing, and restaurant.

Keyboard Lounge
938 W. 4th Ave.
Tel: 276-8131

Live music and dancing.

Anchorage recently began to follow Seattle's lead with a proliferation of coffee houses and espresso joints. Stands and storefronts offer a variety of coffee-based drinks, and a couple of houses feature live entertainment. For example:

Adventures & Delights
414 K St.
Tel: 276-8282

Coffee, pastries, live entertainment on week-ends.

The Java Joint
2911 Spenard Rd.
Tel: 562-5555

Late night gathering place, live entertainment.

Mea Culpa
229 W. Fireweed Lane
Tel: 272-3492

Week-end live entertainment.

South of Anchorage:
The Bird House bar Mile 100.5
Seward Highway

Look for the almost sunken structure on the east side of the road with the huge blue bird peering out. Stop in for a beer, and a visit to a true local landmark. You won't regret it!

KENAI PENINSULA:
Salty Dawg Saloon Homer Spit
Homer

Don't pass up the chance to stop in here for a drink. The place just drips with local color.

Wheelhouse Lounge Land's End Resort End of the Spit Homer
Tel: 235-2500

The bar at the end of the road.

RESTAURANTS
SOUTHEAST:
Alaskan Harvest
320 Seward St.
Sitka 99835
Tel: 907-747-6867
    1-800-824-6389

Fresh and frozen wild Alaskan seafood.

Westmark Shee Atika Hotel
Crescent Harbor overlooking Sitka Sound
Sitka 99835
Tel: 907-747-6241

Fine dining, cocktails

Ginny's Kitchen
236 Lincoln
Sitka
Tel: 907-747-8028

Light lunches, gourmet coffees, homemade pies, desserts.

Silver Lining Seafoods
Box 6092
Ketchikan 99901
Tel: 907-225-9865

Locally caught seafood, fresh, frozen or smoked.

Dejon Delights At Ft. Seward
Box 712
Haines 99826
Tel: 907-766-2505

Smoked salmon, gourmet travel provisions

Hotel Halsingland Ft.
Seward
Haines 99827
Tel: 907-766-2000

Seafood restaurant, salmon bake, lounge.

Ft. Seward Lodge Mile 0,
Haines Highway
Box 307
Haines 99827
Tel: 907-766-2009

Prime rib, all-you-can-eat crab dinners, large deck with panoramic views.

Fiddlehead Restaurant & Bakery
429 West Willoughby Ave.
Juneau 99801
Tel: 907-586-3150

Alaska cuisine, view of Mt. Juneau, live entertainment.

Gold Creek Salmon Bake
9085 Glacier Hwy., Ste. 204 Juneau 99801
Tel: 907-789-0052

Heritage Coffee Co. & Cafe
174 S. Franklin St.
Juneau 99801
Tel: 907-596-1752

Espresso bar, deli sandwiches.

PRINCE WILLIAM SOUND:
Sportsman's Inn
Box 626
Whittier 99693
Tel: 907-472-2352

Restaurant, bar, and motel overlooking the Whittier harbor and Passage Canal.

Oscar's
143 N. Harbor Dr.
Valdez 99686
Tel: 907-835-4700

Breakfast, lunch, dinner, homemade baked goods.

Reluctant Fisherman Inn
Box 150
Cordova 99574
Tel: 907-424-2372

Restaurant and lounge, seafood specialties, view of Cordova harbor.

Ambrosia First St. Cordova
Tel: 907-424-7175

Harbor view, pizza, Italian and Greek menu.

INTERIOR:
Stromboli Deli
1391 Richardson Highway (Across from the visitors center)
Delta Junction 99737
Tel: 907-895-4165

Lunch, dinner, Sunday brunch. Pizza, homemade baked goods, sandwiches, etc.

Tok Gateway Salmon Bake
Box 577 Mile 1313.1
Alaska Highway
Tok 99780
Tel: 907-883-5555

Caribou Cafe Restaurant Mile
186.9 Glenn Highway
"Downtown"
Glennallen 99588
Tel: 907-822-3656

Sheep Mountain Lodge Mile
113.5 Glenn Highway
Palmer 99645
Tel: 907-745-5121

Homemade baked goods and meals, lodge, bar, liquor store, etc. Easy to miss on the highway, so pay attention.

McKinley/Denali Salmon Bake
Box 90
Denali National Park 99755
Tel: 907-683-2733

Just north of the entrance to Denali Park on the Parks Highway.

Lynx Creek Pizza Mile
238.6 Parks Highway
Denali National Park 99755
Tel: 907-683-2547

One mile north of the park entrance.

Sam's Sourdough Cafe
3702 Cameron
Fairbanks 99709
Tel: 907-479-0523

Great sourdough place, hearty breakfasts, etc.

Alaska Salmon Bake Alaskaland Fairbanks
Tel: 907-452-7274
 1-800-676-6925

Pump House Restaurant & Saloon Mile
1.3 Chena Pump Rd.
Fairbanks 99709
Tel: 907-479-8452

Fine dining, great meat and potatoes place, full bar.

The Turtle Club
10 Mile Old Steese Highway
Fox 9712
Tel: 907-457-3883

Fine dining, prime rib, lobster, etc., reservations recommended.

Cripple Creek Resort
Box 109
Ester 99725
Tel: 907-479-2500

Located at Mile 351.7, Parks Highway. Restaurant, Malemute Saloon, entertainment, hotel, camping, etc. Dinner reservations recommended.

SOUTHCENTRAL:
Sourdough Mining Co.
5200 Juneau
Anchorage 99518
Tel: 907-563-2272

Barbecue specialties among restored mining paraphernalia.

Simon & Seafort's Saloon & Grill
420 L St.
Anchorage 99501
Tel: 907-274-3502

Alaska seafood specialties featured, upscale, always something different, interesting, and tasty to be had. Reservations a must, especially during the season.

Gwennie's Old Alaska Restaurant
4333 Spenard Rd.
Anchorage 99517
Tel: 907-243-2090

Breakfast, lunches, and dinners, served in a setting of Alaskana souvenirs and old photographs.

Mexico in Alaska
7305 Old Seward Highway
Anchorage 99518
Tel: 907-349-1528

Authentic Mexican food, as opposed to the usual Tex-Mex fare found most places.

Little Italy Restaurant
2300 E. 88th Ave.
Anchorage 99507
Tel: 907-344-1515

Excellent little out-of-the-way restaurant, Italian and Greek specialties.

Thai Kitchen
3405 E. Tudor Rd.
Anchorage 99507
Tel: 907-561-0082

Excellent family-run Thai restaurant in a most unlikely location- in the back of a convenience store in a strip mall.

New Sagaya
3700 Old Seward Highway
Anchorage 99503
Tel: 907-561-5173

International grocery store, fresh fish market, fresh produce, and a great inexpensive lunch spot if you like Asian food.

O'Brady's Burgers & Brew
6901 E. Tudor Rd.
Anchorage 99507
Tel: 907-338-1080 or
3301 C St.
Anchorage 99503
Tel: 907-563-1080 or
800 E. Dimond Blvd.
(In the Dimond Center Mall)
Anchorage 99515
Tel: 907-344-8033

Excellent burgers, wide selection, beers from all over the world.

Cafe Amsterdam
530 E. Benson Blvd.
Anchorage 99503
Tel: 907-274-1072

Breakfasts and lunches, homemade baked goods, upscale.

Pizza Olympia
2809 Spenard Rd.
Anchorage 99503
Tel: 907-561-5264

Pizza, Greek and Italian food, lunches and dinners.

The Bake Shop
Alyeska Resort
Girdwood 99587
Tel: 907-783-2831

Sourdough breads, breakfast, lunches, pizza, etc.

The Double Musky
Crow Creek Rd.
Girdwood 99578
Tel: 907-783-2822

CAJUN SPECIALTIES
Summit Lake Lodge Mile 45.8 Seward Highway
Moose Pass 99631
Tel: 907-595-1520 Ext. 1

Restaurant, bar, lodge, and gift shop.

Ray's Waterfront Restaurant
Box 1750
Seward 99664
Tel: 907-224-5606

On Seward's waterfront, view of the small boat harbor and Resurrection Bay.

Green Door Cafe
Box 504 Mile 48.1
Cooper Landing 99572
Tel: 907-595-1265

Local seafood, pasta dishes, very good food in an informal setting.

Gwin's Lodge Mile 52 Sterling Highway
Cooper Landing 99572
Tel: 907-595-1266

Burgers, beer, daily specials. Breakfast, lunch, and dinner.

Four Seasons Restaurant
43960 Sterling Highway
Soldotna 99669
Tel: 907-262-5006

Lunches and dinners, homemade breads.

Kitchen Express & Seafood Salon
115 S. Willow St.
Kenai 99611
Tel: 907-283-5397

Fresh seafood, homemade soup, and espresso drinks.

Fresh Sourdough Express Bakery
1316 Ocean Dr.
Homer 99603
Tel: 907-235-7571

Sourdough breakfasts, lunches, nightly all-you-can-eat seafood barbecue. Box lunches for halibut fishing parties available, open at 5:30 AM.

Don Jose's
127 Pioneer
Homer 99603
Tel: 907-235-7963

MEXICAN SPECIALTIES
Cafe Cups
162 W. Pioneer Ave.
Homer 99603
Tel: 907-235-8330

Fresh seafood, pasta, espresso.

POLICE

Police protection within the limits of the larger cities is provided by municipal police forces.

Outside the large cities, law enforcement is under the jurisdiction of the Alaska State Troopers. Villages without police forces employ the services of a Village Public Safety Officer (VPSO), an unarmed resident to handle minor disputes. For police emergencies, dial 911 from any phone, no payment required.

POST OFFICE
Every village has a post office- in fact, only the largest of Alaska's cities have door-to-door mail delivery. The village post offices often function as de facto community centers, providing a place for residents to gather, catch up on local gossip, and say hello to neighbors.

PRIVATE CLINICS
ANCHORAGE:
First Care
3710 Woodland Dr.
Tel: 248-1122
or 1301 Huffman Rd.
Tel: 345-1199

North Care Minor Emergency & General Practice
4001 Lake Otis Parkway
Tel: 562-0033
or Huffman Plaza
Tel: 345-43443

Juneau Public Health Center
3412 Glacier Highway
Tel: 465-3353

Juneau Urgent Care & Family Clinic
8505 Old Dairy Rd.
Tel: 790-4111

Callisto Medical Clinic
212 Carlanna Lake Rd.,
Ketchikan
Tel: 225-4463

Anchor Point Clinic Granross & Anchor Point Ave.
Tel: 235-5284

Family Medical Center
206 Rockwell Ave.,
Soldotna
Tel: 262-7566

PUBLIC HOLIDAYS
In addition to American national holidays, state offices celebrate Seward's Day on March 29. State employees and banks have the day off, but most businesses and federal government offices are open.

SHOPPING CENTERS
ANCHORAGE:
Dimond Center Mall
800 E. Dimond Blvd.
Tel: 344-2581

Anchorage
5th Avenue Mall 320 W.
5th Ave.
Tel: 258-5535

Northway Mall
3101 Penland Parkway
Tel: 276-5520

University Center Mall
3901 Old Seward Highway
Tel: 276-7400

Bentley Mall
32 College Rd.,
Fairbanks
Tel: 456-3900

University Center Mall
3627 Airport Way,
Fairbanks
Tel: 474-3674

Airport Shopping Center
9131 Glacier Highway,
Juneau
Tel: 789-7566

Mendenhall Mall
9105 Mendenhall Mall Rd.,
Juneau
Tel: 789-0090

Nugget Mall
8745 Glacier Highway,
Juneau
Tel: 789-2877

Valley River Center
11431 Business Park Blvd.
Eagle River
Tel: 694-1822

Cottonwood Creek Mall
1801 Parks Highway
Wasilla
Tel: 376-6802

TRAVEL AGENCIES
ANCHORAGE:
Diamond Travel
215 E. Dimond Blvd.
Tel: 907-349-4477
     800-478-4477

Whitsett Travel
715 W. Fireweed Lane, #E
Tel: 907-277-7671
     800-478-7671

Gary King's Travel
202 E. Northern Lights Blvd.
Tel: 907-276-5425
     800-777-7055

FAIRBANKS:
Western Travel
406 Cushman
Tel: 452-1127

Vista Travel
1211 Cushman
Tel: 456-7888

Gray Line of Alaska
1521 Cushman
Tel: 456-5186

JUNEAU:
Southeast Executravel
118 Seward St.
Tel: 586-6883

Juneau Travel
14 Marine Way
Tel: 586-6031

KETCHIKAN:
Ketchikan Travel
217 Main St.
Tel: 225-4400
Fax: 247-4400

Air-Sea Travel
3430 Tongass
Tel: 225-9491
   800-478-7800 (in AK)

KENAI PENINSULA:
Alaska Travel Cache
10767 Spur Highway,
Kenai
Tel: 283-3518

Aurora Travel Agency
158 W. Pioneer Ave.,
Homer
Tel: 235-2111

Chris's Soldotna Travel
35338 Spur Highway,
Soldotna
Tel: 262-2229

TOURIST INFORMATION OFFICES

Alaska Division of Tourism
Box 110801 Dept. 401
Juneau 99811
Tel: 907-465-2010
Fax: 907-465-2287

Alaska Native Tourism Council
1577 C St. #304
Anchorage 99501
Tel: 907-274-5400
Fax: 907-263-9971

Anchorage Visitor Information Center
546 W. 4th Ave.
Anchorage 99501
Tel: 274-3531

Fairbanks Convention & Visitors Bureau
714 4th Ave. #302B
Fairbanks 99701
Tel: 907-456-5774
   800-327-5774
Fax: 907-452-4190

Haines Visitors Bureau
Box 518
Haines 99827
Tel: 907-766-2234
   800-458-3579
(Lower 48 & AK)
Tel: 800-478-2268
(Yukon & BC only)
Fax: 907-766-3155

Homer Visitor Information Center
3735 Homer Spit Rd.
Homer 99603
Tel: 907-235-5300
   (summer)
Fax: 907-235-6557

Juneau Convention and Visitors Bureau
369 S. Franklin #201
Juneau 99801
Tel: 907-586-1737
Fax: 907-586-1449

Kenai Peninsula Tourism Marketing Council
10819 Kenai Spur Highway #103 Kenai 99611
Tel: 907-283-3850
Fax: 907-283-2838

Ketchikan Convention & Visitors Bureau
131 Front St.
Ketchikan 99901
Tel: 907-225-6166
Fax: 907-225-4250

Kodiak Island Convention & Visitors Bureau
100 Marine Way
Kodiak 99615
Tel: 907-486-4782
Fax: 907-486-6545

Mat-Su Convention & Visitors Bureau HCO1
Box 6166J-21
Palmer 99645
Tel: 907-746-5000
Fax: 907-746-2688

Nome Convention & Visitors Bureau
Box 240
Nome 99762
Tel: 907-443-5535
Fax: 907-443-5832

Prince William Sound Tourism Coalition
Box 243044
Anchorage 99524
Tel: 907-344-1693
   (Phone & FAX)

Sitka Convention & Visitors Bureau
Box 1226
Sitka 99835
Tel: 907-747-5940
Fax: 907-747-3739

Skagway Convention & Visitors Bureau
Box 415
Skagway 99840
Tel: 907-983-2854
Fax: 907-983-2151

Southeast Alaska Tourism Council
Box 20710
Juneau 99802
Tel: 907-586-4777
   800-423-0568
Fax: 907-463-4961

Alaska's Southwest
3300 Arctic Blvd. #203
Anchorage 99503
Tel: 907-562-7380
Fax: 907-562-0438

PHOTO CREDITS

Randa Bishop: x, xii, 21 (top), 23, 34, 41, 44, 48, 84, 85, 88, 91, 99, 102, 106, 115, 119, 120, 129, 138, 145, 169, 175, 214, 222, 236, 240, 252/253, 256, 258, 259 (bottom), 262, 266, 271 (top), 272, 280, 283, 286, 287 (top)
Alaska Divison of Tourism/Robert Angell: 66
Lee Foster: 19, 24, 28, 74, 112 (bottom), 116/117, 118, 125, 127, 136/137, 140, 163, 170/171, 176, 178, 190, 202, 210 (bottom), 211, 213 (bottom), 215, 216, 218, 225, 235 (bottom), 248, 250, 274, 276 (bottom), 279
Greg Evans/Miwako Ikeda: 36, 45
Michele & Tom Grimm: xi (top), xvi, 7, 13, 14, 16, 18, 21 (bottom), 42, 55, 64, 65 (top), 72, 77, 78 (bottom), 79 (top & bottom), 82, 89, 92, 96/97, 103, 108, 110, 110/111, 113, 114, 122/123, 126, 128, 141, 143, 146, 148, 164/165, 166/167, 182, 184, 198/199, 199, 204 (top), 205, 206, 217, 221, 223 (top), 227, 228, 233, 239, 241, 242, 244/245, 246, 249, 255, 260, 263, 267, 269, 270, 276 (top), 278, 287 (bottom), 288
Life File/Andreas Rubin: 56, 87, 100, 247
Life File/Joe Oliver: 180/181
Eleanor S. Morris: 15, 124, 130, 131, 193, 194, 195, 197, 200/201, 210 (top), 268, 271 (bottom)
Odyssey/Kevin O Mooney: 6, 32, 49, 53, 54/55, 58, 67, 71, 168, 172, 185, 188, 189, 209, 213 (top), 259 (top)
Douglas Peebles: Backcover (top left & bottom), Endpaper Front & Back, xiv (top), xv, 2, 3, 5, 8, 10, 11, 38, 39, 40, 46, 59, 65 (bottom), 80, 83, 94, 98, 101, 104/105, 109, 112 (top), 147, 150, 153, 154 (top), 155, 157, 159, 162, 177, 183, 186, 187, 192, 208, 226 (top), 230, 232, 254, 257
Ann Purcell: Backcover (top right), xiii (top & bottom), xiv (bottom), 12, 17, 31, 51, 86, 93 (bottom), 154 (bottom), 156, 158, 264, 282
Carl Purcell: xi (bottom), 20, 22, 26, 30, 57, 60/61, 73, 93 (top), 96, 134, 144, 149, 160 (top & bottom), 161, 170, 203, 223 (bottom), 226 (bottom), 234, 235 (top), 243, 284
Tom Reale: 76, 196
VIREO/ S. Bahrt: 68 (top)
VIREO/ A. & S. Carey: 69 (bottom)
VIREO/ Rob Curtis: 78 (top)
VIREO/ W. Greene: 201
VIREO/ A. & E. Morris: 69 (top)
VIREO/ J.P Myers: 62, 68 (bottom), 70 (bottom)
VIREO/ B. Randall: 204 (bottom)
VIREO/ A.L. Sowls: 70 (top)

INDEX

A
Abercrombie Lake, 199
Accommodations, 245
Admiralty Island, 75
Admiralty Island National Monument, 149
Admiralty Way, 143
Adventure, 3, 6, 225
Afognak, 191, 197
Ahtna Arts and Crafts Fair, 114
Airplane, 6, 64, 141, 205, 211, 233, 242, 278
Akhiok, 197
Alaska Airlines, 161
Alaska Aviation Heritage Museum, 117
Alaska Center for the Performing Arts, 211
Alaska Constitution, 19
Alaska Department of Fish and Game, 77
Alaska Federation of Natives, 91
Alaska Folk Festival, 112
Alaska Heritage Library, 117
Alaska Highway, 226
Alaska Indian Arts center, 168
Alaska Marine Highway, 48, 138, 192
Alaska National Interest Lands Conservation Act, 32
Alaska Native Claims Settlement Act (ANCSA), 30, 31, 92
Alaska Natives, 2, 15, 29, 33, 88, 91, 92, 123
Alaska Natural History Association, 210
Alaska Natural Resources Museum, 115, 163
Alaska Public Lands Information Center, 210
Alaska Railroad, 227
Alaska Railroad station, 211
Alaska Range, 52, 53, 54
Alaska Raptor Rehabilitation Center, 160
Alaska State Museum, 119, 145
Alaska-Gastineau mines, 135
Alaska-Juneau mines, 135
Alaskaland, 225, 286
Alaskan Brewing Company, 145
Alaskan Indians, 11
Alcan Highway, 27
Aleksei Chirikov, 14
Aleut, 11, 12, 16, 81, 83, 84, 86, 88, 97, 98, 123, 127
Aleutian, 12, 15, 18, 26, 27, 89, 95, 100, 202
Aleutian Islands, 16, 60, 83
Aleutian Range, 54, 56
Alutiiq Cultural Center, 194
Alyeska Marine Terminal, 177
American, 14, 16, 19, 21, 27, 33
Anan Bear Observatory, 155
Anchorage, 3, 5, 18, 25, 26, 27, 37, 38, 48, 53, 55, 60, 67, 72, 101, 103, 108, 112, 115, 117, 140, 173, 175, 188, 207, 227, 266
Anchorage Fur Rendezvous, 109
Anchorage Museum of History and Art, 211
ANILCA, 33
Archeological, 222
Arctic, 9, 37
Arctic Circle, 49, 61, 228, 230

Arctic National Park, 7
Arctic National Wildlife Refuge (ANWR), 33
Arctic Ocean, 30
Art Galleries, 270
Asian, 9, 44, 191, 273
Athabascan, 12, 13, 14, 83, 84, 86, 88, 130
Athabascan Indians, 81
Attu Island, 27, 60
Aurora Borealis, 241
Avacha Bay, 14

B
Babiche, 131
Bachelor Society, 108
Backcountry, 248
Baidarkas, 84
Bald Eagle Music Festival, 114
Bale Eagles, 153, 203
Ball Games, 261
Baptists, 100
Barabaras, 86
Baranof Island, 159
Baranov Cultural Center, 194
Barrow, 49, 61, 239
Basket-weaving, 127
Basket, 121, 126, 127, 131, 269
Beachcombing, 205
Beadwork, 130
Bear Valley, 176
Bears, 5, 66, 73, 74, 79, 153, 162, 176, 180, 200, 208
Beaufort Sea, 37
Begich-Boggs Visitor Center, 217
Bering, 15, 16, 82
Bering Strait, 9, 27, 81, 89
Beringian plain, 81

Berries, 204
Bethel, 49
Big Diomede, 89
Billings Glacier, 176
Birch Syrup, 277
Bird Creek, 215
Birding, 68, 70, 75
Bolshevik Revolution, 99
Bonanza Creek, 12, 20
Botanical garden, 224
Bristol Bay, 20
British, 155
British Columbia, 13, 170
Brooks Range, 5, 7, 30, 49, 54, 69, 78, 82, 92, 228, 244
Brooks River, 75
Bureau of Land Management, 37
Bus, 3, 6, 64, 225
Bush, 282
Bush pilot, 246
Buskin Beach, 205
Buskin River State Recreation Site, 201
Byron Glacier, 217

C

Camping, 6, 217, 259
Canada, 20, 83
Canada-U.S. Border Crossings, 168
Canneries, 20, 23
Cape Muzon, 60
Cape Prince of Wales, 100
Capital, 4
    Capitol Building, 143
Captain Cook Monument, 211
Captain James Cook, 17
Car, 3, 6, 7, 64, 225
Caribou, 4, 5, 11, 14, 71, 128, 130
Carvings, 123, 125, 269, 270
Catherine I, 14
Catholics, 102
Centennial Building, 159, 284
Chatanika Lodge, 229
Chatanika River, 229
Chena, 228
Chena Hot Springs Resort, 229
Chena River Recreation Area, 229
Chenega, 51
Chester Creek, 208
Chichagof Island, 17

Chilkat Bald Eagle Preserve, 76, 162
Chilkat Dancers, 115
Chilkat dancing blankets, 130
Chilkat River, 162
Chilkat Tlingit Indians, 163
Chilkat Trail, 12, 20
Chilkoot Legends, 115
Chilkoot Trail, 12, 20
Chistochina Fun Days, 109
Chitina, 234, 235
Chugach, 83
Chugach Mountains, 53, 207, 208
Chugach National Forest, 55
Chugach State Park, 72, 208, 212
Chukchi Sea, 54
Circle Hot Springs, 229
Circle Hot Springs Resort, 230
Cities, 2, 3
Clam Gulch, 261
Clams, 261
Clausen Museum, 157
Clothing, 84, 125, 126
Coast Range, 53
Coastal Eskimos, 85
Coastline, 4
Cold War, 27, 89
Columbia Glacier, 177, 186
Concert on the Lawn, 117
Congregationalists, 100
Congress, 23, 26, 33
Cook Inlet, 18, 20, 25, 67, 99, 183, 184, 207, 215, 258
Cooper Landing, 71, 180, 181
Copper, 114, 119
Copper Day, 111
Copper River, 234
Copper Valley Winter Carnival, 110
Cordova, 17, 109, 111, 119
Craig, 154
Crescent Boat Harbor, 285
Cripple Creek Bureau Land Management, 229
Crow Creek Mine, 216
Crow Pass, 214
Cuisine, 273

D

Dall sheep, 5, 63, 72, 180, 208, 215, 270
Dalton City, 115, 163

Dalton Highway, 225
Dalton Trail, 20
Davis Log Cabin, 143
Dawson, 21
Daylight, 5
De Havilland Beaver, 243
Deep Creek, 183, 261
Deer, 5, 67, 196, 197, 200
Delta Junction, 114
Deltana Fair, 114
Democrats, 29
Denali Highway, 227, 231
Denali National Park, 71, 75, 227, 228, 231
Denmark, 27
Department of Fish and Game, 33, 77, 197, 199
Diamond willow, 270
Dillingham, 49, 119
Dining, 3
Discovery Riverboats, 228
Dixon Entrance, 60, 151
Doll making, 126
Dorothy G. Page Museum, 119
Double Musky restaurant, 216
Douglas, 139
Douglas Island, 135, 149
Dutch Harbor, 26, 27
Dyea, 20

E

E. T. Barnette, 230
Eagle River Visitor's Center, 214
Eaglecrest Ski Area, 149
Eagle's Hall, 170
Earthquake, 5
Earthquake Park, 51, 208
Economy, 4
Eklutna Lake, 72
Elk, 197
Elliott Highway, 226
Elmendorf Air Force Base, 211
Elmendorf Field, 27
Emergency, 3
English, 17
Entertainment, 281
Environmentalists, 32
Episcopalians, 100
Eskimo, 11, 14, 84, 86, 88, 123
Ester Gold Camp, 286
Europe, 17
Europeans, 88, 89
Extremes of climate, 5
Exxon Valdez oil spill, 74, 173,

INDEX

194
Eyak, 83

F
Fairbanks, 21, 25, 26, 38, 49, 53, 101, 109, 110, 112, 114, 117, 140, 188, 219, 224, 244, 283, 285, 286
Fairbanks research farm, 73
Fairbanks Visitor's Information Center, 224
Fairbanks-North Star Borough, 219
False Pass, 56
Festival of Native Arts, 109
Festivals, 107, 112
Final Frontier, 1, 2
Fireman's Carnival, 108
First Organic Act, 21
Fishermen, 6, 234
Fishes, 6
Fishing, 6, 7, 182, 187, 194, 201, 232, 234, 235, 248, 267
Fishing Charters, 256
Fishtival, 114
Fishtraps, 131
Fjords, 4, 53, 57
Flattop Mountain, 212, 213
Fly by Night Club, 284
Fly-in fishing, 6
Flying, 242, 243
Forest, 4, 77, 78, 151
Forest Service Information Center, 145
Fort Egbert, 21
Fort Richardson, 27, 175
Fort Seward, 26
Fort William Seward, 168
Fort Wrangell, 101
Forts Gibbon, 21
Fortymile River, 21
Frank Reid, 23
Franklin, 143
Fraser River, 75
French, 17
Friends Church, 100
Front Street, 110, 285
Ft. Abercrombie Park, 201
Fur Rendezvous, 113, 263
Fur Shops, 268
Fur trade, 16

G
Gastineau Channel, 135, 138, 139, 141, 144
Gastineau Salmon Hatchery, 145
Geophysical Institute, 224
George Parks Highway, 188
George Steller, 15
German, 26
Girdwood-Alyeska road, 216
Glacier, 1, 2, 4, 5, 6, 53, 151, 174, 180, 188, 232
Glacier Bay, 146, 257, 258
Glacier Bay National Park, 65, 68, 161
Glen Alps, 212
Glenn Highway, 72, 188
Glennallen, 109, 110, 227
Gold, 20, 35, 123, 135, 155, 169, 170, 192, 221, 283
Gold Creek basin, 135
Gold Creek Salmon Bake, 144
Gold Panning, 156
Gold Rush memorabilia, 115
Gold Rush Revue, 283
Golden Days, 114
Golden Heart, 227
Golden Heart Park, 224
Good Friday Earthquake, 51, 194, 217
Goodnews Bay, 53
Government, 4, 19, 29, 31, 140, 159
Gray Line of Alaska, 146
Great Alaska Shootout, 261
Great Land, 1
Great Tanana River Raft Classic Race, 112
Grey Nuns of the Sacred Heart, 102
Grizzly, 73, 196, 231
Guide Books, 267
Gulf of Alaska, 98
Gustavus, 161

H
Haida, 12, 13, 83, 84, 86, 88, 129, 153
Haida Indians, 81
Haines, 20, 21, 26, 76, 114, 115, 119, 161, 162, 163
Halibut, 41, 43, 184, 191, 257
Halibut Cove, 184, 185
Handicrafts, 121
Harbor Drive, 284
Harrisburgh, 135

Hatcher Pass, 188
Haul Road, 225
Hawaii, 29
Hawaiian Islands, 18
Highest point, 4
Highway, 3, 59, 175, 182, 225, 237
Hiking, 6, 202, 205, 248
Hitler, 26
Homer, 65, 114, 115, 119, 180, 181, 183
Homer Spit, 184
Homer Spring Arts Festival, 111
Hope, 73, 180
Hope Highway, 181
Hotel, 7
Housing, 86
Hunting, 76, 86, 90, 267
Hunting whales, 84
Hydaburg, 154
Hypothermia, 52

I
Ice Age, 9
Ice-hunting, 84
Iceworm Festival, 109
Icy Bay, 151
Icy Cape, 18
Iditarod Awards Banquet, 110
Iditarod Trail Sled Dog Race, 110, 263
Igloos, 2
Illiamna Volcano, 212
Independence Mine State Historical Park, 189
Indians, 123
Inside Passage, 139, 153, 161, 285
Interior, 2, 25, 285
Inupiat Eskimos, 11, 81, 82, 86, 127
Isabel Miller Museum, 159
Ismailof Island, 185
Ivory, 16
Ivory carvings, 269

J
James Wickersham, 23
Japanese, 26, 27
Jesuit priests, 101
Jesuits, 102
Jewel Beach, 205
Joe Juneau, 135
Juneau, 21, 23, 101, 102, 112,

119, 135, 139, 140, 141, 148, 149, 244, 283, 284
Juneau Douglas City Museum, 119, 144

K
Kachemak Bay, 184
Kachemak Bay Shorebird Festival, 111
Kalifornsky Beach Road, 183
Kamchatka, 15, 16
Kamchatka Peninsula, 14
Karluk, 197
Katmai National Park, 75
Kayak, 84, 145
Kenai, 20, 72, 99, 177, 180, 258, 287
Kenai Fjords National Park, 65, 187
Kenai Lake, 181
Kenai Mountains, 53
Kenai National Moose Range, 37
Kenai National Wildlife Refuge, 182
Kenai Peninsula, 17, 21, 28, 37, 48, 65, 71, 78, 173, 191
Kenai Peninsula State Fair, 114
Kenai River, 181, 183
Kenai-Soldotna, 182
Kennecott copper works, 233
Kennicott River, 233
Ketchikan, 28, 60, 119, 146, 153, 154, 285
Kiglapak Mountains, 53
King Salmon, 109, 114, 239
Kiska Island, 27
Klawock, 154
Klondike, 12, 13, 20, 23
Knik, 25, 207
Knik Arm, 208
Kodiak, 20, 26, 72, 75, 78, 96, 97, 99, 108, 109, 114, 191, 192, 193, 200
Kodiak Fisherman, 202
Kodiak Hills, 53
Kodiak Historical Society, 195
Kodiak Island, 18, 72, 82, 191
Kodiak National Wildlife Refuge, 197
Kodiak National Wildlife Refuge Visitor Center, 201
Kodiak Refuge headquarters, 200
Kodiak Visitor Information Center, 192
Koniag, 83
Koniag Yup'iks, 97
Kotzebue, 239
Kuskokwim, 100
Kuskokwim Rivers, 14

L
La Perouse, 17
Lake Bennett, 170
Lake Eklutna, 214
Lake Hood, 117, 211
Lake Hood-Lake Spenard, 283
Lake Spenard, 211
Land bridge, 81
Language, 4
Large Animal Research Station, 224
Larsen Bay, 197
Last Chance Basin, 144
LeConte Glacier, 155, 159
Lemon Creek, 145
Little Diomede, 89
Little Norway Festival, 112, 157
Little Russian Mission, 98
Logging, 44
Lynn Canal Community Players, 115

M
Main Industry, 4
Malaspina Glacier, 17
Mammals, 5, 57, 65, 67, 75, 197, 258
Manley, 230
Manley Hot Springs, 226
Manley Hot Springs Resort, 231
Manley Roadhouse, 231
Manley Trading Post, 231
Marine Mammal Protection Act, 123
Marine Park, 143
Maritime, 48
Masks, 122, 123, 127, 269
Matanuska, 28, 173
Matanuska Valley, 25
McHugh Creek, 215
McNeil River State Game Sanctuary, 75
Mendenhall Glacier, 148
Methodists, 100
Mexico, 17
Midnight Sun Festival, 112

Migrations, 11
Military, 26, 27, 35
Mining, 44
Misty Fjords National Monument, 153
Monashka Bay, 205
Moose, 5, 72, 176, 180, 208, 231, 270
Moose Pass, 186
Moose poop, 268
Moravians, 100
Mount St. Elias, 17, 53
Mount St. Helens, 193
Mountains, 2, 4, 7, 51, 56, 168, 174, 176, 180, 181, 183
Mt. Foraker, 212
Mt. Illiamna, 183
Mt. Juneau, 141
Mt. Marathon, 187
Mt. McKinley, 53, 108, 212, 283
Mt. Roberts, 141, 144
Mt. Spur, 212
Mt. St. Elias, 15
Mt. Susitna, 211, 212
Mukluks, 125
Museum of Alaska Transportation and Industry, 119
Museum of History and Art, 117
Museums, 117, 194

N
National Parks, 4
Native Corporations, 33, 92
Native Regional Corporations, 30, 92
Nelson Island, 73, 125
Nenana, 112
Nenana Ice Classic week-end festival, 109
Nenana River Days, 112
Nets, 131
New Archangel Russian Dancers, 284
Ninilchik, 183
Nome, 13, 21, 108, 110, 114, 119, 239
North American Championship sled dog racing, 109
North and South Peak, 53
North Pole, 110, 114
North Slope, 30, 37, 49, 54, 92, 140, 226
Norton Sound, 82

INDEX

Norway, 27
Norwegian, 157
Norwegian Independence Day, 112
Novarupta volcano, 193
Nunivak, 125
Nunivak Island, 73
Nushagak river, 100

O

Oil, 35, 37, 38, 39, 40, 45, 175, 177, 192, 221
Oktoberfest, 115
Old Harbor, 197
Old Steese Highway, 286
OPEC, 37
Oregon, 21
Oscar Anderson House, 211
Oscar Anderson House Museum, 117
Ouzinkie, 197

P

Pack Creek, 75, 162
Palmer, 114
Parkas, 125
Parks Highway, 226, 227
Pasagshak, 205
Pasagshak River State Recreation Site, 201
Passage Canal, 176
Pearl Harbor, 27
People, 3, 4, 11
Performing Arts Center, 117, 286
Peter the Great, 14
Petersburg, 112, 157
Pier One Theater, 117, 287
Pierce Street Annex, 287
Pioneer Bar, 285
Plaques, 130
Point Barrow, 2, 60, 100
Polar Bear Festival, 108
Population, 4, 26, 27, 139, 140
Port Lions, 197
Portage, 51, 175, 176, 208, 217
Portage Valley, 73
Potlatch, 88, 100
Potter Marsh, 214
Potter Point Section House, 214
Presbyterian, 100, 101
President Carter, 32
President Eisenhower, 29
Pribilofs, 20

Prince of Wales Island, 17, 154
Prince William Sound, 16, 17, 37, 48, 51, 55, 72, 78, 82, 173, 227, 254, 258
Promyshlennini, 95
Protestant, 99
Prudhoe Bay, 29, 30, 33, 37, 49, 92
Public Communications Section, 77
Public Lands Information Center, 224, 225
Public Use Cabins, 178

Q

Quakers, 100
Queen Charlotte Island, 84, 151

R

Raspberry, 191
Raven, 118
Raven Glacier Lodge, 216
Redoubt Volcano, 183, 212
Reindeer sausage, 277
Religions, 4, 95, 103
Republicans, 29
Resurrection Bay, 108, 187
Resurrection Bay Historical Society, 119
Resurrection Pass Trail, 71, 181
Retail, 265
Revillagigedo Island, 17
Richard Harris, 135
Richardson Highway, 71, 73, 226
Richfield Oil Company, 37
River Sports, 251
Rocky Mountains, 54
Roman Catholics, 101
Russia, 14
Russian, 16, 17, 18, 19, 20, 35, 88, 95, 96, 97, 100, 103, 155, 159
Russian Bishop's House, 159
Russian Orthodoxy, 95
Russian-American Company, 16, 96, 98, 99

S

Salmon, 3, 11, 15, 23, 40, 41, 42, 162, 181, 182, 191, 199, 201, 214, 215, 225, 234, 235, 256, 273, 274
Salmon bake, 273

Saxman village, 153
Sea lions, 198
Sea otter, 16, 19, 176, 188, 197
Seafood, 273
Seals, 5, 11, 84, 128, 153, 188, 197
Second World War, 26
Seldovia, 114, 184, 185
Seldovia Blueberry Festival, 115
Seward, 25, 26, 65, 108, 114, 143, 180, 185, 187, 287
Seward Highway, 72
Seward Museum, 119
Seward Peninsula, 49, 100
Seward's Folly, 19
Shakes House, 155
Sheldon Jackson, 101
Sheldon Jackson Museum, 159, 169
Shelikov-Golikov Company, 96
Shellfish, 41, 42, 275
Ship Creek, 25, 211
Shopping, 6, 265
Shoreline, 5, 6, 201
Shumagin Islands, 100
Shuyak, 191
Shuyak Island State Park, 200
Sightseeing, 6
Silver Hand, 267
Sisters of Providence, 102
Sisters of Saint Ann, 102
Sisters of St. Joseph of Peace, 102
Sitka, 17, 19, 20, 21, 23, 88, 99, 108, 135, 159, 160, 284
Sitka National Historical Park, 159
Sitka Summer Music Festival, 112
Skagway, 20, 22, 112, 119, 161, 283
Ski, 262
Skiing, 6, 262, 263
Snowshoes, 131
Soapy Smith., 22, 169
Soldotna, 180, 181
Sourdough, 273, 276
Southcentral, 139, 173
Southeast, 89, 254
Southeast Alaska, 17, 20, 27, 78, 83, 151, 207
Souvenir art, 123
Spanish, 17
Spanish-American War, 22

Sport fishing, 171, 199, 234
St. Elias Range, 53
St. George Island, 98
St. Lawrence Island, 82
St. Michael, 98
St. Michael's Cathedral, 159
St. Nicholas Orthodox Church, 144
St. Paul, 14
St. Paul Island, 98
St. Peter, 14, 15
Stan Price State Wildlife Sanctuary, 75
State bird, 4
State Flower, 4
State Legislature, 4
State Office Building, 144
State song, 4
Steese Highway, 226, 229, 230
Sterling Highway, 185
Stikine River, 155
Stikine River Trail, 21
Stikine Tlingits, 155
Stikine-LeConte Wilderness Area, 155
Subsistence, 83
Summer Arts Festival, 114
Summit Lake Lodge, 181
Super Cub, 243
Surimi, 43
Susitna Valleys, 173
Swan Lake, 181
Swanson River, 37, 181

T
Talkeetna, 283
Talkeetna Historical Society Museum, 119
Talkeetna Moose Dropping Festival, 112
Talkeetna Wilderness, 107
Talkeetna Wilderness Women's Contest, 107
Tanana, 228
Tanana Valley State, 114
Tanana Valley State Fair, 114
Tanner Crab, 41, 191, 275
Taste of Homer, 115
Taxidermy, 270
Telegraph, 21
Temperatures, 2, 47, 49, 50, 51, 193, 219, 224
The Southeast Alaska State Fair, 114

The Three Saints, 96
The World Eskimo Indian Olympics, 260
Thorne Bay, 154
Tidal bores, 215
Time zones, 4
Tlingit, 12, 13, 81, 83, 84, 86, 88, 98, 129, 153
Tok, 114, 188
Tongass Island, 20
Tongass National Forest, 55
Totem Bight State Park, 153
Totem Heritage Center, 153
Totem poles, 102, 122, 129, 154, 155, 129
Tourism, 45, 139, 192, 223
Tourists, 213
Tracy Arm, 146
Trans-Alaska Pipeline, 177
Treadwell, 138
Tundra, 4, 63, 78, 151, 189, 203, 231, 248, 249
Turnagain Arm, 52, 67, 181, 207, 214, 215, 217, 258, 259
Two Bears, 267

U
U.S. Coast Guard, 195
Ulu, 128
Umiaks, 84
Unalaska, 99
United States, 19, 21, 27, 89
University Museum, 224
University of Alaska, 73, 109, 224
University of Alaska Museum, 117
Ursuline Nuns, 102
US Fish and Wildlife Service, 33

V
Valdez, 17, 21, 30, 37, 51, 92, 119, 175, 176, 227
Valdez Glacier Trail, 21
Valdez Museum, 177
Veniaminoff Cultural Center, 194
Veterans' Memorial Highway, 149
Vitus Bering, 14
Volcanoes, 5, 54

W
Wales, 119

Washington, 21, 23, 29
Wasilla, 25, 119, 188
Westchester Lagoon, 208
Wetlands, 56
Whale blubber, 128
Whalebone, 16
Whales, 6, 153, 161, 188, 197, 215, 257
White Fang, 163
White Pass Summit, 13
White Pass Trail, 12, 20
White-water rafting, 6
Whittier, 50, 51, 175, 176
Wickersham House, 144
Wild Berries, 79
Wild flowers, 79, 202, 203, 267
Wild game meat, 277
William Seward, 19
Willow, 140
Willow Creek, 189
Windsurfing, 215
Winterfest, 109
Wood Campus Center, 224
Wrangell, 20, 119, 155
Wrangell Narrows, 157
Wrangell-St. Elias, 232

Y
Yakutat, 50
Yukon, 13, 14
Yukon Quest, 263
Yukon River, 21, 102, 226, 230
Yukon River bridge, 225
Yukon-Kuskokwim, 99
Yukon-Kuskokwim Delta, 56, 82
Yup'ik, 86, 98, 127
Yup'ik Eskimos, 12, 81, 82

INDEX

315

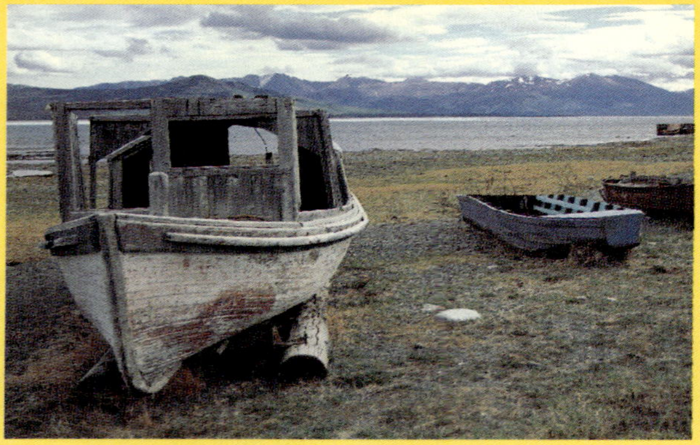